BREAKING GROUNDS

THE JOURNAL OF A TOP
CHINESE WOMAN MANAGER IN RETAIL

BREAKING GROUNDS

THE JOURNAL OF A TOP
CHINESE WOMAN MANAGER IN RETAIL

Bingxin Hu

Translated from the Chinese by

Chengchi Wang

HOMA & SEKEY BOOKS
PARAMUS, NEW JERSEY

First Edition

Library of Congress Cataloging-in-Publication Data

Hu, Bingxin, 1950-
[Bo qu di yi. English]
Breaking grounds : the journal of a top Chinese woman manager in retail / Bingxin Hu ; translated from the Chinese by Chengchi Wang.—
1st ed.
p. cm.
ISBN 1-931907-15-3 (hardcover)
1. Hu, Bingxin, 1950- 2. Businesswomen—China—Biography. 3. Shopping centers—China—Wuhan. 4. Retail trade—China. I. Title.
HF3834.6.H8A3 2003
338.092—dc22
2003016847

Published by Homa & Sekey Books
3rd Floor, North Tower
Mack-Cali Center III
140 East Ridgewood Avenue
Paramus, NJ 07652

Tel: 201-261-8810; 800-870-HOMA
Fax: 201-261-8890; 201-384-6055
Email: info@homabooks.com
Website: www.homabooks.com

Editor-in-Chief: Shawn X. Ye
Executive Editor: Judy Campbell

Printed in the United States of America
1 3 5 7 9 10 8 6 4 2

For My Daughter, Xuan Wang

Contents

Preface to the English Edition

*B*reaking Grounds, a record of my growth after setbacks and of my exhilaration with my success, was published in February, 1999. To my surprise, this book not only resonated in the Chinese business world, but also became popular among businesses with foreign investment, which bought hundreds of copies at once. Mr. Xinming Wang, Chairman of the Board of the Wuhan Branch of the Shanghai Pepsi Cola Co., Ltd, bought 200 copies and distributed them to the management team, from the CEO to middle management. Upon inquiry, I was told that many international companies predicted in the late 1990s that investment in China would see a boom in the 21st century. *Breaking Grounds* was the first book then that presented a detailed description of the growth to success of a joint venture in China with Hong Kong investment. The real-life cases in the book truthfully reflected the clashes of new ideas with old concepts, the growth of new corporate cultures against the old ones, the psychological transition among the Chinese staff… The book functioned as an excellent course book for understanding Chinese businesses and the Chinese culture, and for achieving the goal of localized management.

My daughter Xuan Wang, who was then a junior business student at the Boston University, strongly recommended having the book translated and published in English. She was desperately aware of the sketchy knowledge among the American public and American businesses of the elaborate and profound Chinese culture. Unfortunately, I was too busy then to add this project to my agenda.

Later on, I got acquainted with Shawn Ye of Homa & Sekey Books in New Jersey through Chengchi Wang, the translator of the book. An enthusiast in Sino-American cultural exchange, Mr. Ye expressed strong interest in publishing the English version of the book after reading it. At the same time, Mr. Louis B. Barnes, a distinguished Harvard Business School professor, agreed to write a foreword for *Breaking Grounds*. Then my decision to publish the English version of the book in the U. S. was finally made.

It is my sincere wish that the English edition can promote the cultural and business exchange between China and the U. S., and add to the knowledge of Chinese businesses by international companies interested in investment in China.

I would like to express my hearty thanks to Professor Louis B. Barnes who wrote the Foreword for the English edition, Chengchi Wang, translator of my book, Shawn Ye, publisher of Homa & Sekey Books, and, last but not least, my husband Jiang Wang and my daughter Xuan Wang, who have always been so understanding, helpful and supportive.

Bingxin Hu
July 18, 2003
Guangzhou, China

Foreword

*B*reaking Grounds is an autobiographical account of a CEO's life in a large Chinese retail organization. But it is more. The CEO is a woman who was referred to by her associates as "Chief Hu." She came from an unlikely background of factory, hospital, and Communist Party work and completed the Chinese edition of this book in the spring of 1999.

Her business organization was the path-breaking, joint-venture Wuhan Plaza in China, a large retail shopping complex within a new 48 story building. Bingxin Hu (or Hu Bingxin as she is known in her native land) moved from state-owned enterprises into China's new private sector as the market economy took over much of China's reform economy. She moved from her 1988 job as a Communist Party section chief (in the Organization Division of the Party's Commerce Committee) to the CEO role in this major entrepreneurial enterprise in less than a decade. To do this, she had to voluntarily "go down" to the grassroots levels of what was then a low-status world of business and commerce in 1988 rather than continue in the Party bureaucracy. It was a bold move at the time, but one that paid big dividends for her and reflected China's rapid transition into modern times.

Ms Hu initially joined the Wuhan Department Store in 1988 under the tutelage of General Manager Mao Dong Sheng who seemed impressed by her initiative and persistence. Within a short time, she had moved from Mao's Number 6 Deputy to his First Deputy, and Mao would remark to others that "only Bingxin understands me."

But that was not enough. Ms. Hu did more than understand Mao. She had ambitious career plans and artfully designed her future career around a set of unyielding values that will remind American readers of a cross between a military campaign (as portrayed by Sunzi's *The Art of War*) and 19th century Protestant Ethic edicts —

unstinting hard work, attention to details, and continuous study. She was an avid reader (every evening for hours) on mostly work-related topics and apologizes for the lack of time spent with her family. Some of the section headings in her book chapters include:

- Play Tough
- Look into Every Detail in Person
- Group Assault Before Dawn
- March in the Forefront of Revolution

But Hu had more than militaristic toughness on her agenda. As she notes at one point when faced with the dilemma of accepting Mao's offer to become Executive General Manager of the parent company (the Wushang Group) or, alternatively, heading up the company's newest crown jewel, The Wuhan Plaza. With regard to this choice, Hu says:

I was in pursuit of a meaningful life. I wished to break into a new world of China's retail trade with my own hands. The Wuhan Plaza was said to be virgin land. I believed it promised more. My feeling was that it had its special mission, independent of the Wuhan Department Store and all the other similar shopping centers in China. "Special" not in the sense of its physical make-up, but in the sense of its spiritual and cultural contents. These contents were probably totally new, different from any tradition or foreign beliefs.

Such values and ambitions helped lead to the design and building of the giant 48 story Wuhan Plaza, begun in 1996 and opened for business in September of 1998. The retail operations became an immediate success and continued to grow. Ms. Hu became the first General Manager of this 76,000 square meter organization with 3,000 rigorously trained employees. But in some ways, the above quotation also captures a paradox built into Ms. Hu's ambitious person and programs. On the one hand, she argues that "affection" (as well as discipline) is a cornerstone of the Wuhan Shopping Center's employment policies and practices. On the other, because "Business is War," sales clerks and floor managers were required to stand at attention or keep walking during all hours on duty (no chairs in offices on the shopping floors), including throughout frequent training sessions. Because of her strong devotion to, and belief in, computer technology, Ms. Hu refers to the importance of management by "mathematical modeling and to the values of "scientific" management, possibly not realizing the negative history attached to that term (a la Frederick W. Taylor) in the western world.

But as the reader will see, Ms. Hu's real aspiration for herself and for Chinese businesses is **professionalism** at all levels. "Professionalism before profits," the Wuhan Shopping Center's General Manager proclaims, and in this vein, **Rules are Higher than the General Manager**. The rules of professionalism demand continuous and disciplined training which reflect competence and courtesy within the organization and by its employees. As Ms. Hu declares at the end of her fascinating book, China will never reach its full potential until it reaches high enough to develop a class of professional General Managers. Hu's very powerful declaration of war on traditionalism and lethargy marks an all-important step in that direction for her compatriots in China and a strong warning to managers in general.

Louis B. Barnes
John D. Black Professorship Emeritus
Professor of Organizational Behavior Emeritus
Harvard Business School

Introduction:
This World and I

> We are part of history;
> history favors competition.
> — Author

The idea of writing this book came in the summer of 1998. It was very hot and the sales of air-conditioners saw a sharp increase, which blew a cool breeze into my heart. Data from the Computer Center showed that we were running far ahead of our competitors in all the business indices. It was then that someone said, "Chief Hu,[1] why not write down your sweet-bitter experience in the past few years, to put a full stop to it?"

I have never thought of a full stop for my life because my career had not exhausted all the potentials. What I needed was at most a "dash." I took note of this punctuation when I took courses in the Chinese Department of the Dianshi University, and found that it had the interesting function of connecting two sections. It suddenly dawned on me: Why not throw a bridge to connect the past and the future by writing a book? A dash, a book... A decision was made then.

I began to collect and sort fragments of my previous writing, only to discover that it was not as easy as I had thought. Questions kept coming up: Why should I write this book? Except for summarizing my personal experiences, who else was this book intended for? Past events came back thick and fast, and fantastic reveries streamed into my mind. Those past events were like old photographs one on top of another, some colorful, some black and white, and it was so hard to find out a clear path through them. The fantastic reveries were like wild music without a title. There was the clarinet as smooth as a feather, the trombone as powerful as a thunderbolt, as well as the rumbling drums. I couldn't let myself get lost. So I washed my face in cold water. The theme crystallized in the following calmness — to compile the mental journey of a general manager, recording her pursuits, hardship, perplexities, accomplishments, and the appeals that she had wanted to make from time to time.

I don't want to be obsessed with myself. I am very career-oriented. I spend most of the 24 hours working and studying. Career is my first consideration.

Besides, China is in need of a powerful general manager class in order to develop its economy rapidly. In view of this situation, I wanted to write about the thoughts and acts of a general manager.

I am a member of the society. This book should belong to the society, too, as part of the answer sheet filled out for the century.

Talking about competition in the century, a past event came into my mind. In 1996, I went to the United States on a fact-finding trip and visited a gigantic distribution center. Only the Americans could have the guts to build it! It was a warehouse so huge that jetliners could pull into it. Inside the center, goods piled up mountain-high and were arranged orderly in squares, leaving enough space for passages. To my surprise, this center, which supplied food to the eastern U.S., had only a dozen workers, with computerized management. More shockingly, computers even generated precise workflow procedures, stipulating specifically the exact amount of goods a worker should handle each hour and each day, routes and timing for the forklifts, and delivery time range for trucking.

I detected a silent challenge right on the spot, a war without gun smoke. On my way home, I had a heavy heart. Out of the plane window was the deep blue water of the Pacific Ocean. As the jetliner gained altitude, the water and the sky faded out, giving way to patches and piles of white clouds. The clouds were soft as cotton fiber, light as feathers, calm as a dream and spreading as the boundless grassland covered with snow. They had a relaxing and soothing effect. But all this was just a false impression, because right at that moment, through the speakers, a flight attendant asked the passengers to fasten the safety belt as thunder and lightening had been brewing in the clouds.

I was suddenly caught by a sense of anxiety, my mind turning to the world under the clouds. Were there any hidden dangers in the world, under these poetic clouds? Any false sense of safety would be dangerous. We were facing a life-or-death battle, in the retail business that I knew so well, for example.

While we were still overjoyed with the increasing size of new department stores, great changes were taking place in the world. While we were still intoxicated by one opening ceremony after another, waves after waves of revolution were surging outside China. We believed that department stores would never disappear, yet foreign companies had already started to modify its structure. Warehouse-style cash-and-carry stores, networked chain stores, enormous shopping centers and online shopping supported by computers all swarmed to the Chinese market with their ideas, approaches and smiling shopping guides. Our stores could not compete in size. The total sales revenue of the 150 biggest department stores in China was $3 billion per year, while the annual sales revenue of the American company Wal-Mart reached $120 billion. Our stores could not compete in management either. While most of us were still complacent with our cash registers, Wal-Mart was already using its own satellites to keep track of its global purchase and sales.

The gap was enormous. We had no reason to be complacent. We must fight on.

In a battle, the rule is to know our foes as well as ourselves. The first question is: Who am I?

My name is Hu Bing-xin. But my original name was a little different in Chinese spelling, with the last character *xin* to mean "continuous fragrance" rather than "heart," although they sound the same. My father, a man of learning, picked this birth name to show his everlasting affection for his daughter. But it had too many strokes in Chinese spelling, hard to write for a primary school girl. I later changed it to the homophonic *xin* and my father tacitly consented.

Bing-xin is a good phrase, meaning "crystal heart." I like this name, which is very feminine. It is good to be a woman and I enjoy the female role, exquisite and gentle, rich in personal feelings and gorgeous colors. From the bottom of my heart, I don't have much favor for the current popular buzzword of "iron woman."

Besides, the name implies a calm pursuit of noble virtues and personal career. I am a career person.

What does "career" mean in the 1990s? According to my understanding, it is not blind labor like oxen plowing through the fields, or lightheartedness like horses galloping carefree. It requires endurance of another kind: learning, thinking, positioning, planning and following up.

This means that I should be efficient during daytime, handling critical business operations, and persistent in the evening, buried in books and pens.

Ever since I took the position of the Deputy General Manager of the Wuhan Department Store in 1988, I have made a point to read for at least one and a half hours everyday, however busy or tired I am. I see it as "re-charging." My husband said there were three sounds in our home deep into the night: chairs creaking, pages turning, and the clock ticking. He is humorous from time to time. In my opinion, however, the sound of the clock ticking is no humor. Whenever I pass the clock counting down to Year 2000 at the foot of the Tortoise Hill, the constant changes in seconds always shake my soul. I feel as if it were telling me: That is the time left for you. Are you ready for the new century? You should always keep the next round of competition in sight. It is a nerve-racking reminder that time determines life or death, victory or defeat. I was aware of it when I was in the Chinese Department of the Dianshi University. I understood that before Christ, the Yellow River civilization had developed in pace with the ancient Greek civilization; during the Qin and Han Dynasties (around 200 AD), the Chinese civilization was more advanced than the European civilization; even in the Ming Dynasty, China outpaced England in capitalist development. We fell behind later on because we didn't seize the chance. We became late-comers.

I am part of my own people. For our under-development, we all should feel the acute pain, like a knife cutting through the skin, and we should try to catch up day and night.

We should never leave behind painful historical records again, because —

"Moscow doesn't believe in tears."[2]

But once I nearly burst into tears when my daughter disappeared behind the window of a Boeing jetliner. She was leaving to study in the U.S., an unfamiliar land on the other side of the ocean with different time zones. Their night is our day time.

At that moment, a sense of regret surged through me. I was too busy. I had always wanted to watch TV with my husband, visit my parents in the hospital, and stroll around the streets with my daughter. But I had to ask them to forgive me for not showing enough affection. I had only 24 hours a day.

I was choked with sobs, and let my daughter fly away. I had to overcome a mother's reluctance and sorrow at the moment of departure.

I wouldn't let my affection get in her way. She had to understand her mission for studying in the U.S. — to obtain the "passport" for the Chinese people to become world citizens in the next century. It is believed that global integration will take place then, with all the human beings living in a "global village." Americans moved fast, many of whom have already become world citizens. So did many of the Japanese and the Korean. Take the world renowned LG Group for example. Its birthplace was South Korean, headquartered in Seoul. But its business reaches out to the entire world, its staff shuttling on international airliners. If they can succeed, why can't the Chinese? Every year, selection is made of the 500 top enterprises in the world. We should have a place in it. We should compete in the world.

It is time to toss out the old saying "Children mustn't leave home while their parents are still alive." Keeping children around would only spoil them; true love for them would mean encouraging them to contribute to the country.

We are quite some distance behind the developed countries. A large number of professionals are needed to fill in the gap.

Knowing the world is a required course for us, a process of "understanding your rivals." We took the course in the past few years as we went abroad on fact-finding trips, searched through foreign reference materials, browsed the Internet, looked for the point of intersection with the world and created the Wuhan Plaza model.

I looked up to gaze after the Boeing airliner, which sewed up the clouds like a silvery needle and flew away, leaving behind a stream of lingering thoughts.

It really feels good to fly by plane. Yue Xiaodong, Professor of Psychology at the Hong Kong City University, wrote a book named *Feeling of Ascending into the Sky*.

I was visiting Hong Kong on business when I ran into Yue Xiaodong by accident. After reading his book on psychology, I had often felt the desire to ask him questions on psychology.

What stimulated this desire was a past event, which happened when I was working in the countryside of Xiangyang after graduating from high school. One day, I was told that the human race had launched a spaceship to the moon and astronauts had taken a few steps on it. I looked around for newspapers to learn more details. Unfortunately, there wasn't any in our small mountain village.

That night, there was no peace with me any more. What a difference between landing on the moon and fixing the Earth![3] What did the Earth look like as seen from the moon? A pale china dish, or a fresh orange?

It turns out from satellite photographs that the Earth is neither a china dish nor a fresh orange. It is a light-blue pellet, wrapped in white vapor. Our huge earth is but a tiny particle in space. "Huge" and "tiny" are relative, though. The boundless space should not intimidate us into inaction on the tiny Earth, and the small size of the Earth should not keep us from searching for the infinite.

In this view, landing on the moon is as meaningful as fixing the Earth. We shouldn't worry about our own insignificance; what is disturbing is lack of lofty aspirations. We should not overlook the details in the search for the big picture. Our job is to strike a balance between the micro and the macro, and find our position in the society.

Positioning is critical. It will determine the coordinates of our life and the orbit of our movement. It is the starting point of all our endeavors.

We must fully appreciate the importance of positioning at this particular point, because history, the horizontal axis for our positioning, is developing ten times faster, whereas our society, the vertical axis, is expanding at the same speed, too.

Any mistakes or delays would result in consequences ten times as serious.

Our only hope lies in our willingness to take on any risks for our cause, with a positive attitude, the courage to challenge, and the sensitivity which can perceive the slightest sign of momentum.

(Endnotes)

[1] "Chief" is the common title that Chinese use to address general managers.

[2] This is the title of a Russian movie popular in China.

[3] It is a black-humor phrase referring to farm work.

1

Call of the Shopping Plaza

Past is history;
Future brings the promise.
— Author

1. I Yearned for a Change That Year

A day in the office began with cleaning up and fetching hot water.

Here, everything followed a certain order, step by step, calm and uneventful. Even workers walked around on their tiptoe.

Familiar things and routines were nice to have: they led you cruising comfortably down a destined track. No worries, no risks.

If this track represented the "regular moves," what, then, were the "variations?"

I remembered my grandfather once explained "variations" to me. I was too young to truly understand it then. All I could recall was that he enjoyed playing *weiqi*[1] and often lost himself in the fierce battle between the black and white *weiqi* pieces. Thread-bound *weiqi* manuals were his favorite. He took the game seriously: each time he won a game, he would elaborate on *weiqi* tactics. He would even gesture to me, then a young kid, saying, "You think I win by the manuals? No way! I count on my variations."

At that time, I took "variations" to mean "swift adaptation to the ever-changing circumstances." It was hard to tell whether this was good advice or not. Looking back on it, I realize that making variations is actually more difficult than solving riddles. The timing of change is determined by the overall consideration. The overall consideration grows out of insight – a combination of perception, judgement, courage and adventurous spirit. Also contributing to it are one's intelligence, education and personal quality. People generally avoid talking about changes, because to change involves enormous efforts. Planning to change when all is unclear poses an even greater challenge.

But there come things that force one to think about change, such as the events in China in 1988. That was a subtle time, when the Reform pushed from the countryside to the cities. There was news that Nian Guangjiu, who had made a fortune by selling Fool's Melon Seeds, was arrested, accused of profiteering and capitalist business practice. I checked him out in newspapers and magazines, and found that he was like a weather balloon, signaling changes of the political wind with his ups and downs.

On the other hand, I also sensed that people were becoming very impatient. They couldn't wait anymore. Migrant workers from the rural areas took the lead. Wave after wave, they stormed the cities, even bringing along their own bedding rolls. They streamed into railway stations and packed in trains like sardines on their way to find jobs in Southern China. Against the human torrents, goods made in the South surged northward and swept the backcountry. This head-on clash of human torrents and commodity flow stirred up a huge commotion. The railway system sounded alarms under the pressure. The media cried out loudly. The whole nation was thrown in shock, everyone feeling unsettled and listless. Despite all the outcries and interventions, the turbulence grew more and more violent, gushing on with unprecedented fervor and power.

I was shocked: What was going on all around?

My knowledge in political economics advised me that great changes would result from a large-scale commotion in the society.

Then I wondered: What would be the impact?

From my experience of nation-wide travel and then work in the countryside during the "Cultural Revolution,"[2] I could predict that the calm over China's dead water would be shattered, and that everyone would be thrown into this turbulence, willingly or not.

To plan for changes in advance? The variations?

This question haunted me.

Honestly, I didn't have to change. I had a nice position, working as a section chief in the Organization Division of the Communist Party's Commerce Committee in Wuhan, capital of Hubei Province.

What is the function of the Organization Division? It is the Party unit to administer Party officials, which meant that I was guaranteed a bright future.

I could continue along this track, because I had good qualifications. In 1968, I was sent to do farm work in the countryside of Xiangyang. In 1970 I started to work in a factory there. In 1975, I was re-assigned to a hospital in Wuhan and soon began to attend a two-year study program at the Medical College of the Concorde Hospital at my own expense. Several months after my daughter was born in 1978, I started to attend the Hubei Dianshi University and was one of the top students. Later, I was elected to Deputy Director of the hospital by a unanimous vote from all the 44 middle-level managers, to take charge of finance, logistics and plant construction. I did a good job, joining in the Chinese Communist Party in 1980, soon promoted to a section chief position in the Organization Department of the Party's Commerce Committee. The section chief was only a step away from the Division Director position. Should I go on, promotion to that position was within reach.

But promotion was my least concern then. It was nothing in light of the great events in China.

The choice I had to make should have a big impact on my life. Becoming a certain director appeared so trivial.

China had come to crossroads. The whole country was changing. Should I change, too?

I yearned for change. However, before the dust settled, I had to watch my steps.

I must consider how long the push for change would last and how strong it would turn out to be.

It was hard to predict. After all, I was just one among the grassroots masses.

For a time, all sorts of thoughts and ideas swirled in and out of my mind. Sometimes they were just a book or a line. More often, they were heavy memories.

Hometown lanes in the rain in Southern Jiangsu Province, the narrow path in the countryside of Xiangyang, and the noisy workshop in the factory — all these flashed by in vivid pictures.

The countryside of Xiangyang where I had worked[3] appeared in a gray picture. A few scattered clay huts squatted around the fields, like old women who had not washed their face for days. Women in their 30s looked like grannies, and men couldn't hold their waist straight before they reached 40, all battered by hard life. They would fight over pennies, on the winding and muddy road after the rain.

The road ended at the air compressor factory, and the scene changed to the workshop where glasses were blackened by soot. Dust-covered workers were busy at the grinders, and sparks flew up with dust in a bright shower. At dining time, long queues filled the dining hall. People were hungry for food and craved for meat, just like me when I was in the countryside.

In the village that I had been sent to, the best food was noodles mixed with sesame leaves.

No books, no entertainment. Under the stars, I could only play some lonely tunes on my *pipa*[4] on the threshing ground.

I wanted very much to visit my parents in Wuhan. But I seldom made the trip. Short of money, I had to save every penny.

Memories of sorrow, of backwardness, of poverty — they overwhelmed me. Past memories flashed by one after another, like movie montage. I gave out a loud cry – this had to change!

Change or perish.

This might well be the cause of the fanatic torrents of the rural workers, and the ultimate driving force for reform.

With this driving force, the power and life span of the Reform were beyond any doubt.

I decided to embrace the variations, and to expand myself in the looming storm.

2. Break away from Mediocrity

One more day in the office started, with cleaning up and fetching hot water.

But when I walked in, my colleagues said that I had brightened up, in high spirits. They asked whether I had any good news to share.

Not really. I didn't have any good news to share. I looked inspired because an important statement was about to burst out from me. It made me excited and miserable at the same time, since I was attempting to hold it back for the moment.

I had read another wonderful book the night before.

The book was about the American entrepreneur Harmer. The most interesting part was his journey to the Soviet Union after the October Revolution in 1917. At that time, factories in the Soviet Union were closed down, fields were strewn with bodies of those who died of starvation, and rebellion was spreading like wild fire. He was the first Western entrepreneur to visit the Soviet Union. He told Lenin during a meeting that he wanted to invest in the Soviet Union. Lenin said there would be risks. He smiled lightly: risks went hand in hand with opportunities.

Harmer made a big fortune in the Soviet Union. What mattered was not the fortune he made, but his unique insight, which enabled him to see the tremendous economic opportunities in difficult times. While I was reading the book, it struck me that we had a similar situation. The thread of thought became crystal clear: backwardness would lead to large-scale economic development, which in turn would call for tens of thousands of business professionals. This was the opportunity.

Suddenly I couldn't sit back any more. I stood up and threw the windows open. My husband heard it and asked what I was up to. I said, "Would you support me if I decide to start all over again?" He was a little shocked, with his eyes wide open. After that he mumbled, "It's up to you. I'm on your side whatever you do."

My husband knew that I wouldn't settle for a mediocre life.

Indeed I can't tolerate a mediocre life. I admire Japanese cherry blossoms. It is said that cherry blossoms are most spectacular in the Japanese city of Nara: when they are in full bloom, they decorate the landscape in rows and patches, like bright red mists. Then the whole city will turn out to marvel at the spectacular view. The Japanese admire cherry blossoms for their aspiration, not just for their looks. These flowers show up in full glory and retreat in splendor, expressing a powerful urge for accomplishment. I thought that grass went through but one spring, and man had but one life. Humans should feel the urge for glory and accomplishment, too.

This desire for glory and accomplishment might have come down from my family, in other words, from my upbringing. My ancestors lived in Anhui Province and later on moved to Jiaxing in Zhejiang Province. Both were fertile lands which produced great talents. My great grandfather gave the family motto of "Books are personal treasure, and scholars are most distinguished guests at the dining table." My maternal grandfather was a scholar of great learning. I still clearly remember the huge antique-looking bookcases in his room, loaded with awesome volumes. Once I thumbed through some of them without asking for permission and got slapped in my hand. In his last years, he acted upon Cao Cao's[5] lines, as "an old steel resting in the stable, still aspiring to gallop a thousand miles; the ambition of a hero in his old age still as strong as ever." He served on the Political Consultative Committee in Nantong, Jiangsu Province. At the age of 76, he started on the math book *Simplified Calculation of Multi-Digit Multiplication and Division on Abacus*. But he passed away before finishing it.

I was brought up in the home of my maternal grandparents. They had six daughters and one son, most with some accomplishments. One became a university professor. Others were head-nurse, teacher or school physician. My uncle Wang Ji is a well-known translator. The O. Henry short novel anthology that he translated, *The Cop and the Anthem,* has been very popular among the Chinese readers.

My father was mistreated by fate but remained strong. To me, he always appeared overpowering, profound and dignified, like a mountain. These qualities may have grown out of setbacks in his life. He was a man with great learning and should have gained some prominence. Unfortunately, he joined the military during the Anti-Japanese War, serving as a driver on the Yunnan-Burma front for the nationalist government. Because of this "historical blemish,"[6] he was never given the opportunity to bring out his full potential. In spite of the difficulties and hardships, he never gave up hope. He learned English and Russian by himself, to the level that he could substitute for teachers in schools. He ranked among the best during a test for accountants from all the commercial organizations in Wuhan.

One day, back from his work, he sat by a window in the slanting sun, exhausted, saying to me slowly, "The most dreadful thing is not poverty, but mediocrity, like stopping after a little gain, or giving in to one's own fate. Don't feel bloated for becoming a petty official."

I thought, what could I hope for except for being a petty official?

At that time, the topic of "downsizing" had surfaced in the Reform. The government was looking for ways to cut down on its structure. The army was considering how to reduce its size. The media were debating whether to eliminate redundant staff in enterprises. Among all these rapid developments, "going down" became the buzzword.

I was excited, knowing that "down" was the way to go.

Frankly speaking, a life in dead water was not my dream. It would be too boring.

My uncle once wrote me a line, "Too confident to be submissive; too proud to take pity from others." Even when I was a child, I would give up anything in order to come out on top. I competed with boys as well as girls. I played all the boy games, such as the football, cards and marbles. Later on, when people began to see me as a boy, I revolted again. I washed three basins of clothes a day, and forced myself to sit down and tried my hands on the *pipa*. I also learned embroidery, designing very attractive patterns.

At school, I competed in sports as well as in academics. I was picked by the school team for my skills with the basketball. I never gave up. When the Xiangyang Air Compressor Factory recruited workers, I was rejected the first time. I found my way to the factory.

I told them that I was a good basketball player and they could use my talents in sports. This turned them around. I had no fear for difficulties, either. The leftist policies before the Reform made it very difficult for me to get anywhere, because I was born to a family with "historical blemishes." I said to myself: OK, there would be light at the end of the tunnel, no matter how winding the tunnel was. I would work my way through. I would triple my efforts. I joined the Communist Party at last and even found a job in the Organization Division. I took things seriously. To graduate from the Dianshi University, I wrote a bold thesis, after burning the midnight oil day after day, titled "Taking Social Origin into Consideration But Not Subscribing to It." It was published on the internal edition of the *Liberation Daily* at the recommendation of Chen Xiucheng, former Deputy Editor-in-Chief of the *Yangtze Daily*. I enjoy singing, dancing, playing the bowling and tennis. People gossip that I am over-active, and so cannot stay on the same job day after day.

Well, I am not over-active — I often feel exhausted. But I hate to waste myself in a mediocre life.

I had read *The Red Rock*[7] and *How Steel IS Made*.[8] I remembered Osterovski's famous remark, "How should we spend our life? We should not end up feeling ashamed because we wasted it, or regretting for having achieved nothing."

I told Liu Haisheng, Director of the Organization Division, that I wanted to talk to him.

He was a man of principle, yet warm-hearted and considerate. He agreed to the talk promptly.

I went into his office. The door shut behind me. Suddenly I realized that I could not back out now.

I smiled. It felt wonderful, the determination of not turning back. It would mobilize every cell in my body, which would finally expose and elevate my true self.

I was not nervous, and reported my thoughts without any disguise or exaggeration. I recall presenting the following reasons for going down to the grassroots units: first, I talked about a shameful case that had been haunting me, which happened during the historical event called "Counter the Right Wing's Attempt to Reverse the

Ruling."[9] At the time, out of my love for the Party and my enthusiasm for work, I spent days and nights organizing the hospital staff to put up wall posters criticizing Deng Xiaoping and to prepare shows for the "counterattack." I sincerely believed that it was good for the nation. As time went by, it turned out to be a fiasco, much to my surprise and dismay. Before long, with his critical role in the Reform, Deng Xiaoping fully proved how ridiculous we were. A feeling of being fooled had been haunting me ever since. I decided that I would do some solid work instead of getting wasted in shadow boxing games.

Another motivation for me to quit came from the on-going nationwide discussion on establishing a system which would give managers and directors the rights and responsibilities to manage their organizations. I sensed that this discussion alone was an indication that changes in the economic system were getting more and more substantial. Now that the whole nation was going to focus on economic development, which in turn called for hands-on exploration and responsibility taking, why not go down? Was I going to wait till rounds after rounds of conclusions were made, till gray strands crept into my hair, and then to spend the rest of my life in regret?

The talk was more relaxed than I had imagined, although the topic was serious and somewhat strange — at that time, few people would volunteer to go down to the grassroots.

When I went out of the office, I found the sky was clearer and bluer, as if it had been cleaned with water; high and profound, giving out the sense of the sea and the charm of a poem.

3. A Golden Law

I read about the sea in poems by Pushkin and Lemontov, on its crystal blue and its splashing waves. I have always loved the beautiful Russian literature. Whenever I read its descriptions of the sea, I always have the impulse to drink a handful. Sea is a free element, representing immensity. Soon after I "plunged into the sea,"[10] however, I discovered that chanting poems about the sea was totally different from plunging into it. It did not bring any imagined poetic flavor.

When I informed my relatives and friends of my decision to go down to grassroots units from the Organization Division of the Party's Commerce Committee, I found myself heading into a storm.

First, an uncle made a call from Shanghai, asking in surprise, "Do you really want to become a business woman?"

I had great respect for my uncle from my childhood, because he was one of the few senior tax experts in Shanghai, a person of excellent character and great learning. His opinions had never been taken lightly in my family. He did not seem to be pleased with my choice.

His question sounded as if I had done something very outrageous, disgraceful to the family and to the ancestors.

I knew I had let the ghost out of the bottle: I was going against an attitude.

This ghost was the popular prejudice against businessmen. China basically remained as an agricultural society. For thousands of years, agriculture was prioritized over commerce. The common belief was that businessmen had nothing on their mind but profit-making, that they were snobbish and mean, stinky with the smell of copper coins. After Liberation,[11] social classes were listed as "workers, farmers, soldiers, students and businessmen," with businessmen hanging at the bottom. It was under such circumstances that I talked about business, and even gave up my Party official position for it. This could only bring about an outcry.

When I tried to explain my point of view, skepticism came from another direction: "It's nice and comfortable to hold a Party position, with a bright future. Common wisdom says it is better to stay than to move. Why bother to change?" There were also gossips: Hu Bingxin had to move because she had lost favor with her boss. She just couldn't stay on.

I was dumbfounded.

A person's choosing a different way of life would suggest that she could not carry on in her old position?

I saw that I was running against the "popular wisdom," a combination of conservatism and "petty citizen"[12] mentality. It did not stop there, though. More vicious remarks drifted in: Hu Bingxin wanted to take up business because she was the least favored among the three section chiefs in the fight for the Division Director's position when the Director retired. She knew it all along, and so adopted the tactics of retreat in order to advance.

I felt the urge to clear my name. But then I thought better. Why waste my time on rumors and slander?

I believed in this motto: stick to your own path, whatever others might say.

I tried to reason against the popular wisdom. I discovered that I was not only on the right track, but fairly forward-thinking as well. As far as I could tell, all the modern social structures favored a small government supported by a large economy. In the U.S., a municipal government only administered city planning with a few dozen workers. In contrast, many companies were multi-regional and even multinational. Our tomorrow probably would resemble their today. We had been dragging our feet for a long time with the burden of overstaffed organizations. Logically, the next step would be downsizing, driving most of the staff down to the grassroots units.

Better to go down sooner than later – I justified my decision. With this justification, I buried myself in books, all sorts of books. My favorite one was *Think and Grow Rich* written by Napoleon Hill, a student of Carnegie. His theory was regarded as philosophy of economics, a theory different from that of Socrates, Plato and other western philosophers.

The book pointed out ways not only for people to rise above poverty, but also to build a perfect character and rich life. The theory grew out of his visits to 500 celebrities. It could be summarized into 17 rules. At the core was a formula: success = correct thinking + conviction + action. "I must have a conviction; I must stick to my conviction," I thought while reading it.

Further reading brought me to what Napoleon Hill called correct thinking, a golden law named PMA, i.e., a positive attitude.

It went like this: "Today, I am going to compete with others; today, I am going to compete with myself; today, I am going to do more work; today, I am going to break the record of yesterday."

I took it as my motto and wrote it down in my notebook. I understood its teaching as willingness to meet challenges.

Suddenly, I realized that to spin a cocoon around oneself was the worst thing in stormy times. The most terrifying confinement in the world was the closure of one's mind.

With my mind at ease, I started on things that I should do.

After I adjusted my attitude, the world opened up before me. This adjustment was also made possible with the help of Liu Haisheng, Director of the Organization Division of the Commerce Committee and Mr. Kai, Director of the Organization Division of the Party's Municipal Committee. When one feels lonely, kindness from others is especially appreciated and remembered. I can still recall the talk with Jiang Hongqi, Director of the Municipal Foreign Trade Committee, right in his office.

Mr. Jiang was a scholarly leader, having written a play called *The Dear Ones*. As a scholarly official, he often had unique perspectives. He was open-minded, active and sharp in perception.

I entered his office. He didn't say anything when he saw me; he only smiled. That smile was like warm sunshine.

Soon he started talking, not on anything specific. Instead, the topics spanned thousands of years and thousands of miles, showing his great eloquence.

Suddenly, he changed the topic to me: "I was told that you wanted to go down and work in business. That's a great idea! The superstructure is like hair, and the economical basis is like skin. If there is no skin, where can hair attach? So the skin should be our focus." With this theorizing, he gave his approval to my decision.

Then he put forward a suggestion. Businesses in foreign trade were short of management people, especially those willing to explore and pioneer. He asked whether I would like to go.

This took me by surprise. I wasn't prepared for it.

But it opened my eyes. I felt the need to narrow down on my choices. I also discovered that not everyone was against my decision!

4. Starry Sky and Lamplight

Success = Correct thinking + Conviction + Action

With conviction, my initial idea to go down to grassroots pulled through the hardest period and gradually materialized into action.

I had several choices. Few people in government organizations would go down on their own at the time. There were plenty of opportunities to choose from, unlike the situation today.

Since then, the administrative structure has been compacted time and again, and the staff reduced accordingly. Many are crying out in panic, "No more good positions left! I would have gone down had I known better."

Their panic proved that my choice was correct. To be fair, it was not easy to go down. Take the businesses under my consideration for example. They were all generating profits. They all possessed well-known brands. But what would be a real good business for me? I believed that "good" could only be relative. "Good" meant "the right one."

I was searching for space to maneuver in, a big stage to play on.

Hopefully, in this space, my individual development could keep up with the development of the society.

I turned it over and over in my mind: "Where's my position?"

A line in Tagore's poem gives a perfect description of my mental state then. He lamented that there were stars in the sky, but the lamp in his room was not yet lit. The image of lamplight actually brings my thoughts to a pair of headlights. It is proof what a prudent move I had made. It happened on a rainy night a couple of days ago.

I went out of the Wuhan Plaza and took a taxi.

Wipers were sweeping back and forth on the windshield. In the headlight, the street was littered with fallen leaves. The fall season was taking its toll.

Under the faint light inside the taxi, I could see the driver was a handsome man in his 40s. I started to chat with him.

He was not the owner of the taxi. He didn't have the money to buy one. So he rented it from the owner.

After graduating from a vocational school, he had been assigned to Wuhan Oriental Bed Sheet Factory and worked as an assistant engineer there for more than 10 years. He had his own plans and ambitions all along, but never put his thoughts to action, for fear of leaving the familiar way of life. Now he was so regretful! The factory closed down, putting the workers out of work, when he had just passed his prime age. He tried to find another job, but was told that he was too old.

"Wash and sleep at 40; go to the neighborhood committee[13] at 50," he quoted a popular doggerel, smiling bitterly while shaking his head. His voice sounded husky.

From his bitter smile came another revelation to me: whenever the society moved a step forward, it would leave behind muddy footsteps and casualties.

To avoid falling down as casualty, precautions and, more importantly, actions had to be taken. Life sometimes was determined by just a few steps, taken at crucial moments.

Life was no dancing. One couldn't backtrack. To take the crucial steps, one must be brave, and, in the meantime, be cautious.

Cautious I was. Now that the desired position looked more like the result of chance than of targeted search, I decided to reach out and look for more opportunities. Talking about opportunities, my heart warms up when I recall a person. I got to know him several years ago but at first it was just a nodding acquaintance. More exchange began at the Municipal Commerce Committee HR Reform Seminar held by the Municipal Commercial Committee's Organization Division at Puqi in 1987.

Leaders of the Commerce Committee and managers of the major enterprises took part in the seminar. I presented my thesis on a system to give managers and directors their rights and responsibilities for management.

My presentation ended with a loud applause. It left a deep impression on one of the participants.

This gentleman wore a pair of glasses, with a square chin and full forehead. I had read his personnel file. After Liberation, he was Secretary of the Youth League[14] Committee at the Commerce Bureau. In 1957, he was labeled a "Rightist" because he sided with Ma

Yinchu's[15] theory on population growth. In 1959, he was banished to the Friendship Department Store (which later on was renamed Wuhan Department Store) as a laborer. During the Reform, he was appointed as the General Manager of the Wuhan Department Store, and was once cited as National Model Worker on the Commerce Front.

While I read his file, he struck me as talented (he served as Secretary of the Youth League Committee when he was very young), independent-minded (he dared to side with Ma's theory), tenacious (he made a comeback after pulling through all the hardships), and capable (the Wuhan Department Store was sailing full steam ahead under his leadership).

This man was Mao Dongsheng. We didn't talk during the seminar. That night, the meeting room was changed into a ball room, where we met. He did not have a partner and so invited me to join him for a dance. I told him I didn't dance. He promised to teach me. We only danced for a while before feeling well acquainted.

This acquaintance brought him to my mind when I searched for opportunities.

Coincidentally, the Municipal Commerce Committee called a meeting to plan for the work for the second half of 1988. Managers of various enterprises got together once more. I met him again.

I went to him directly during recess since we already knew each other.

I said, "Chief Mao, I heard that the Commerce Committee is putting together a company for foreign trade. I plan to go. What's your suggestion?"

"Why do you want to go there? Come to my company and give me a hand." In my memory, that was the way he put it.

His answer was crisp, with an authoritative tone. Only people with authority could speak in such a confident, undisguised manner.

"I'm serious," I said.

"Me too" was his reply.

Coming home from the meeting, I told my husband about the encounter. I said that my sixth sense told me that the Wuhan Department Store had a huge potential, a big stage that I had been long looking for.

It was the largest shopping center in Wuhan, with the latest facilities and concepts, and the highest sales revenue and profit. Most importantly, it was a pioneer in the reform of Wuhan's commerce system, exploring business diversification on a large scale and experimenting on stock options.

This meant that it was keeping up with the overall development of the times, full of vigor and capable of growth. If I committed myself to it, I could possibly bring my dream to reality.

My husband smiled at me, saying, "Let's turn the dream into reality."

After obtaining the support of my husband, I went to Chief Mao's home after dinner a few days later. His home was close by.

Once seated, I cut to the point right away, saying, "Chief Mao, I would like to get your confirmation. Did you mean what you said the other day?"

"Of course," he confirmed.

"But I don't have the slightest clue to the business." I thought I must be open about it.

He waved his hand and said, "Don't worry. It's easy to learn, as long as you work hard."

I smiled. I was hard-working. Then we took up the next topic.

"If I can come," I said, "I would like to work on management. I was in general admin and finance. Now I want to do the real thing."

He paused for a while and then patted on the desk, "All right."

This closed the deal, which again revealed his fascinating authority.

Because of this, I thought I should no longer hesitate.

I should seize the opportunity. I told myself that around a man like this, my career could well take off.

With this goal in mind, I became the last of the six deputy general managers of the Wuhan Department Store.

5. "Come on. Give Me a Hand!"

For my career, I chose to follow Mao Dongsheng, General Manager of the Wuhan Department Store.

The next day, I went to the Wuhan Department Store as a customer. I strolled around, browsing through the commodities on display, from the perspective of a picky customer as well as of a sharp observer. I exhausted myself in the end – never in my life had I spent so much time strolling in a shopping center.

I discovered for the first time that the Wuhan Department Store, which I had thought I knew well, was smaller than I had imagined. Its tall building appeared somewhat worn-out, and its light-blue ceramic tiles looked tarnished. Although still live with ambitions, it had entered its middle age, or even old age. It looked dwarfed amid the jostling crowds in the streets. From another perspective, it was bigger than I had imagined. It was accommodating so many customers and so many commodities. How much brain power would it take to remember all these items and know their routes of circulation?

I couldn't help recalling Chief Mao's wish, "Come on. Give me a hand!" I asked myself, how could I help him? I didn't know anything about business, which the store was all about.

I could therefore appreciate his perception of me, feeling thankful for his decision. Honestly, he was running a risk in making the decision.

But I was equally sure that he was not going to pay any price for it.

I soon plunged into action. I sent in a request for transfer. Liu Haisheng and Zhang Huixiang, Director and Deputy Director of the Organization Division of the Commerce Committee, went to the Wuhan Department Store twice to arrange for the transfer. My colleagues made fun of me, "Go and get some candies, Bingxin. We will marry you off." On the day of my departure, I really looked like their daughter being married off, with my colleagues displaying my "Deputy General Manager, Operations" appointment letter on a poster, and sending me off in a car.

Outside the department store, Chief Mao welcomed me in person.

I was deeply moved by the sending-off and welcome. But as soon as I entered the Wuhan Department Store, I felt I had lost something.

What was it? I searched in the bottom of my heart, to find that it was peace of mind.

Leaders of the Commerce Committee had coached me in person, step by step, for so many years. Now that I had left them, I felt I was deeply indebted.

When Chief Mao showed me around all the departments, the sense of loss built up: I would need a lot of coaching from him, too.

It seemed that Chief Mao went out of his way to make me feel at home. With a smile on his face, he introduced me, his new Deputy General Manager, to everyone we met.

I felt very grateful to him. In turn, I greeted all the staff that we met with modesty. In fact, I couldn't have done otherwise. When I came back from the various departments, I found myself quite uneasy. No sound in the office, no sound from my desk. Only the voices of the customers and sales staff poured in, mingled with nonstop telephone rings. I couldn't answer phone calls, because I wouldn't know who was calling or what they wanted. I wouldn't know what was going on. I could only ask for help. Out there in the business area, counters, shelves and sections were all confusing and mind-boggling. They reminded me of the mountain peaks in a poem describing Mount Lu, which changed shapes and size depending on the viewer's location in the mountain.

At that moment, I felt that there was still the issue of positioning.

I had to find my place. This was the first thing to do in my new job.

I brightened up, and sat back to analyze the Wuhan Department Store. It was first built in 1959 under the name of Friendship Department Store. In 1983, it expanded to a large-scale shopping center. As in all old enterprises, there was a mixture of old and young in the staff. This age gap was reflected in the gap in management.

I was neither old nor young. In my middle age, I could fill this gap.

Mao's "Come and give me a hand" was probably a wish for complement and interaction, in age, seniority and style (due to gender differences), and in transition from past to future.

I was looking for a place to bring out the best in me; he wished to build a team to maintain the momentum: there was also an interaction between the two of us.

Interaction was only desirable. This was the professional relationship we must establish.

Based on this consideration, I gladly accepted Mao's assignment - managing the General Merchandise Department.

General merchandise was the most stable business in the department store. By this assignment, he minimized the risk to the whole store, while allowing me time to try my hands on the business, a period for me to warm up.

Call from the department store. My career in business set off in a low profile. I preferred the low profile because it was in accordance with the cognition theory. To be a teacher, I should first of all be a student.

There was nothing shameful about starting low. Some foreign millionaires chose to have their children start as blue-collar workers. In ancient China, generals were selected from among the soldiers. Low profiles could lead to high profiles. Yet, being a student, or a blue-collar worker, or a soldier, was not a pleasant experience.

Up till the late 1980s, Chinese businesses did not have any idea on workforce diversification. For dozens of years, people would work in a business till retirement. And their sons would take over. Then the grandsons. The only choice was to stay in the same place, day in and day out, year in and year out, till getting promoted. In the General Merchandise Department, there were people who wanted to get promoted, and those who might eventually be promoted. Suddenly, here I came, an outsider blocking their career path. Do I need to describe their feelings?

On this issue, I could only sincerely wish for their understanding. If my arrival impacted their career, it was not on purpose. In the meantime, I hoped that they could open up their mind. Outsiders hopping in would be the way to go. The system was changing, so should old concepts, which had formed in the old-fashioned businesses.

I was in my 30s, a woman's ripe season. I was tall, brisk-walking, and well-dressed. I considered proper dressing an absolute necessity, because it revealed the mental state. It also showed respect for people around.

I should say that people in the Zhejiang-Jiangsu area have a long tradition of decent dressing, in order to look in good spirits. They might live on pickled greens to go with their rice, but would never forget to press their folded trousers under the pillow at night, to have lines on the trouser legs when they appeared in public the next day. I don't see this behavior as a sign of vanity. Instead, I consider it a dress culture. They would see these lines as representing tangible orders, to guide themselves, so as to elevate to some mental freedom. To clarify myself, I am elaborating on dressing here because I wish to be seen in the right light: I was decently dressed for mental freedom.

But it was difficult to feel free at first, for Chinese businesses at the time didn't have a system or function for training. For new hands and re-assignees from other positions alike, there was no one to offer systematic training. They had to ask around. Sometimes it turned out to be embarrassing. In addition, trade secrecy was still quite common.

I knew the reason for trade secrecy. It resulted from the shortage in merchandise in a planned economy. Under that system, whoever knew how to get commodities had the biggest clout. Channels and relations were the guarantee for jobs and decent positions. They were the life line.

Let's further trace the origin of trade secrecy. The circulation of merchandise never had a chance to fully develop in China. The existing commercial system was built from small shops and stores. As such, it was never free from the narrow-mindedness of small business and trade guild behavior.

The circulation system after Liberation contributed to the growth of trade secrecy. For more than 30 years, the commercial structure could be summarized as "first, second, third, zero," which referred to the first order wholesale, the second order wholesale, the third order wholesale and retail. The aim of the whole mechanism was to set up blockades. It was these blockades that produced privileges and power.

Having learned about all this, I still couldn't bring myself to a compromise. It was not the right way for managing a modern business.

What I found unacceptable did not stop there. There was the more elusive attitudes of indifference, contempt and gloating towards me. Some gossiped, "Hu Bingxin has a big mouth, but the department store is not a forum. I bet she will pack up and leave in half a year."

I felt upset, but I didn't want to tell Mao about it. He was too busy.

Moreover, I was still an outsider to business operations. I was the root cause of the problem.

I was fully aware that the general attitude towards me was more challenging than welcoming. To convince the challengers, I had to challenge myself, my self respect, my knowledge and my energy, before I could finally rise above them.

In order to rise above the challengers, I probably had to hold back for some time. In other words, I must learn to lie low.

All the challenges were backed by some forces, so I had to lie low.

All the challenges must be answered with my success. Only by lying low, could I concentrate on my achievements and convince people with them.

Lying low did not have to be negative. The old saying goes, "The Tao of both military and civil undertakings is tension alternating with relief." Napoleon said that he was sometimes a lion, sometimes a rabbit. The key to bringing out the positive side of low lying was study and improvement.

I had a strong personality. Meanwhile, I believed that real power did not come from words, but from the mind.

To build up my mind, I read all the books that I could get hold of on business management, marketing and sales, and business accounting, evening after evening, until the clock struck midnight.

In addition, I went to the counters and asked experienced sales assistants in private about the buying behavior of customers and the circulation of merchandise.

Chief Mao said, "It's easy to learn, as long as you work hard." I followed his advice to the word. Only I myself know how many vendors I visited, how many sales leads I followed up and how exhausted I was.

I found that I could talk on more and more issues, and that my words were carrying more and more weight.

The lady who predicted "I bet she will pack up and leave in half a year" gradually changed her attitude, too, to "she is getting somewhere," "she is pretty good" and "she beats me."

Public opinion was a good indicator. It proved that I was accepted after roughing it out.

Getting accepted was a good thing, although it sounded insignificant.

6. Hone up Sensitivity

Chief Mao sat intensely at the head of the conference table, listening to my work report.

The pens of other deputy general managers were passing over their notebooks, revealing a sense of concentration.

When I finished, Mao said, "Bingxin, you kept silent for half a year and then shocked the world with an amazing call."[16]

He meant that my report was quite convincing. I drew a deep breath. I knew at that moment that I had taken root in the Wuhan Department Store.

I had pulled through all the frustrations and hardship in the break-in period. I was feeling lost, though. Was taking roots good enough? What could I do to help Mao? I remembered my father once said, "Bingxin, even the Japanese businessmen are looking into *The Art of War* by Sunzi. When you have time, browse through it and learn the art of war."

"In military strategy, there are regular and irregular moves. Regular moves are a show of force, while irregular moves lead to victory." This part of the book struck me as an important strategic concept.

I scored 96 in the test for Classical Chinese Literature at the Dianshi University, and had no trouble understanding *The Art of War* by Sunzi. I read on and ran into "Good attackers hover in nine heavens; good defenders hide beneath nine grounds."

What were "nine heavens"? I knew it referred to the profoundness of the sky, but my thought was led away, by the image of the boundless sky.

I recalled watching the night sky on the flat roof with my mother when I was young.

My mother played a big role in my growth. If my father was like the mountain, she was like the sea. I felt my mother was a typical Chinese. She was born into a big family in Nantong, in the "water country" in Southern Jiangsu. My grandfather was a scholar, and as such, believed in education. His seven children all received good education. My mother studied in the Shanghai Nurse School after middle school, and then chose nursing as her career. For all her life, she modeled on Nightingale in caring for her patients.

In the difficult days of the Cultural Revolution, she never blamed my father for our hard times. She took care of all the household chores, and struggled to bring up her three children. Her care went to such details that we never had to wear clothes with patches on them. This accounted for our habit of decent dressing. Her care was mixed with education, for example, telling stories about stars when we watched them in the summer night.

I remembered her looking up into the sky, saying in a poetic tone, "Stars look all mixed up, but each has its own name and position."

"How can we locate them?" I asked.

"Put the sky into a grid in your mind; then you can locate stars in the grid."

"Why do I need a grid?" I asked.

She was amused by my answer, and patted me gently, "for positioning."

I didn't understand the weird concept of "positioning" at the time. But now I was alerted, thinking of the starry sky while reading *The Art of War* by Sunzi.

Suddenly I realized that I was so tied down to daily operations that I forgot the most pressing issue: positioning.

As a general manager, closing in and zooming out were equally necessary. Getting buried in the specifics all the time would get me nowhere.

Digging into the specifics was necessary at a certain point of time. But doing this forever would blind me and lead to errors.

I must find out where my strength was.

I could only win by maximizing my strength and minimizing my weakness. My strength lay in my love for reading and the knowledge coming with it.

What is knowledge? It is the abstraction from numerous individual examples and the generalization from numerous experiences; therefore it can be a good guide in overall planning.

Knowledge offers an additional eye and an additional brain, so to speak. It broadens narrow personal experience and propagates individual learning.

It is information condensed, replacing slow individual accumulation with the entire treasure of human civilization.

Swiftness, the ability to generalize, the ability of comprehensive perception.

These were the qualities a general manager should be equipped with. I was going to bring them into full play.

I began to shift my mind into full gear in search of opportunities. In the first half year of 1989, I seized one that seemed to have little chance of success. We went to Guangzhou to take part in the annual trade show of the National Trade Association. At the newly opened corner on the third floor of the Nanfang Mansion, I found an Italian artificial jewelry counter from Hong Kong .

Although it was not a well-known brand then, its display counter presented a new world. It was a real eye opener for me.

"Introduce it!" I found myself saying. Suddenly I realized it was exactly the business opportunity I had been looking for.

Having locked up my target, I sprang to action.

I should say this operation was a combination of coincidence and mishap, a test of patience and will-power. I intended to introduce this brand, but the company's owner Mr. You De happened to have headed back to Hong Kong. I made a call to Hong Kong, only to find that he had flown to Australia. I called Australia and finally caught up with him.

He was pleasantly surprised. His products were on sale in Guangzhou only on a trial basis. His next move was Shanghai. He had been to Shanghai twice, and twice he had been turned down by a big department store. Later on he admitted that he was thinking of giving up on China. I persuaded him to come to Wuhan and give it a try. His artificial jewelry caught right on soon after it made its appearance, and set the record of RMB 80,000 in sales on a single day.

This successful case of honing my sensitivity cheered me up. Meanwhile, I felt I shouldn't stop there. Instead, I should follow up, to develop more cases. I was not talking about You De's brand. In fact, after our success, department stores all over China were competing for his business. It was storming the Chinese market in a big way. What I meant by "follow up" was this: Could we replicate its unique sales counter? Could we develop some kind of feature shopping?

This inspiration struck me like lighting. In case the idea would vanish, I took it to Chief Mao, as if I were holding the only key to a large fortune. Obviously I needed his support. Implementing the idea would call for extensive remodeling, or even temporary closedown of some sections. I was quite nervous when presenting my plan to him, for fear that he would reject it.

Well, he didn't. He just smiled. He had his own business sense, which enabled him to pin down opportunities. My plan was accepted and put in action.

I remember we began the project right away. Bringing their tools, the project team made their way into the shopping center to renovate the business areas. After the renovation, the new feature shopping sections became an immediate success. The Wuhan Department Store was the first to market feature shopping in Wuhan, and it sent a shock wave across the city.

Did I stop there? No, my imagination knew no limits. When the renovation for feature shopping was in full swing, I realized that I was devising some marketing plan. The idea of marketing plans was truly wonderful. It was high time to break away from the sales model based on experience only and manage business on rational thinking.

That year, we conducted featured sales promotions in front of the Wuhan Department Store. Traditional promotions started by putting up signs like "Woolen Sweater Autumn Show." This time everything was different. We had integrated planning, ad catchwords, artwork, a complete promotion plan and budget. Two 5-ton Dongfeng trucks were brought in and placed side by side, to form a stage in front of the building. Professional models gave an eye-opening fashion show. This type of promotion unprecedented in Wuhan's retail business sent another shock wave through the city. The promotion was a huge success, opening up new channels for sales.

I never stopped pushing on. Based on "planned marketing," I followed my thoughts. I asked myself, now that promotion could be planned, could I plan for featured products? With this idea, I visited both the Shashi Thermos Bottle Company and its joint-venture branch company in Shenzhen. I found that thermos bottles, which did not change much in the past 30 years, came in with dazzling designs in the joint-venture. I was convinced by the vitality of joint-venture companies, and decided to materialize it into concrete events: exhibits of featured products from China's joint-venture companies. We were the first in Wuhan to introduce the Hong Kong Product Show sponsored by the Trade Development Bureau of Hong Kong, and the Shishi Product Show, to improve the product structure of the Wuhan Department Store. We ran the exhibits for 3 successive years, formalizing the events into a system later on. From that system, I reflected on product rotation. With all the new products streaming in, there was no reason to keep the old ones.

This issue was so important that I zeroed in on it as soon as it sprang up. We were the first in Wuhan to implement commodity rotation. As a result, the Wuhan Department Store became known for the good quality and new designs of its commodities. Customers believed that there were always eye-openers at the Wuhan Department Store. Our business soared. It was probably at that time that Chief Mao believed that I had matured.

For the first time, he made the comments on me, "When Bingxin came over, she was like a piece of blank paper. What was regarded as right and proper, she dared to change."

These were highly positive comments. That year, I was promoted to the First Deputy General Manager from the sixth one. I answered the call from the department store. From then on, I was destined to make my way in the merchandise world, sharing its ups and downs, and its joys and sorrows.

(Endnotes)

[1] A Chinese board game.

[2] A movement from 1966 to 1976 launched by Mao Zedong to "purify" the ideology in China.

[3] After the Cultural Revolution, millions of high school graduates in Chinese cities and towns were sent to the countryside to be "re-educated by the peasants."

[4] A Chinese musical instrument like the mandolin.

[5] An ancient Chinese statesman and ruler known for his military and poetic talents.

[6] After the Communist Party took over the power, those who had served in the Nationalist army were considered politically unreliable.

[7] A Chinese novel describing the life in prison of some underground Communist Party workers arrested by the Nationalist government.

[8] A Soviet novel by Osterovski describing the life of a Soviet hero, very popular among the Chinese till about two decades ago.

[9] This refers to a political event in the 1970s, when Deng Xiaoping

was criticized for attempting to reverse the ruling on him by Mao Zedong as a "rightist."

[10] "Plug into the sea" is the popular metaphor for engaging in business activities.

[11] This is a common term describing the victory of the Communist Party in 1949.

[12] This is a Chinese term referring to uneducated and short-sighted urban inhabitants.

[13] The neighborhood committee is an organization for looking after the neighborhood, usually staffed by retired and elderly people.

[14] It refers to the Communist Youth League, an organization for young people affiliated with the Communist Party.

[15] A Chinese scholar who advocated population control, against Mao Zedong's belief in population growth.

[16] This comes from an ancient Chinese poem describing some birds as "stayed silent for 3 years and then shocked the world with their calls."

2

Seize the Opportunity

> The use of military force is the great-
> est matter of a state, a matter of life
> or death, survival or extinction. It
> has to be studied with absolute care.
> — Sunzi

1. Jump out of the Ring

The Wuhan Department Store had hardly built a foothold when a
violent storm rolled in from the distance. Starting out in the
information industry, the storm brewed in the 1980s, intensified in
the early 1990s, and then pounded the whole world with all its might.
It changed the manufacturing industry and the service industry, rapidly taking the human race into a service-oriented society. For the
first time in history, service workers in the U.S. outnumbered manufacturing workers, reaching 36 million, and accounting for 27% of
the total workforce. Japan and Europe followed up soon afterwards.
The explosion of the service industry touched off a violent competition. In this competition, the retail business, which is part of the
service industry, was thrown into a startling battle. In an effort to
grab market share, various business operations emerged, backed up
by sophisticated planning and fresh, appealing concepts. As the battle
intensified and territories shrank, methods such as consolidation,
integration, networking and cross-industry operation were employed

against each other. National boundaries were limits no more. The whole world was now a battle field, and internationalization the Tao to survive. The warring parties started to turn to foreign lands.

China was the best choice in this territory flagging campaign. Lufthansa and SciTech in Beijing, Yaohan and Sincere in Shanghai shot up in the frenzy. China met the challenge with its Reform. At the beginning of 1992, Deng Xiaoping went on an inspection tour to South China, further pushing for reform. The eastern breeze brought in the spring season. China's reform movement spread from the coastal areas to the Yangtze River valley. People were excited all over the country. New projects sprang up everywhere. Everyone was trying their hands on business. The media claimed "900 million out of 1 billion people are doing business" in a "business frenzy." The Chinese set their mind on business in the hope to get rich overnight, ignoring the expertise required. Rampaging across the land was the fervor for small-scale production grown out of the small-scale agriculture economy in the past thousands of years, as well as the mass psyche to follow the crowd.

Blindness and craziness were on the rise. No one ever considered the possible result of the internal fight and the fragmentation of customer base caused by too many suppliers. No one cared to investigate measures to meet international business challenges. In the messy battle, heroes from all camps were trying to fight to the top of the hill. Among this confusion, various economical entities set out to violently attack the traditional state-owned commerce. On another front, the traditional state-owned commerce was under attack from real estate companies, financial institutions and even businesses run by government agencies, with their abundant financial resources and connections. The traditional state-owned commerce was facing troubling times. Foreign businesses were closing in from outside, and competition was intensifying inside. How to jump out of the besieged city was the most pressing issue at the moment.

Mao proved to be a true entrepreneur at the critical moment. He calmly planned the next moves. He smoked more and looked exhausted. Unfortunately, his plans ran into the wall in execution from time to time. And for the few words he uttered and wished to talk about, he usually couldn't find a listener.

Lack of communication was leading to delays and misunderstanding, which worried him.

The inability to communicate effectively and to exchange ideas in depth was threatening the future of the Wuhan Department Store.

Mao often said at that time, "Only Bingxin understands me."

I was proud of being an "understanding friend," but I was not happy. Just like Mao, I was heavyhearted, in no mood of feeling optimistic.

I faintly sensed that a crisis was looming in the glory. We were reaching the climax of an arch and would soon face the danger of slipping down. Judging from economical cycles in the past, frantic surges would always lead to rapid retraction. The excitement of rushing into massive actions was not far from the pain of ensuing adjustment. How to seize the opportunity and expand amid the rush, and how to stand tough during the economic adjustment became our new tasks. We must have new thinking and new strategies, I pondered.

This idea was confirmed in the Spring Festival of 1992, when Qian Yunlu, Party Secretary of the Wuhan Municipal Committee, and Zhao Baojiang, Mayor of Wuhan, came to the Wuhan Department Store to give their New Year greetings, with a group of officials from the Party's Municipal Committee and the Municipal Government. On that occasion, Qian Yunlu asked Mao, "In your mind, how long can the present trend last?" Mao answered without hesitation, "Half a year."

A good answer, which confirmed my thought.

Now that we had only half a year, we must act quick.

Acting quick meant intensive exploration. When our competitors were busy shattering the traditional business, we were venturing out on new paths; when they were learning the basic rules of business, we were planning the strategy of expansion.

This meant we should not stop at simply countering the moves of our rivals. We would jump out of the ring.

At the critical moment, Mao made the move to jump out of the ring — the Wuhan Department Store would set up a Business Diversification Department.

Mao had talked to me about establishing a Business Diversification Department on three occasions, and finally appointed me, then the Deputy General Manager of the Wuhan Department Store, as the Director of the Business Diversification Department.

It was an excellent move of precaution, and a surprising tactic in the business war, which might help the Wuhan Department Store disengage itself from the present tangled warfare, to reach a new height. When Mao came to me to talk about the Business Diversification Department, I believed it was a golden opportunity for the enterprise's development and probably the spring board to the world.

Mao knew that I understood his intention. That prompted him to say, "Only Bingxin understands me."

I was not trying to please him. I indeed had the same opinion. Once more, this case proved to me Mao's vision and thoughtfulness, to see the chance amid confusion. The chance was remote and intangible, but it promised a brighter future than the Wuhan Department Store. However, I didn't jump on the wagon on the spot. Honestly, I felt honored because I was chosen, but at the same time I felt quite lost.

Business diversification was the strategy that Mao placed his hope in. It was out of his appreciation of me that he had chosen me to carry out his strategic plan.

But the profit generator of the whole Wuhan Department Store Group (Wushang Group) was the Wuhan Department Store. I had just got my hands on its operations, promoted from the sixth position to the first among the deputy general managers. Turning to the unknown territory of business diversification would involve risks as well as loss of interests.

These were secondary considerations, though. I did not promise at once because the prospect was not clear to me yet. I did not want to tumble, to the detriment of others as well as myself. That was the point.

But in my mind, I already fell for the job of business diversification. I like challenges.

I did my own homework.

I talked with my relatives, friends and my husband, who used to work in foreign trade, to learn about ways and procedures for bringing in investment.

Before I knew it, I was already cruising in the field of business diversification. I had a serious talk with my husband one day. He also voted for it.

I called Mao immediately and told him without any hesitation, "Chief Mao, times are difficult, but I have decided to take on the job anyway."

2. Grab the Chance While Moving Along

When the Business Diversification Department was set up, I acted as its director, in addition to my capacity as the Deputy General Manager of the Wushang Group.

The department was rather primitive, with only one office, several old desks and an old car. But I realized that it was the platform for the Wushang Group to make a strategic breakout.

A platform for strategic breakout should be guided by strategic policies. We decided on "Diversification, Modernization, Internationalization, and High Profitability." The tactical principle was to "grab the chance whiling moving along."

From the very beginning, we followed the working guideline of "thinking big while working on details."

It is easy to talk about this guideline now, but it was extremely hard to push for it years ago. Before anything could be done, rumors started to circulate, such as "Mao has banished Hu Bingxin," and "a demotion disguised as promotion." I was deeply hurt. I discovered that in China, you could never complete a mission without going through humiliation.

Soon after I took on the function of business diversification, my office looked deserted, with few visitors. Since I had left the circulation of commodities, nobody would care about me. I saw the underside of the world. This made me sad and, at the same time, challenged me on. I knew that the Business Diversification Department was to be a decisive battlefield for me. Should I fail, I would be the loser after being a hero.

Acting with a strong will and tenacity as before, I shifted my mind into top gear for processing and perception.

Business diversification. Large as the world, huge as the populace, I had no clue to the approach. There were no on-going projects, no thread to follow up, and I didn't know any foreign businessmen. I stormed my brain till it was about to explode. Finally I concluded that I should weave a big network as well as follow every little thread; keep a high profile as well as a low one.

In the high profile, I went out of the way to contact government agencies in charge of foreign trade, and sought every opportunity to participate in overseas trade events for bringing in investment. Meanwhile, staff members were sent out in a planned fashion to domestic territories in search of investment.

In the low profile, I hung out in the street like a peddler, to collect news about promising programs or foreign/Hong Kong businessmen, trying to set up a meeting through such contacts. No clue would ever slip by.

The high profile saw camera flashes, cocktail, light music, news releases and signing ceremonies. Eye-catching and graceful.

The low profile meant begging, time and again, for a meeting, waiting by the gate sunny or windy, and emptying glasses of alcohol drink down the throat. Disheartened and depressed.

My experience at that time can be summarized as "exhausting both the heaven and hell." My description of those tough times is "unspeakable difficulties, uncountable words and unrelenting efforts." Today, the comment on my success then consists of only one phrase: I removed the parentheses from "Wushang (Group)."

When the Wushang Group first started, the word "Group" was put in parentheses. National regulations specify that a "group" must have a number of subsidiaries, but at the time, Wushang had only the Wuhan Department Store. To add "Group" to "Wushang," we cut some corners: we upgraded departments to companies to expand the size, and to stay within the regulations. Simply put, the "Group" was faked. The real start of the Group would rely on the aggressive and relentless work by the Business Diversification Department.

In the spring of 1992, conferences for bringing in capital and investment were called by the Hubei and Wuhan governments in Hong Kong and Singapore. Wushang took part in the conferences, which turned out to be the prelude to removing the parentheses around "Group." The China International Broadcasting Station reported that "Mr. Mao Dongsheng, General Manager of the Wushang Group and Ms. Hu Bingxin, Deputy General Manager, attended the conferences. They signed contracts with the Japanese Yaohan Group, the Hong Kong Hudson Group, the Hong Kong Longshun Group and Hong Kong Aowei International Real Estate Company." "The total investment reached 1 billion U.S. dollars." Media in both Hong Kong and Singapore also ran special reports. "Wushang is a hit," they reported.

When the China International Broadcasting Station ran the story in its newspaper, it published a photo, in which Mao, I, and some foreign businessmen were standing together. In the flash of cameras, the moment was captured. Captured forever. That moment was indeed historical, but whenever I see the picture now, I have the feeling described in a woeful line from a song — "How much pain is there behind the success?"

The routine work of the department was not as colorful as the media reports. Smiles in the spotlight were accompanied by hard work, worries and sweat. The persistent pursuit for a new future and the never-ending search for projects were built on daily bits and pieces. Every bit must be handled carefully. Here are some records.

Record one: Wushang Parkson Cash and Carry Store, an inevitable result growing out of pure chance. That day, Sun Huaiyu, Director of the Municipal Foreign Economy Committee and Li Pan, Secretary-General of the Wuhan Municipal Government called me, saying that the Malaysia Goldlion Group had arrived in Wuhan, and that Pang Sai Kwong, who was in charge of the retail business of the Group, was among the visitors. We immediately found out that the Goldlion Group had assets up to 2.1 billion in U.S. dollars.

In Malaysia, it owned banks and rubber plantations, ran more than 30 cash and carry stores, and built a high-tech industrial park jointly with Taiwan. I told my staff that we wouldn't let the chance slip through our fingers: Get the paperwork ready for investment and we would sit down to negotiations. When we dined with the Goldlion Group, we hit on the topic of cooperation as we were well-prepared and the Malaysia group was looking for projects to invest in. We hoped that they would invest in the second phase of the Wuhan Department Store renovation project. But they said they had something better to offer: the cash and carry store. They invited us to go on a fact-finding tour if we were interested. I grabbed the opportunity , saying that since we were going to Singapore the following week, why not go on to Malaysia which was only a few hours' drive. They were amazed at my swift decision-making and gave their invitation right on the spot. A week later, we went to investigate the cash and carry store never known to us before. Upon returning to Wuhan, I wrote the feasibility study and submitted it to Mao for final approval. The formal contract was signed in half a year. The total registered capital of the program was 12 million U.S. dollars, with our side taking 50% of the stocks.

Record two: Wuhan Yongan Children Amusement Center Co., a case of success under pressure. It was an unusual story. Mr. Quek Chi Shun, a businessman from Hong Kong, was referred to us for cooperation. He was a graduate from MIT and intended to repay his motherland. For some reason, the top management of the Wushang Group couldn't reach an agreement on the project and was about to give it up. Mao asked me to have the last round of talks with Quek. I met him at Qingchuan Hotel in Hanyang. We reached an agreement on the project. We would provide the space, and he would pay a generous rent. I reported to Mao, saying that we would recoup a large amount of cash and introduce an advanced management system at the same time. We would kill several birds with one stone. Why not go for it? Mao adopted the suggestion of the Business Diversification Department and approved the program. The program was accomplished in due time, and the top-notch children center opened on April 28th, 1993, featuring shopping, dining and amusement for children of all ages, the first of its kind in China.

Record three: Huaxin Real Estate Development Co., an outcome after many twists and turns. The whole thing was very dramatic. The second phase of renovation for the Wuhan Department Store brought in an engineer from the Architecture Design Institute. He in turn introduced a Mr. Situ for the decoration part of the project. Situ invited Mao to a dinner, but Mao sent me over instead. At the dinner table, Situ told me that his company was backed by the Hong Kong Hudson Real Estate Co. I expressed my wish to have a talk with his Hong Kong boss. Mr. William Choi, the Hong Kong boss, arrived soon after and we had the first round of talks. I further checked out his business when I went to Hong Kong in 1992. When I came back, I gave a two-hour presentation to Mao. The program got a green light immediately. Both sides put down their investment to develop Wuhan Plaza's real estate business. The program's registered capital was 12 million U.S. dollars, while the total investment reached RMB 900 million. Our side took 49 percent of the total shares. The project was among the top-priority projects in Wuhan. The real estate company built the Wuhan Plaza Mansion in 1996, with 85 percent of the floor space sold. The Wuhan Plaza Shopping Center occupied the bottom eight floors.

Record four: Oriental Express Fast Food Co.

Record five: Dongshun Real Estate Development Co.

Record six: Wuhan Plaza Management Co.

We had many records like these. They were stories of non-stop endeavors.

Looking back, I now feel that if movement is the key to life, it is also the key to seizing opportunities.

At the time, I moved around to such an extent that nobody saw me in the department store for half a year. Gossips rose. "Where's Hu Bingxin? Who knows what she is up to?"

Mao knew what I was doing. In the meantime, I felt that our business development work needed to be acknowledged: not to acknowledge my personal achievements, but to acknowledge the strategy of challenging the future through business development. For that purpose, I organized a strategic development seminar for the Wushang Group.

The seminar was attended by Zhang Peigang, tenure professor of the Huazhong University of Technology and a leading scholar of developmental economics in China, and many well-known professors from Wuhan University. They spoke highly of our development strategy. At the same time, an article by Mao and myself on the same topic appeared in *China Securities News*. After the seminar, at Mao's suggestion, the Business Diversification Department organized a tour for the middle management to one of the projects we had developed. They were totally convinced.

Only then did I feel some relief. The world was moving fast. Only by moving fast could we catch up with it, grasp it and interact with it. These interactions brought about opportunities. I was finally able to seize the opportunities.

I got myself accepted with my achievements — seven joint-ventures, with foreign investment of 60 million U.S. dollars. This was a solid start for the Wushang Group, which is now composed of seven joint-ventures, ten holding enterprises, twelve fully owned enterprises and five chain stores.

In the vast world made up of numerous people, I gave the Wushang Group a big push along its track of development.

The track brought the Wushang Group to a new height and put me in a miraculous land.

3. Find the Cooking Pot to Cook Meat

This miraculous land was the Wuhan Plaza.

Now, the towering 48-story building, with its sparkling multi-facet glass walls, its smooth and skyscraping outline, its hustle and excitement during the day and glittering neon lights at night, is proudly presenting its beauty and magnificence.

In 1995, it was a huge construction site; in 1994, it was a deep excavation for the foundation; in 1993, it was a garment market of sheds made from corrugated iron sheets. Looking back into the history often brings on philosophical thoughts.

The history presented itself as a string of footsteps, which formed a logical development: Mao's decision led to the Huaxin Co., which in turn gave birth to this building. This building formed the foundation of the Wuhan Plaza. Chief Mao started everything, with our participation.

Mao Dongsheng, Chairman of the Board, is truly a business master. Following his plan, the Wushang Group established the joint-venture, Huaxin Co., with Hong Kong's Hudson Group, to deal in the Wuhan Plaza building's real estate. The net profit of this operation was RMB 300 million. With this money and a little more, we purchased the bottom eight floors of the building. This meant that the joint-venture contributed the value of the Wuhan Plaza's real estate. We did not stop there, though. Instead, we set up the Wuhan Plaza Management Co., again with Mr. Choi, using the real estate as our investment, and had this company rent the real estate property. This masterful manipulation of capital by Mao was acclaimed in the media as "Wushang's Theory on Capital."

Our business gradually took on human characteristics. When we planned the Wuhan Plaza Management Co. with Huaxin, I felt like a mother just starting her pregnancy. I could feel its growth day by day, feeding it with the nutrition in my blood. Suddenly, I found it was taking shape. The shape was as vague as the universe at its very origin, but I knew I wanted it.

I was excited. I decided to return to the solid ground from the vast sky. I went to Mao and asked him to give the program to me.

Mao was somewhat hesitant. He would like me to take the position of the Executive General Manager of the Wushang Group. He told me to think it over.

What would I think about? I was in pursuit of a meaningful life. I wished to break into a new world for China's retail trade with my own hands. The Wuhan Plaza was said to be a virgin land. I believed it promised more. My feeling was that it had its special mission, independent of the Wuhan Department Store and all the other similar shopping centers in China. "Special" not in the sense of its physical make-up, but in the sense of its spiritual and cultural contents. These contents were probably totally new, different from any tradition or any foreign belief.

To understand my point, some knowledge of the background would be helpful. After Deng Xiaoping's tour of South China, the Reform made further headway, and the force that stood in the way of ideological liberalization suffered setback. In the meantime, innovation and new breakthrough were urgently called for. People were still blinded by the good feeling of the traditional commerce, believing "I'm No.1 under the sun." They were too carried away by this feeling to sit down and plan for the future. Old business structures, old concepts and old management methods were used repeatedly, as if they would never grow out of date. With regard to all the changes that foreign capital brought along, they were not sober enough as they should be, thinking that foreign investors were just after money in China, and that foreign ideas and concepts would have little impact on daily operations. This led to a huge gap in the retail business in China.

This gap lay between the past and the future, between foreign and Chinese business operations.

And the Wuhan Plaza was born to this gap.

This meant that I could make experiments vital to the retail trade in China.

In my opinion, the experiments would be conducted sooner or later. It was an honor as well as a challenge for me to engage in them.

Frankly speaking, I had long felt the impulse for these experiments. The impulse resulted from my feeling about and comparison with the outside world.

The world had become very fascinating. It was the most striking impression I had after coming to work at the Business Diversification Department. I went abroad on several fact-finding business trips during this period, and observed the world with my own eyes. All the descriptions in books looked so pale against my personal experience. Book descriptions were flat and static, but the real world was forever moving with energy.

I cherished the fact-finding business trips and was very serious about them. I insisted on mindful observation or role participation, as opposed to mere physical presence, or just strolling foreign streets and purchasing a few nice things to take home with. As for those who only loved foreign luxuries, they were simply despicable.

I read a book about Katsu Wada, President of Yaohan. The book recorded a visit he had made to Singapore. Instead of heading directly for the hotel upon his arrival, he went to lay flowers at the local monument for martyrs in the Second World War, to apologize for Japan's crime of invasion and to win over local people. His approach was well worth learning, especially his constant awareness of his professional role and his entrepreneurship. Those who never forgot their roles became outstanding figures. Some of those who went on such business trips eventually lost out simply because they did not care about their roles.

Then how did I do my own fact-finding? I went out of my way to contact top-class international companies. I believed that we should aim at the best in the world. If you aim at the best, you could at least end up in the middle; if you aim at the middle range, you would end up in the lower range in the worst scenario. But if you aim at the low end, you would probably get nowhere. Aiming at the best would ensure that we could at least reach a certain level.

Efforts would surely bring about rewards. On those fact-finding trips, I observed some systems and concepts totally new to me.

For example, when I strolled around the huge blocks of commercial skyscrapers in Causeway Bay, the commercial center in Hong Kong, I understood what "clustering" meant. When I roamed in the chain of Yaohan Department Stores in Hong Kong, I saw "retail chains." In some big companies, I witnessed a modern scientific management system in their rules and regulations for the staff. Sitting in their offices and observing their ways of dealing with problems, I could feel their meticulous management concepts.

When I was turning these concepts over in my mind, I told myself, "Hu Bingxin, on these trips, remember to focus on people as well as things, and on their inner thoughts as well as their external behavior. Probe behind the appearance, like stripping bamboo shoots to the core."

In this continuous probing, I came to the conclusion that the outside world was indeed fascinating. I thought, "Why should we act like an ostrich, closing our eyes to the strong points of the outside world?"

We should be as magnanimous as the Han and Tang Dynasties, as inclusive as the Wei and Jin Dynasties, and learn to "steal fire." As Lu Xun[1] put it, "Use other's fire to cook one's own meat."

That reminded me of another point: We needed a cooking pot to cook the meat.

What was my cooking pot? The Wuhan Plaza.

Traditional old enterprises were not the best pots for cooking meat. They had too much sediment and were mixed with many strange smells; soot under the bottom was too thick, so much heat would be lost in cooking. They had cracks here and there, so the cream of the broth would leak out.

I would need a new pot, so that I could put in it quality commodities from the world in addition to Chinese specialties. With these, I would cook fresh and delicious dishes. In the course of cooking, I would tackle two urgent problems that the Reform had to solve: the integration of the new and the old, and the integration of the Chinese and the foreign.

The Wuhan Plaza would be my new pot. I decided to submit my bid.

Just then, Mao picked me after elaborate discussion and consideration. I remember that he was hospitalized for an operation on his thyroid gland. When I visited him, he announced his decision from his hospital bed, with sincerity and high expectations.

As an entrepreneur, one of Mao's outstanding skills was selecting the right person for the right job.

4. Copy = Death

In 1994, I was transferred to the Wuhan Plaza as the Chinese representative in the operation. The representative from the Hong Kong side was Mr. William Choi.

Mr. Choi was an old friend of mine, but I knew that between us, interests and concepts would outweigh personal relations. In fact, we represented two different worlds. Breaking-in and even colli-sion would be expected.

I was excited by the possible breaking-in and collision, because in this process, my personal identification would fade out, and a new generation of Chinese entrepreneurs that I represented would become internationalized.

I took office, but where was the Wuhan Plaza?

In the sand-table model, it was as small as a pocket toy. You could take it away in your sleeve and put it in that deep hole next to the Wuhan Department Store. In reality, when viewed against the towering Wuhan Department Store, the bottomless excavation ap-peared intriguing and mysterious. I had never seen a pit as large, as deep and as frightening. I felt it was more like a big mouth, making silent inquiries about its future to humans and to the heaven.

"How is my luck in the future?"

"Hello, Big Hole. You are needed for a building as high as 48 floors. Its height is based on your depth. You will see a network of stakes very soon, and the building will grow up quickly, finally becoming a giant."

"And then?" it asked.

"It's hard to say. Maybe you will die very soon. But most prob-ably you will turn into a monument."

I talked silently with the deep pit as I smiled. Then I entered the office with the sign Wuhan Plaza Project Office. I couldn't help feeling amused. The office was on the ninth floor of the Wuhan Department Store. A single room of several dozen square meters. With bare cement floor and unpainted ceiling, it looked like an old warehouse, pertaining to the hard journey of the ground-breaking work. I couldn't help feeling amused because I had changed my office three times in just six years after I took up business.

The first time, I was transferred from a Party branch to the office of Deputy General Manager; then I moved to the Business Diversi-fication Department; now, here I came. I was so restless!

But I was happy with the changes. The second change had actu-ally fulfilled my expectation of transition and brought me to the Wuhan Plaza, a window of the century.

Could the Wuhan Plaza become the window of the century? Certainly. Otherwise why was I here?

But I did not anticipate different opinions on how to manage the Plaza when it was still a deep excavation.

Hong Kong's Causeway Bay is a well-known retail center in the world. Three skyscrapers carve out the market share and customer base. They take the lion's share of Hong Kong's retail revenue. When Mao looked up to them, his admiration was beaming out from behind his glasses.

This was real achievement! This was real courage! This was real modernity! Mao didn't say anything, but I understood his expression.

I knew why Mao appreciated all this. The Wuhan Department Store was one of the 3 major buildings in Wuhan dedicated to the 10th anniversary of the People's Republic of China. It had been enjoying a booming business since 1959, handling up to 200,000 customers everyday. The issue of overcrowding had been brought up time and again, and the answer from the Wuhan Department Store was to expand continuously. Mao's greatest desire was having several buildings like the Wuhan Department Store in the neighborhood, to create a clustering effect.

I knew Mao had an ambitious plan: clustering these shopping centers with the neighboring Youzixiang Mansion, World Trade Plaza and Concorde Plaza, to turn the area into a treasure land for retail business in mid-China and a world-class commercial center like Causeway Bay.

I was fully convinced by Mao's sweeping ambition. I felt that I should give him another hand in working out the blueprint step by step, so that each individual in the cluster would exhibit its own characteristics and together they would generate more profits through complement instead of head-on clashes.

I began to look into the issue of complement as opposed to clashes. I thought it was crucial to the success of clustering, and was well worth studying. Soon came the chance for discussion, out of Mao's initiative. When we were discussing the management of the Wuhan Plaza, Mao suggested following the business model of the Wuhan Department Store in filling the business floors with commodities. He meant to ease my work load and psychological pressure, but I was disturbed by the suggestion.

It was not really what I wanted, and was out of step with the current and future business development.

If the Wuhan Plaza were to copy the Wuhan Department Store, both would probably lose some ground. Due to historical reasons, the Wuhan Department Store had a commodity structure based on the principle of "guaranteed supply." On the other hand, supply of commodity was quite abundant now. If the role of a guaranteed supplier were to be repeated and expanded, these suppliers would soon begin to fight for customers and divide the customer base.

Clustering was needed, but the cluster should be sorted into distinct groups, each group with its own individual features. Cooking all the ingredients in a single pot would spoil the dish.

So, when Mao said the Wuhan Plaza could model on the Wuhan Department Store, it occurred to me that we needed to exchange views on the issue.

For some years, people had been quick to act, to the extent of losing their mind. Take commerce for example. When the government called for circulation of goods, the whole nation jumped onto the bandwagon. Everybody rushed in: government agencies, social organizations, joint-ventures, individuals, manufacturing companies, farmers, herdsmen, fishermen, real estate developers... The battlefield spread all over the country. They acted fast because speed was a decisive factor in battles. In the frenzy, we ignored a fundamental question: what department stores should be built? Commerce did not mean loading goods in stores, recruiting some sale assistants and ordering uniforms for them. It was a serious subject requiring serious study.

We paid a huge price for it but we seldom learned our lesson. We never thought whether the 170 large-scale department stores were too many for Beijing since New York had no more than 20. We never thought whether we were killing each other when our commercial streets sold the same items. Sometimes we were too free and lighthearted. If we didn't do well, we would dismiss it lightly with "It is a tough time for business" and write off the loss with "We just paid our tuition."[2]

Since when did we change the motto of "careful planning" into "pay tuition?" It is said that "pay tuition" has been in use for a while, but "careful planning" has an even longer history. Why not do careful planning to avoid paying tuition? Is cost no longer important for business?

I believed in cost control. We should plan before doing anything. Although the business was not mine, the career was.

I told Mao that the Wuhan Plaza had to be managed in a different way. The old model wouldn't work.

Mao was open-minded and let me choose my own plan.

His management style was laisser faire. That was fine. It would give me a free hand.

5. March in the Forefront of Revolution

The new plan for the Wuhan Plaza featured four new aspects: new management concepts, a new management mechanism, a new management style and a new employment and salary system.

These four new elements were necessary. I never liked to follow suit. Besides, we had a new organization: the Wushang Group set up the Wuhan Plaza Management Co. with Huaxin. Chief Mao served as Chairman of the Board, Mr. William Choi as General Manager and I as Deputy General Manager in charge of day-to-day operations.

But what would be new? Frankly speaking, I did not have a clue at the very beginning.

Our quest for the new model was a hard journey.

We began by looking into reference materials. I browsed through books after books, documents after documents, web pages after web pages, which I had printed out. In search of the new model, I ran into a book about the Martha Department Store in England when I was browsing in a bookstore in Hong Kong. I bought it as a treasure and made many copies of it, to be distributed to the staff. I sailed through the sea of information for a long time and made my discoveries at last. I was able to chart the historical development of the retail trade.

The development was quite clear: there were six revolutions all together.

Each revolution was tied to the increase in productivity. New methods of production led to new patterns of distribution. This in turn brought about revolution in the retail trade.

The first revolution took place at the beginning of the slave society. With more and more surplus products, bartering was no longer feasible. Markets appeared and currency was born. Professional merchants became a distinctive social group.

These professional merchants walked the streets, with bags of goods on their back, or drove their caravan everywhere in search of profit. By and by, they found that it was a waste of time and money to transport and sell goods at the same time. So they settled down, transforming from traveling peddlers to stationary merchants. Bags of goods gave way to shops. This way, the second revolution in retail trade was accomplished at the beginning of the feudal society.

More and more shops appeared as the society moved forward. Then industrialization broke out. The most prominent feature of industrialization was the abundance of commodities, which in turn called for a new type of shopping space. In 1852, Bon Marche, the first department store in the world, opened in Paris, introducing the arrival of the third revolution. It caught the attention of the world right away because of its spacious and graceful shopping floors, its variety of commodities, its openly marked prices and its easy access.

This was an enormous revolution, the result of which has been preserved up till this day. But just as the department store was having its day, there came the "single-price" store. "Single-price" stores were the offspring of modern industrial standardization, as well as the outcome of compromise and competition in the commercial war. It emphasized standard pricing and equal profit sharing. The appearance of the "single-price" store marked the end of the fourth revolution.

But this revolution had a short life. The information industry soon boomed and networks became popular. Networking not only brought about reorganization of information and production, but also revolutionized distribution. This revolution saw the emergence of a great number of chain stores and the prevalence of large-scale operations. The fifth revolution in the retain trade represented by chain stores accomplished the following: discount stores, cash and carry stores and supermarkets were organized into chains. The chain stores of Wal-Mart, king of the retail trade in the world, numbered as many as 3,000, with the annual sales revenue reaching $100 billion.

The sixth revolution arose almost at the same time as the fifth revolution. Like chain stores, it was based on the information industry. However, while chain stores emphasized networking, it focused on centralized processing. This revolution produced gigantic shopping centers. They usually had titanic structures with a space of 60,000 to 200,000 square meters. They integrated all kinds of specialty stores, department stores and supermarkets. To this, they added entertainment, dining and exhibiting functions, to form the service center for neighboring areas.

These revolutions in retail generated a great number of by-products: self-service markets, discount shops, cash and carry stores and flea markets.

Diversification and frequent revolutions were the two features of the modern retail trade.

While the application of high technology and intensive knowledge characterized the general development, centralization or chain operation stood out as the trend in our times.

Centralized operation had many advantages. Statistics showed that the top 50 retail enterprises in the U.S. took up to 22% of the total market share.

The world was moving ahead at full speed, with a sense of urgency. It was said that returning to nature and pedestrian-only commercial districts were on the rise, giving life to the seventh revolution. On the other hand, Internet shopping was heralding the eighth revolution.

For the time being, we were not concerned about Internet shopping and pedestrian-only shopping districts. Were shopping centers with centralized management the new form we were looking for?

We did not jump to the conclusion. We had to keep a cool mind. Closing the books, we decided to check out the new form in China. So, when stakes were being hammered into the foundation of the Wuhan Plaza in 1994, we set out quietly. Winds blew hard on the east coast, and it was freezing in Beijing. We went to Beijing and Shanghai, to learn about the commercial war.

What we saw everywhere were mostly department stores, whether small as a sparrow or large as a dinosaur. It was known that the first department store in China was opened by Russians in Harbin in 1900. The store was called Qiulin Co., and its impact could still be felt today. Despite the various luxurious facades, these department stores were all the same inside. Selling commodities was their main function. The medium and small ones were doing fine, but the large ones were already having a hard time.

I looked into the cause and found that they had fallen behind by two orders, still staying with the fourth revolution.

While they were still focused on commodities, our foreign counterparts were already working on network (chain store) management, property management and capital management (shopping centers). In short, their focus had shifted to management and its concepts.

While our Chinese colleagues were still pre-occupied with the circulation of goods, our foreign counterparts were concentrated on supervision and integration. The daily management of chain stores was to supervise every franchiser, and that of shopping centers was to select, configure, coordinate and eliminate the various participating units.

The big department stores in China hadn't realized the point yet, stilling holding onto the old system. As a result, the sales revenue of Beijing's Modern Plaza was similar to that of Guiyou Center, which was 4.5 times smaller, and the profit was RMB 37.85 million lower than the latter.

Foreign experience showed that department stores could survive with a floor space of less than 20,000 square meters. If the floor space went above 20,000 square meters, they would fail with no exception, because they would be drowned in the numerous goods. To avoid getting drowned, subcontracting would be necessary. Then you would see inventory and sales spinning out of control, and profit and efficiency getting lost.

The Wuhan Plaza had a floor space of 75,000 square meters. The department store model was out of the question.

I believed that we had to do away with the department store model. If we could not find a new model, we might as well quit now.

On this fact-finding trip, we learned more lessons than success stories, with a greater sense of loss than of accomplishment.

The new model was indistinct and elusive. It had to be found, though. We decided to continue probing.

Around 1994, several foreign-owned and jointly-owned shopping centers sprang up. They introduced many new business forms. We turned our eyes towards them.

I still remember the difficult days of those visits for information. For example, I contacted a foreign-owned department store in Shanghai through my networking, and was received warmly by its Chief Accountant. But management and operation were off the topic. We weren't even allowed to take photos.

To meet a senior manager of a department store with Hong Kong investment here in Wuhan, we had to act secretively, as in underground operation.

Most hurting was the attempted meeting with a Chinese Deputy General Manager of a foreign-owned department store in Beijing. My secretary went to make an appointment for me but was stopped by the security guard. I had him obtain the telephone number, but he was blocked again by the company restrictions. I finally lost my temper and shouted at my secretary, "You must get his telephone number today, whatever happens!"

The secretary was astonished and felt hurt.

I was speechless, too. I suddenly came to my senses: why should I need that number now?

I decided to turn away from these foreign-owned and jointly-owned businesses, which presented a mysterious, serious, and dignified front. According to my information, they didn't have any cure-all either.

They couldn't stop the Chinese from catching up with the latest development in the world, nor would they be able to put down the new generation of Chinese entrepreneurs.

I had never backed down in adverse situations. Rather, when forced into a corner, I would put up a fierce fight. When this happened, I was often blessed with inspirations.

That day, I suddenly thought of a conclusion by Peter Shaw, an American sociologist. He believed that the top challenge in the future was going to be competition initiated by new organizations.

Revelation struck me right then and there. "The new model" we were searching for should be a new form of organization. It should stay in the forefront of the sixth revolution. Its main component should be a shopping center.

I slumped into a sofa, telling my subordinates to stop poking around: we were heading home the following day.

6. Develop Human Resources

When I was back in Wuhan, I brought together all the investigating teams and initiated elaborate discussions among the decision-makers. The operating model of the Wuhan Plaza was finalized: it would primarily be a shopping center, complemented with some functions of the department store. We would take to the road of modernization in the Chinese context.

Several years later, when I was evaluating the initial decisions, I drew a comparison chart for myself.

Listed on the left side of the chart were the functions of foreign shopping centers and department stores. Shopping centers had the following characteristics: with a floor space of more than 20,000 square meters; property management; vendor integration; business support (including communication, account settlement, security, cleaning and logistics), comprehensive services (general merchandise, dining, entertainment, and exhibiting). Department stores had the following functions: sales management, and customer service.

On the right side of the chart were the functions that the Wuhan Plaza had already implemented: the Wuhan Plaza, with an area of 76,000 square meters, property management; vendor integration; sales management; business support; customer service; comprehensive service; and personnel training.

From the chart the Wuhan Plaza looked like a hybrid. It combined the achievements of the sixth revolution with the heritage of the fourth revolution; the latest foreign development with conventions in Chinese retail business; the mainstream in the world with Chinese tradition. With this cross-breeding, functions of the Wuhan Plaza exceeded the sum of functions provided by each parent model, that is, "1+1>2." It was proved by our operation that the cross-breeding was successful and that we achieved hybrid advantages.

In retrospect, the advantages are obvious. But when we planned for the model, the advantages were just theoretical, not factual. The opportunity to test the model out in operation was yet to come; and the team to bring the model to fruition was yet to be organized. I felt a desperate need for the team. I couldn't charge into the battle single-handed, like a commander without soldiers!

There were only four workers in the project office of the Wuhan Plaza: myself, a secretary, a typist, and an assistant. All the staff were my devoted followers, coming over with me from the Business Diversification Department of the Wuhan Department Store to the Wuhan Plaza Project Office. Two of the three had never been involved in business operations. On the other hand, I needed a large number of senior managers with an advanced knowledge structure to comprehend and support the operations of the pioneering system at the Wuhan Plaza. They should have abundant practical experience, able to plunge into work right way. They should have beliefs and a strong desire for achievement, charging on without any thought about their own safety.

I went to Mao to ask for more people. It was a hard decision for him. The Wuhan Plaza was still under construction, its future unpredictable. Many employees at the Wuhan Department Store were wary about jumping over. Moreover, transferring many middle managers would deplete the Wuhan Department Store of its human resources.

Mao wouldn't give up the cream of his staff at the Wuhan Department Store. On the other hand, I wouldn't settle for anyone less qualified. I made my own move and went to the Lighting and Decoration Department of the Wuhan Department Store to look for Zhang Xurui. Zhang was a manager who had spent dozens of years at the Wuhan Department Store. I elaborated on the future of the Wuhan Plaza for him and encouraged him to join me. I then added, "I'm short-tempered and strong-minded. Think it over before telling me your final decision."

Zhang came back to me the next day, saying, "I'm willing to work for you." I was truly grateful to him. At the moment when the future of the Wuhan Plaza was still uncertain and some staff members in the Business Diversification Department asked to be transferred back to the Wuhan Department Store, he gave up his secure position with no hesitation and joined in the Wuhan Plaza.

Never before had I felt the acute shortage of management talents.

When I was walking through the streets against bustling crowds, a thought might strike me out of the blue: "Vast as this ocean of human beings, who can give me a helping hand?"

People were the primary resource of any business. I remembered an American entrepreneur's concern. He said the greatest risk for him was losing his people. Nothing in the office could move except people, who would leave at the end of the day. Without them, the office remained deadly silent. This meant that the business would be dead if people didn't show up the next day.

I also remembered comments by Ivester, Chairman of Coca Cola, that a modern talent embodied a mobile office with all the auxiliary technologies.

Humans used to be treated as a working force, a means to work on resources. The greatest discovery in the 1990s was that humans were resources themselves.

The desert would constitute a view only with a line of traveling footsteps and a tiny human figure in the distance; the sea appeared boundless only with a human sail; deposits became mines only through human digging; and businesses generated profit and added value only with human participation.

Man was the magic wand for all the miracles. In other words, everything became miraculous because of man.

I was in search of miracles, but where could I find the people I needed?

Where to look for them? I found myself running into stone walls in every direction.

While we were pursuing every lead all over the place, I was puzzled: "How come professionals are so hard to find in China?"

Professional workers, like professional soldiers, had their own values, professionalism and sense of leadership, which were developed through long-term training. They understood rules and disciplines, duties and responsibilities. They knew professional office technology and would be fully functional wherever you sent them.

Sometimes I couldn't help forcing a smile when I lost myself in these daydreams. It seemed that we, who were in desperate need of professionals, could obtain them only through our own training.

As luck would have it, a university teacher named Zhuang Xianming was recommended to me while I was daydreaming. He had a pair of glasses on a square face, looking just like a scholar. He headed the Industrial and Commercial Business Management Section at the Huazhong University of Technology, with an MBA degree from a program jointly sponsored by the Huazhong University of Technology and University of Toronto. He was also granted the National Award for Special Contributions and had just been assigned a two-bedroom apartment.[3]

He sought me out because he wanted to find a land of experiment for his theoretical knowledge.

I had the land. I needed people to cultivate it.

We were right on. I talked about the importance of practice for business management education, about reform in education, about the vision that education should provide in our new age, about the Wuhan Plaza, and about the meaning of life.

He listened quietly. Later on, he said that he decided to come over to the Wuhan Plaza because of me and my powerful character.

On hearing this, I was pleasantly surprised: my powerful character? It was another way of describing my persistent pursuit of my career.

I was very honest with him at the time. I told him, "You will have to take some risks when you come. Your employment will be based on contracts, and your personnel files will be left with the Human Resources Management Center,[4] and your two-bedroom apartment may have to be returned."

An average guy might hesitate at these conditions, but he just blinked once. I came to the conclusion that he was not only a scholar, but also a person willing to give up everything for the career.

I needed these people who would give up everything for the career. His will power would provide a strong backing for his career goal.

With Zhuang joining us, the Wuhan Plaza had a master degree holder for the first time. And he gave me very good advice on the use of computers and on enterprise culture. Moreover, his changing over started a chain reaction, leading to the arrival of two computer engineers.

These two engineers were recommended by Zhuang. One of them, Pan Hanlin, was a graduate from the Huazhong University of Technology and had worked on computers for more than 10 years. He was directing a national research program at Jianghan Oilfield.

I seized the chain reaction by inviting Pan to join us. When his organization brought us to court, I decided to take on the case. They asked for RMB 40,000 as compensation, which I agreed to. Pan's value was much higher than RMB 40,000.

During the Three Kingdoms, Cao Cao gave up five top generals in exchange for Guan Yu. Shouldn't we have the same boldness in our search for professionals?

Maybe my sincerity moved God, or maybe my persistence was winning the heart of people. By the end of 1994, most of those who have now become senior managers had shown up. They came from everywhere, with selfless enthusiasm, getting together in the Project Office with bare cement floor and paintless ceiling. We set sail from here determinedly, like a bunch of travelers in the fifth-class cabin.

We were convinced that we were sailing towards success, because more and more people joined our ranks.

This did not happen because they were simply following the crowd. It was the result of our philosophy in human resource management.

We made it clear to everyone: the philosophy of the Wuhan Plaza was "Human assets first, profit second." People were what counted.

We did not depend on temptations or promises, either. It was our attitudes to our staff that worked.

For example, for the veteran members from the Wuhan Department Store, we made full use of their ability and experience; for new graduates from business schools, we provided strict training.

I told them that no one was perfect, and that people were to be managed through rules and regulations. We believed in the power of rules and regulations.

They felt that it was a fair system. They were happy with it. It meant that they were given the right to compete on an equal basis, as well as the space to develop themselves.

I believed that as a type of resource, human assets needed to be deployed, managed and protected as well.

In the mean time, as a type of resource, human assets also needed to be enriched and expanded.

Based upon this consideration, we spent RMB 100,000 on a newspaper advertisement of job opportunities on October 12, 1995. It had a striking effect on the community. For the 80 management positions, we received 1,208 applications; for the Financial Controller position, we received more than 200 applications. I was present at nearly all the interviews and saw with my own eyes how disappointed people were when they were disqualified and how elated they were when they got the position.

All these reactions, disappointment or elation, confirmed our values in human resources.

I believed that our human assets represented an excellent opportunity. With these assets, the Wuhan Plaza was well on its way to success.

Now the point was how to optimize the human resources, to expand our human assets and break through barriers.

There were still many barriers: minefields and traps.

7. Market Orientation on Weak or Strong Markets

My trap was market orientation.

Adam Smith, representative of the British school of classical economics, compared market to an "invisible hand." My experience was that the hand could raise you up into the sky, or strike you down into the dust.

How to handle the hand became an issue of life or death. China had been searching for an answer for the past twenty years. All the businesses were working on it.

The critical point of this issue was the "invisible" part. You thought you were approaching the issue, but it was just a blurry vision; you thought you were safely away from it, yet it gave you such pain. It left you in suspense and you couldn't do much about it; it made you feel like walking with unsure footsteps forever.

This was because market orientation was forever a strategic challenge for businesses. The strategy must be clear, and its presentation concise.

I suggested that the strategic market orientation of the Wuhan Plaza be different from that of the Wuhan Department Store. The goal was individualized consumption, to "collect quality merchandise and serve the masses." This strategy would enable the Wuhan Plaza and Wuhan Department Store to complement each other.

My reasoning was as follows: the Reform made some people rich, which provided financial basis for a higher level of consumption; the Reform created a relaxed atmosphere, which provided social basis for individualized consumption; centralization was giving way to diversification, which provided cultural and psychological basis for individualized consumption; for a long time, only the basic needs in consumption were met in the society, and we had the responsibility to meet the demands for a higher level of consumption.

When expressed in common language, these reasons did not sound very convincing.

There were enough reasons to be skeptical. The business perspective for the brand-name merchandise was uncertain. Small stores and specialty stores could afford to take the risk because "small boats could turn around quickly." The Wuhan Plaza was so large that even selecting the brands would be an enormous job.

The risk was tremendous. General merchandise had been known to both the consumer and the vendor. The preference for brand names, on the other hand, was highly individual. If the wrong brands were selected and customers didn't happen to like them, business would run into a dead end.

And the market was weak. People had money, but they didn't have the desire to spend it.

The market was indeed weak. I would not deny that. The Wuhan Plaza was not born to golden times. That was why our strategy was so hard to formulate. The Chinese economy started periodic adjustment in 1993. The main tasks included slowing down the overheated economy, reducing projects, controlling consumption, and tightening monetary circulation. The general economic condition had an impact on consumers' spending behavior. Meanwhile, after the overstocking frenzy by consumers in 1988, the shortage economy turned into a surplus economy. The seller's market became the buyer's market. Hot spots had disappeared from the market. All businesses complained about the tough time.

Where was the new hot spot in the market? No one could tell.

When would the economy turn around? It was hard to predict.

At such times, it was advisable to be cautious. "Cautious" meant "conservative."

But I was strong-minded and not conservative. I enjoyed challenges, never giving up on my commitments.

Of course I didn't follow my thoughts blindly. Strategic issues called for extra care. Out of this consideration, I often went window-shopping, visiting the specialty stores on Nanjing Road and Chezhan Road at Hankou, as well as the Wuhan Branch of Hong Kong New World Department Store, which specialized in brand-name merchandise. Browsing among the superb collection of beautiful commodities, I did some careful observation. I found that their business was booming. In the meantime, Lufthansa and SciTech had already started their business in Beijing. The Oriental Bazaar, The Pacific Department Store and Isetan had sprung up in Shanghai. Investigators we sent over brought back the message that their business was on the rise, too.

I felt assured. I saw myself facing a most precious commercial opportunity.

The market was weak, but the brand name business was flourishing. Wasn't this foretelling the arrival of a higher level of consumption?

Besides, given the lack of hot spots on the market, a more precise description was that there were no hot spots for general merchandise. It did not mean that new hot spots would not occur again.

"Hot" and "cold" were relative. Old things were fading out, while new things were stepping in. I had just arrived at the junction of life and death.

Still, as a measure of precaution, I reported to the Board of Directors on several occasions. After elaborate discussions, the Board finally sanctioned our strategic orientation for the Wuhan Plaza: assemble brand names and serve the populace. I elaborated on the concepts when the strategic orientation was finalized. I said that brand names referred to new and well-known products of a higher grade, as opposed to today's general merchandise. They didn't necessarily have to be more expensive. "Serve the populace" meant meeting consumers' demands for a higher level of consumption and for diversified and individualized service. The service did not have to be limited to providing for the most basic needs of the consumers, which would be an underestimate of their purchasing power.

With market orientation established, we began to look for vendors. The construction of the Wuhan Plaza was not finished yet, and it was little known to the outside. Moreover, Wuhan was not among the most appealing cities in China. When our sales people ventured to Beijing and Shanghai, a sudden remark would be thrown at them: "How big is Wuhan?" Besides, the weak market made vendors more cautious.

"It is hard to succeed in the wrong times," I often repeated this line then.

But I already jumped on board the ship. It had to set sail.

In a crisis, we have a better appreciation of our own existence; this in turn leads to an awareness of our potential capabilities. When I recall our efforts to bring in vendors, I realize that if you strongly believe in your success, your mind would clear away all the obstacles, and arouse all the intelligence and energy to help you reach your goal.

Take a simple example. When we were laboring our brains for ways to boost our popularity, an idea suddenly occurred to me. The Chinese believed "blooming flowers inside a compound send their scent outside the wall." Why not make some moves, to work out our popularity abroad and then re-direct it back to the domestic market?

Seizing upon this revelation, I immediately reported my thoughts to the top management and started detailed preparations. From September 7 to September 11, 1994, the Wuhan Plaza sponsored a three-day event to release the news and recruit vendors at the Regent Hotel in Hong Kong. The event was quite heated. Qian Yunlu, Secretary of the Municipal Committee of the Communist Party, Dong Shaojing and Sun Zhigang, Vice Mayors of Wuhan, Chen Yuanlin, Secretary-General of the Wuhan Municipal Government, and Li Pan, Deputy Secretary-General, took part in the event. Representatives of world-famous department stores from Britain, Canada, Singapore and Malaysia, and about 500 industrial and commercial celebrities from Hong Kong came for talks and negotiations. This event ended with several contracts and boosted the popularity of the Wuhan Plaza. With this foreign trump card in hand, we soon began the second round of promotion — to import our success back to the domestic market.

From October 18 to October 21, 1994, we presented another event at the Jiangcheng Hotel in Wuhan for Chinese businesses, to release the news and recruit vendors. Across the street, the Wuhan Plaza building was rising higher day by day. Li Meifang, Director of the Municipal People's Congress, Dong Shaojian, Vice Mayor,

Hu Zhaozhou, Deputy Director of the Political Consultative Conference, and He Hanxiang, Chairman of the Municipal Labor Union, showed up at the event. Vendors swarmed in. Friendly reporters from the news media pitched in, too, to help us boost our popularity. More than 200 contracts were signed at this event. There were comments that the Wuhan Plaza made aggressive moves before it opened its doors.

Aggressive moves? They were far from adequate.

The 200-some contracts could not satisfy our appetite. Our plan called for more than 200,000 kinds of commodities when the Wuhan Plaza opened. 55% of them should be unknown to other retail businesses in Wuhan, 10% to 20% should be foreign brands well accepted in China, and 20% should be from top ten quality products from Chinese businesses.

Some people commented on this plan in disbelief, saying, "Hu Bingxin, you have a big appetite. This plan will burn you out."

I answered that I would not mind overwork in my quest for perfection.

I was so tired that I would doze off whenever I got in the car. I could manage to put up with physical exhaustion, but I could hardly carry on with a totally exhausted mind. Yet I had to carry on. How many chances did one have to bring out one's full potential in a lifetime? In this complete physical and mental exhaustion, I gave rigid orders to my staff for the number of vendors and contracts they were supposed to clinch. No one should return without meeting the target.

Recalling those days, I still feel very grateful to Zhang Xurui and Li Lifen. To get vendors interested, they went through so many hardships, walked so many miles and spoke so many nice words. I am also very thankful to Zhao Defa, General Manager of Operations at Shanghai's Hualian Plaza, and Wan Wenying, Deputy General Manager of Beijing Lufthansa. Thanks to their support, we finally made it through.

But I couldn't announce that we had made it through. Instead, I continued to press my staff. In July, 1995, I asked Li Lifen to head for Shanghai with four other employees to look for vendors. I gave them a "must-do" number before they left. They combed Shanghai for a week, and signed 12 contracts. Right at that moment, Shanghai was hit by a typhoon, and four out of the five in the team fell sick. Li was very upset. She called me in a stormy night, wondering whether they could return since they were approaching the target.

Her phone call disturbed me. I could imagine how hard it was for them, and the word was on the tip of my tongue to bring them back.

But, squeezing the handset hard, I heard myself say, "Li Lifen, if you come back now, you'll be fired from your position."

I added forcefully, "If you come back, I'll go to Shanghai to replace you."

No doubt this was pushing her into the corner. I could hear she choke when she spoke.

I thought, maybe she was crying; maybe she was complaining that I was cold-blooded.

But without pressing, we would get nowhere. I myself was under great pressure, too.

The pressure came from my dedication and a sense of urgency. It reminded me that I was facing an enormous task. I had to take every precaution.

The familiar line rang up again: "Moscow doesn't believe in tears."

8. Overhaul the System

After the phone call, Li Lifen stood in the wailing wind and weeping rain for a long while.

She didn't return to Wuhan. Instead, she went to Zhao Defa, Deputy General Manager of Shanghai's Hualian Plaza the next day, for his help in locating vendors.

She and the four buyers returned with 45 signed contracts, way above my target.

Pressure might bring out people's potential. By the way, I resorted to the traditional "rule by man" in this particular case.

However, "rule by man" had its own limitations. Because of this, we started to design the management structure of the Wuhan Plaza when we were still looking for vendors. This was as important as designing the Wuhan Plaza building, and more crucial than recruiting workers or looking for vendors. The design of the building provided a physical form for our company, while the designing of the management structure would build blood vessels and a circulation system into it. Manpower and merchandise were the metabolism of a business. The management structure, on the other hand, provided the control mechanism. I once worked in the Organization Division of the Party's Commerce Committee, and later on as Deputy Director of a hospital and Deputy General Manager of the Wuhan Department Store. I had the chance to observe the traditional management structure from above and from within. I had such a bad experience with it that I decided the first thing to do when running an enterprise was set up a new management structure.

Now I had this opportunity. I took to action immediately, looking for a reference system first, to see what others were doing. "You wish you had read more books when starting to put them to use."[5] In the process of seeking a feasible model, I discovered that only two department stores in Wuhan kept a little management data, which were far from systematic. They were tainted heavily with planned economy and traditional management, lacking in modern scientific management concepts, and disconnected from the reality of competition in the market economy. In short, they couldn't invigorate us.

But we needed vigor, which was represented by two elements. One was a simple but efficient operating structure, the so-called *ti* (body); the other was a scientific and practical control system, the so-called *zhi* (control). To invigorate our business, the management system should be complete, flexible and workable. It should also integrate the past experience with modern international practices. It should be able to stand the test of time, stable and forward-looking.

I discovered that this train of thought would lead me to the edge of knife, the summit of height, and difficulty. I would have to burn more mid-night oil to complete this highly difficult maneuver with the limited means, but I had no choice. The Wuhan Plaza must present an advanced management model to our trade, as well as quality consumer merchandise to the people. I therefore made a list for myself.

On the left side of the list were topics to be dealt with during our design; in the middle were requirements; on the right was current malpractice to be avoided. I wanted the design to be supported by computers. I stipulated the design method. *Ti*, the operating structure, was to be decided on by the upper management, while *zhi*, the control system, was to be formulated by a taskforce. And the leader of the taskforce should be an outsider to the retail trade. This would enable him/her to stay away from the old routines.

My list was as follows:

Ti (operating structure):

Top management level: no deputy positions, to avoid unnecessary disputes and weakened power;

Management structure: one-level management, flat-structure, to avoid interruption;

Middle management: no deputy positions, to avoid bickering over responsibility;

Retail teams: managed vertically by each department, to avoid losing control.

Zhi (control system):

Human resources management: all employees subject to promotions and demotions, hiring and dismissal, rewards and punishment, to avoid life-long positions;

Finance management: one-level accounting, to avoid withholding and careless disbursement;

Commodity management: separation of purchasing and sales, to avoid corruption and embezzlement;

Business management: rotation, to avoid stagnation;

Service management: zero distance, to avoid alienating customers;

Floor management: always on the move, to avoid being superficial;

Training management: continuous and diversified, to
avoid treating it as a mere formality;

Property management: adding value, to avoid property
depreciation.

After drawing up the list, I looked it over out of prudence. I felt
that I would run into resistance. The topics were clear; the requirements in the middle of the list required new thinking; and the problems to be avoided on the right side were current malpractice to
fight against. It meant that there was no tight-rope to walk on, no
balance to be made — the new system would have to be built among
strong conflicts.

Predicting potential upcoming conflicts, I started to look for evidence. The taskforce for formulating the control system began to
operate, expanding their search to every corner. I made a bold decision, and asked Ms. Choi, Deputy General Manager representing
the Hong Kong side, to purchase documentation on management in
Hong Kong. We did this because from the very beginning, the Wuhan Plaza needed to be internationalized, aiming at the advanced
level in the world. Hong Kong was a world-famous commercial
capital. Ms. Choi got in contact with a gentleman who had worked
in management positions in several international shopping centers,
with easy access to information. He proposed a shockingly high
price. Still, we would do anything to achieve top-class management.

Meanwhile, we started to look for reference for the operating
structure. We visited the Wuhan Office of Coca Cola, the Sino-French
joint venture Shenlong Automobile Co, and the New World Department Store. We discovered that their top management was extremely
simple in structure, with a chairman of the board or general manager on the foreign side, and a general manager or a deputy general
manager on the Chinese side. But for the need for power balance
between the two sides, there could be only one general manager in
this structure, with no deputy positions. I liked it because it centralized the management of all the activities in the business in an efficient manner, free from the defects of setting up many deputy posi-

tions, such as overstaffing, constant bickering, self-importance and power draining.

We prepared a report, suggesting that, in addition to William Choi, the General Manager who was based in Hong Kong most of the time and Ms. Choi, Deputy General Manager who worked in Mr. Choi's capacity in his absence, the Chinese side be represented by only one Deputy General Manager (myself) in charge of daily operations. No other deputy positions would be set up.

Mr. Choi read the report carefully when it was submitted to him. He gave his full support, saying that the proposal was in line with international practices.

Then the report was submitted to the Board of Directors.

I remember that the Board meeting lasted forever, starting with an intangible pressure in the silence.

Chief Mao lit a cigarette and spoke calmly. He thought the Chinese side should provide at least four deputy general managers. How could Hu Bingxin take care of everything? She wouldn't even have time for all the meetings.

Chief Mao was showing his care for me, but, remembering all the problems of deputy positions, I said that this problem had an easy solution. We could set up several assistant positions for the general managers.

The difference between assistants and deputy positions was this: when the general manager was absent, one of the deputy general managers could take over the function. In contrast, assistants could only take assignments. When the general manager returned, deputy general managers would resume their own responsibilities. Assistants would never function in a management position; they would only offer helping hands.

On hearing this, Mao didn't say anything and sank into thinking. I understood that this structure was widely different from the traditional one, which he had spent his whole life in.

The discussion on the operating structure ran aground, and the issue of the control system didn't fare smoothly, either. The management documents that had cost us tens of thousands of Hong Kong dollars were sent over. When I looked into them, I found that they were full of details, without mentioning the underlying principles, like a tree with only leaves but no trunk. Without a trunk, leaves had nothing to attach to.

We had to find other alternatives. We bought many management books from the Business School of Harvard University, and got hold of a set of ISO9000 Quality Management and Assurance documents that had been sanctioned according to international standards. I believed that we could borrow the expertise from other industries. We reorganized the taskforce. Outside experts were still playing the leading role. In the meanwhile, people from within the retail trade were added. We required them to investigate every set of rules and regulations as a special subject. They were to follow this procedure: formulate rules and regulations in a specific field, discuss the draft with the people or departments involved, update the draft, bring them to discussion again, until they were perfect. In this way, the various versions of the documents, from the preliminary draft, to the second draft, to the third draft, on and on, piled up in a room.

The amount of work was not hard to imagine.

The difficulty of the work was not hard to imagine either.

I believed that truth could be reached only after laborious journeys, and that creativity could be stimulated only in a persistent pursuit.

In this spirit, a Board meeting was called again for the operating structure.

Before the meeting, we listened to some comments. The major opposition was that without deputy general managers, supervision would be weakened, arbitrary decisions and corruption could occur, and it would not help bring out the initiative from everyone. On hearing this, I felt a chill through my body. Why did traditional thinking only focus on personal relationships, but not on the work itself? I wondered how bickering deputy general managers could bring out the initiative from everyone, how these deputy general managers, each with their own controlled domain, would contribute to supervision, and whether power sharing by the deputy general managers would not lead to other interest groups or corrupt cliques. At that moment, I saw with my own eyes the social and historical inertia, and deeply felt the difficulty of acting with sincerity and integrity, and the even greater difficulty of trying to do things. Ms. Choi, Deputy General Manager from the Hong Kong side, felt rather troubled when she learned about this. She hated entanglement in personal relations. She believed that businessmen must concentrate on business and do whatever was good for business.

When the Board of Directors met again, Ms. Choi made her position clear: "If additional deputy positions are set up, I'll withdraw from the cooperation."

Astonishment. Silence. All turned their eyes to me, with a grave look.

Ms. Choi went on, "I trust Bingxin. I don't think she is power hungry. As her compatriots, don't you..."

These remarks were quite stern. I felt sad but soon raised my head. I realized that this was not just my personal matter. It would determine the fate of the new management model. I had no choice but to tough it out.

9. Bring in High Tech

Chief Mao proved to be a reform-oriented businessman once more. At the critical moment, he lit a cigarette and smiled, giving his endorsement to our proposal.

I understood that he had placed the responsibility on his shoulder, for the new operating structure, and for me. Only by bringing the Wuhan Plaza up could I pay him back for his support and trust.

I buried myself into the establishment of the structure and system. A few months later, we finished the 220,000-word document *Comprehensive Quality Management of the Wuhan Plaza*.

This was the law of the company, a heavy and thick handbook. It included big topics such as the overall structure and system of the company, and specifics such as the *Employee Handbook* and the *Handbook for Sales Assistants*, which provided guidelines for the staff. It was proved in the subsequent business practice that this document was the key to the Wuhan Plaza's profitability, and a management classic highly acclaimed by our colleagues in the retail business.

The operating structure was established, and the control system was also in place. What we needed now was a computer system to support them. I didn't know much about computers, often feeling awed by them. If those who didn't know how to work on computers were functional illiterates, I was almost among them. I felt the rapid development of modern technology and the urgent need for knowledge renewal. While the "self-importance syndrome" was ridiculous, I didn't feel inferior either. I believed I could learn.

Mao knew me well. When he saw I was worried about computers, he told me to take it easy, not to put too much pressure on myself. He said it would be great if the computer system could be set up. If not, they could at least be used as cash registers.

The computers to be used just as cash registers? I was the type that the more I was trusted, the more I wanted to accomplish.

Right at that moment, my assistant Zhuang Xianming repeatedly reminded me never to use computers as cash registers. Modern businesses must be supported by high technology.

I was impressed by an essay on the race between the rabbit and the tortoise. It went like this: usually people believed that the tortoise defeated the rabbit by accident, because the rabbit took a nap. Judging by their ability alone, the rabbit could never be defeated, unless we assumed that it would take a nap. It was not scientific to base any prediction on assumptions. It would not only exaggerate the spiritual power of the tortoise but also encourage the dangerous belief of leaving things to chances.

The essay went on to say that we should follow a different path, i.e., to completely neutralize the advantage of the rabbit. The rabbit was still a rabbit. It didn't take a nap either. But the tortoise managed to find a car. The car extended the legs of the tortoise and helped speed it up. The race would take on a new sense of drama, and the outcome would be factual and solid, not based on an assumption.

When reading the essay, I thought: if the tortoise could win with the help of a car, what could we do?

After browsing all the data I had obtained, and recalling all the overseas shopping centers I had visited, I came to the conclusion that, in order to win in the current and future commercial wars, we must increase the investment in high technology.

Let us increase the investment, then. The top management of the Wuhan Plaza was in consensus. We were not short of funding. What was needed was mental commitment.

Now came the time to commit our heart and soul to technology.

I began to bury myself in books, seek out data and design a feasible plan based on the characteristics of the Wuhan Plaza. We followed up every clue, visiting almost all the big shopping centers in China that had installed computer systems, as well as some top businesses in Hong Kong. But after all this, I was confused. Each business had its own system. Which one should we take up? Life was usually paradoxical: it would be too simple without any choice, and too difficult with too many choices.

Presented with so many choices, we had to go through rounds and rounds of comparison, balancing and evaluation.

The time was not spent in vain. The strategy crystallized in the evaluation: our starting-point must be high, the scope of application must be wide, the technology must be new, the function must be complete, and the operation must be stable. The system must remain competent for at least 3 to 5 years.

With the strategy ready, other pieces fell naturally in place. We found the Chinese distributor of IBM, the best hardware manufacturer in the world, and negotiated repeatedly with their general manager for better pricing.

This general manager had discovered that the Wuhan Plaza still under construction would become the leader in using computers in China's retail business. Out of his confidence in this market perspective, he signed the contract, although he emphasized on several occasions later on that I was the most demanding and competent negotiator he had ever met in Mainland China.

I had to be competent, because Zhuang Xianming had told me that there was an important concept in computer application – the Leadership Law. It meant that in order to represent the requirements and plans of the leadership in the computer system, the leaders of the business must get involved in the design and development of the application. Software, a dazzling maze, looked highly complex and mysterious to me. It was obvious that I couldn't master software applications overnight, but I believed that I should suggest their operation modules based on the needs of the Wuhan Plaza. These new modules must have something revolutionary in them.

I needed a good software developer who could turn my requirements into reality.

We contacted many foreign software developers. To my dismay, most of them were foreign to the Chinese market, and their applications were not fully localized. In addition, the mature applications were all modeled on the platform of the department store + branch stores.

A department store model? No way! Ours must be totally new, a unique model.

We then turned to domestic software developers and made three criteria for selection. The starting-point should be high, the price should be low, and it should be able to provide a one-package solution to both hardware and networking.

The Hong Kong side in our top management was quite skeptical.

In compromise, we selected two companies so that they could compete on an equal basis. We then would choose the winner.

The Hong Kong side recommended a trusted foreign company. We picked Shanghai Coms Business Computer Co, Ltd. The foreign company turned up their nose at Coms. We thought: "Well, we will see who will make the kill in the competition."

We gave both companies three months to prepare. Coms took it seriously, dispatching a big team of technicians to Wuhan right away. They researched our requirements and worked overtime everyday. In contrast, the foreign company only contacted us a few times by phone and fax.

Underestimating the rival? Yes, it did.

There was a dramatic turn in the development. It turned out that the brand name was not the only decisive factor in the competition.

When open bidding started three months later, it was obvious that the foreign company was unable to perform up to the criteria. Their software was localized into Chinese, but without rigorous testing. As a result, "gross profit margin" became "profit margin gross", a wrong order in Chinese.

In contrast, Coms was commended by all the reviewers because of its rigorous and detailed program design.

I remember that I wrote the software evaluation report for the company myself. I spent a whole night on it. Many computer experts commented that the report was beautifully written, with good theory and clear logic, as if written by an expert. On hearing this, I smiled, not out of my vanity, but for the achievement I had made in learning the computer. The praise was like a score report, representing the reward for my efforts. An even bigger reward was the savings for the company. We had planned to spend RMB 30 million on the computer system; we ended up using only 8 million.

We bought a premium product for 8 million! It stood the test in later business operations and proved to be perfect.

Besides, it is still taking the lead in China now. It is the largest computer system with the latest technology, the most complete functions and the highest reliability in China's retail business.

More importantly, it provided comprehensive supervision and support for merchandise, finance, human resources, decision-making, information, and property management.

Now we had the backing to compete with any powerful rivals!

10. Build a Soul of Culture

Now it was time to build the soul of the business.

We had the brain, which was the business strategy; the body, which was the building; the blood vessels, which were the operating structure and the control system; the supporting skeleton, which was high technology; the energy, which was the human resources; the metabolism, which was the commodity. The only thing missing was a soul.

What role does the soul play? It is the values, ethics, self-discipline, and moral guidelines. It is the motivation and driving force.

Man builds everything in the world. As such, he imprints his characteristics on his accomplishments. The highest form of human characteristics is what is called the "soul."

The term "the soul of an enterprise" appeared early. I checked out its origin. It was also known as "enterprise culture." It came from the U. S., although its origin could be traced back to Japan. It evolved from the term "organizational features," which was often the focus in Japanese enterprises. According to my research, the founder of the theory was Chester Barnard, an American management expert. When discussing the manager's functions in 1938, he stated that the role of a leader was to create a set of values through the power of the organization, and guide the enterprise with the values. In his opinion, the most important job of a general manager was to preserve the values of the enterprise and get them accepted by all the members of the organization through his personal exemplification and instructions. In his book *The Practice of Management* published in 1954, Peter Drucker provided some basic principles on the enterprise culture: people were resources, not expenses; people must be managed; management was an art; management was an ever-changing practice; while concerned with the achievements of the organization, the manager should look inward, focusing on the structure and values that facilitated personal achievement. Comparative management studies intensified in the 1970s, and cultural power was given more weight than economic power. Having looked into the success stories of 62 outstanding enterprises in the U. S., American economists stated eight laws in the book *In Search of Excellence*. Enterprise culture, which emphasized values as a driving force, was listed as one of the important economic laws. It was generally accepted that an enterprise without enterprise culture was spiritless.

Of course we needed spirit. We needed the soul for the enterprise.

The whole organization should act as one entity, demonstrating the corporate will and values.

I wanted to turn our team into a self-motivated army, not only restrained by discipline, but also inspired by heroism, team spirit, a sense of success and mission. These would lead us to success.

But how could I summarize our characteristics, will power and values in concise language? This was a tough issue.

I discussed this issue with many people. Each had their own ideas. Some even suggested soliciting enterprise culture slogans with a prize offer, much in the same way as advertisement tag lines are solicited these days. This idea was feasible, but I felt that this issue should be approached with careful deliberation, not with fanfare. The language must deliver our corporate characteristics, specific and tied to the retail trade.

I received my inspiration from the remarks of an American retail expert. He said, "The retail trade is about details." Not long after, when I talked with Chang Kuo An, an elderly Taiwan businessman, a comment from him further deepened my understanding of "details." He said that there was nothing big in the retail business. If details were taken care of, the job would be all done. A revelation struck me. Yes, our enterprise culture ought to focus on details.

"Details" best described the nature of our business.

Meanwhile, if we were successful with all the details, how could we mess up the big picture? The big picture was pieced together from the details.

Previously, people had been taken to empty talks in discussing the enterprise spirit. Our concentration on details would make us distinctive, like a gentle, refreshing breeze.

I worked swiftly, but I always attended to all the details. Now we would highlight "details!"

As a result, we decided on "make every detail perfect" as the primary concept of our enterprise culture.

Perfection is the highest level in our life and career. By choosing this level, we were destined to put in more work and do better than other businesses.

We must go higher and do better. Otherwise what would become of the Wuhan Plaza, and how could we win out in the fierce business war?

Every detail with perfection. When this principle was formulated, I enforced it among all the employees. On some occasions, my standards were highly demanding, but I felt they were helpful in overcoming bad habits such as laziness, carelessness, inadvertence, and low efficiency.

For example, we demanded that the first thing an on-site supervisor should do everyday was to check whether all the lights were on.

Another example. One day I found the cover of a junction box was missing in the elevator. I brought together all the senior managers into the elevator and asked them whether there was anything unusual, to guide them to details.

As a result of our focus on details, 98% of the lights were in working conditions, and the floor was always spotless. Once, the owner of a famous brand in Hong Kong came to look for business opportunities. He felt the back of the escalator handrail — it was clean. He felt the wall tile — it was clean, too. Very impressed, he said, "Since every detail is handled so well here, I will trust my brand to you."

Our attention to details won over manufacturers and vendors, who signed contracts with us. Moreover, the cause and effect relation between the details and the whole was tested out in our work.

By then we had only one value for the enterprise culture. Was it specific enough?

I further developed it into a system, which was made up of several concise slogans, very easy to remember.

The first slogan was the management principle: "Rules are higher than the General Manager"; the second slogan was the staffing principle: "Close but with some distance, using people with suspicion"; the third slogan was the business principle: "Top quality service, with customer orientation."

These three slogans were all aimed at "details." The first one provided a policy basis for details; the second one created a cultural context; and the third one pointed out where detailed work would be applied.

Later I heard comments that these three principles were against the tradition. I smiled. They were specifically made to correct traditional shortcomings. In the past, the interpersonal relationship was put above policies in our enterprises, and the rule by law gave way to the rule of man. The president of a big company in Malaysia said to me, "Chinese enterprises are not doing well because of their management problems. They prefer this order: relationship, reason, and law." Now I intended to reverse the order to "law, reason, and relationship." "Law" referred to company policies; "reason" was based on rational considerations; and "relationship" was motivation and rewards. No one violating company policies should be excused, not even the general manager. Company policies worked out laboriously by the management team were not to be brushed aside or violated. Besides, the company was a work place, where the relation between the employees should be strictly professional, not based on favoritism or nepotism. Favoritism and nepotism left many enterprises disoriented and paralyzed, entangled in endless in-fight. I had to turn it around. "Close but with some distance, using people with suspicion." This simplified human relations in business. We were all co-workers, related to each other in our work, like links in a moving chain. Favoritism and nepotism had no place in our business, and no time or attention should be given to solving human rivalries or internal friction. I believed these crisp lines embodied modern concepts of human resource management. They were to be imprinted in the minds of the employees, to guide them in self-discipline.

The principle of "top quality service, with customer orientation" did not seem to go against the tradition except for focusing on the relation between the seller and the customer. The seller should always put him- herself at the service of the customer.

"Orientation" meant an attitude of service, to help customers find what they really wanted, and refine their consumption and behavior.

Going against the tradition was not totally bad or beyond comprehension. Our society was in the process of transformation. Transformation meant, in a sense, turning away from tradition.

Now experts are calling for building a support system, which would include a set of new concepts, when the structure of the market economy is being constructed. I believe that this set of values in our enterprise culture was the support system for the Wuhan Plaza in the commercial war.

Out of these considerations, I didn't try to shy away from the label of "going against the tradition." On the contrary, I continued to generate some new concepts from the values of enterprise culture.

For example, "Only the result counts, not the process"; "The order of the superior is the order from the company"; and the "Cup Theory" stating that "the cup is broken because you didn't handle it properly."

These ideas seemed harsh, but they were highly necessary. They would contribute to an enterprising spirit in our company.

We valued affection. I myself was taken by affection from time to time. But I knew that in the challenging time and intensifying commercial war, we must train and discipline an army that would obey the order uncompromisingly, charge ahead regardless of their own safety, and remain invincible under all circumstances.

(Endnotes)

[1] Lu Xun was a very famous Chinese writer in 1920s and 1930s.

[2] "Pay tuition" has been used frequently to mean "learn at a cost."

[3] Government employees in China, including university teachers, used to have free housing as part of their benefits.

[4] China maintains a centralized system of tracking people with higher education. Those who join the private sector often leave their confidential personal files with the Human Resources Management Center in each city.

[5] This is an old Chinese saying.

3

Dig in Feet to Achieve High;
Stretch out Hands to Embrace Hope

> I am not regretful, though I have lost my head over you.
> — "A Thousand Paper Cranes," Japanese folk song

> There is a small city named Zilang in Southern Jiangsu, I miss it from time to time. I miss its peaceful lanes, And the fragrant flowers on pagoda trees...
> — Author

1. Play Tough

It was too early to tell whether it was a win or a loss. One thing was clear, though. I was now stranded, like Zhou Yu before the Battle of Chibi,[1] who had prepared a battlefield of a hundred miles and was waiting for nothing but winds from the east. East winds now were the Wuhan Plaza building, which was to be packed with concepts, management systems, goods and staff. The building was really a pain in the neck. No sooner than the huge site was excavated than a geological subsiding occurred. Construction went on and off up sluggishly. Everyday we ran back and forth to the site. We asked the Property Management Department to tighten the rope by sending written requests to the developer, to hurry them up. Yet the numerous written requests fell on deaf ears. The building was still like a child retarded in growth, leaving its parents heart-broken.

Matching the sluggish progress of construction were the auxiliary projects. This huge building had to be powered by a transformer substation, and the expenses were to be shared by several consumers. We paid our share, but the others wouldn't. The substation then went up in smoke. The whole building was hanging on only one temporary power line, the electricity from which couldn't even be used to tune the escalators. Up to this moment, the chance to efficiently implement the original plan had vaporized. We could only slowly climb up the stairs.

We had come over many hurdles. According to our plan, the Wuhan Plaza was to open its doors in October, 1995. All the work was laid out with this target date in mind. But it turned out that we had to put off the grand opening to March, 1996. March was the spring time. We hoped that the arrival of spring would bring along good luck. Unfortunately, "spring winds cannot blow beyond the Yumen Pass."[2] The doors had to remain closed by then. In April, 1996, the sun was shining quite hot already, and we became fish in a dried rut.[3]

We very much wanted to swim swiftly back to the open sea, but the path to the sea was blocked. The only cause was our inability to control the construction schedule. If this was allowed to go on, the progress of construction would become a guessing game.

But remaining closed was no game. We had to inform the vendors time and again of the delay. By doing so, we lost our credit and risked losing the vendors we had taken so much pain to lure over.

"The morale can only be boosted, not depleted." The repeated delay could even disappoint and scatter the project team.

For each single day we remained closed, we incurred expenses without generating any revenue; we were throwing away thousands of dollars. This was not my money, but I should feel my responsibility for the investors.

These aside, the most critical issue was the grave challenge the Wuhan Plaza was facing — we were missing the vital business window, much to our woe.

The spring of 1996 was not a favorite season for the retail business. The weak market continued to remain weak. The newspapers were just celebrating "huge department stores going wild in Beijing" when Chinese department stores began to collapse. According to some statistics, from 1994 to early 1996, nine department stores in Shenzhen closed down. On May 1, 1996, Beijing's Xinte Shopping Center shut its doors forever, seven months after it started business. In the same period, large shopping plazas went out of business one after another, including Guangzhou's Guofeng Department Store and Shenyang's Concord Department Store. Disasters brought about chain reaction like domino chips. In 1996, 199 out of 212 large shopping centers in China showed red in their books.

The grave situation put us in jeopardy. If we didn't act fast and powerfully, the Wuhan Plaza would probably come to an end before it saw its day.

When I finished reading the statistics, my first reaction was to bring together the senior staff for a meeting.

I required the department managers at the meeting to gather information overnight and list the loss of delay in detail.

We had to present the grave situation to the Board of Directors. Moreover, I had to find a way out of this dried rut.

One night, I went to the Wuhan Plaza's construction site. It was a cool spring night. The Wuhan Plaza building towered high against the dark blue steely sky. It still looked miserable, wrapped in scaffolds and safety nets, the glass sheets yet to be installed, exposing the structure inside. The spot where "Wuhan Plaza" in Li Tieying's handwriting should be embedded showed nothing but cement. The central entrance was blocked by walls. Inside the walls was a tower crane rising up into the sky. A crescent moon hung under the crane's arm. In the moonlight, the surface of the square lay bare, with no pavement. Trash piled up here and there, in a place that should be clean and bright.

The whole square looked like a waste land, and the building resembled ruins.

But, wait — I saw tiny golden flames flickering on every floor.

These were lights. Workers were working under these makeshift lights in order to meet the deadline for interior decoration. I asked the people around. They told me that more than 500 workers were already working on interior decoration, and that another 500 could be brought in if necessary.

1,000 workers. It suddenly occurred to me that there was an excellent chance to explore, which in turn led to one idea after another.

A few years later, when our ideas were mentioned, some people still considered them as crazy. As I remember, when I told Mao about my worries and he began to make his arrangements, a writer asked me, "Are you a little bit paranoiac?" I asked back, "Have you read Andrew Grove's *Only the Paranoid Survive*?" He said not yet. I told him that there was a well-known remark from this President of the world-renowned Intel Corporation, to the effect that in business management, paranoia was absolutely necessary. I also told him that Grove believed in paranoia because at many subtle or critical moments, popular opinions and conventions couldn't be relied on to handle the situation. Only the paranoiac had the overwhelming power. I added that I was at a critical moment now and I couldn't follow the routine and wait. We had to go paranoiac.

He said to me cautiously, "As I understand it, it's life or death for you."

I smiled, "We are fighting with our back to the wall."

"You guys are tough!" he remarked.

I replied, "Of course. Business is warfare. We have to be tough in a war."

In fact, our idea was very simple. We would ignore the unfinished exterior. Instead, we would launch our grand opening as soon as interior decoration was done. This idea was based on the following reasoning. The Wuhan Plaza building was 48 stories high. The top part was still under construction at the time. If we followed the conventions, we would probably remain closed for another year. In a year, the general economic climate might change, and competition within the trade might intensify. We would be pushed into a corner. We couldn't afford to let go business opportunities for one more year. To grab market share, the only choice was to press on.

Viewed from another perspective, however, this idea was simply ridiculous. We had no electricity, no water (not connected to the water mains), no toilet (not built yet), no dining facilities (staff canteens were still under construction), no imposing exterior, even no name (the shop sign could not be installed in time). A grand opening with so many No's — ours would be the only case in China and in the world. We were not a roadside shop. The Wuhan Plaza was a huge shopping center with an area of 76,000 square meters. Our case could probably be entered into the Guinness record.

Entered into the Guinness? That would be fine.

This was quite a challenge. I carefully thought over all the issues in question and reported to Mao.

Mao proved to be an entrepreneur indeed. He had been deliberating on the grand opening plan for some time already. He said to me, "The Wuhan Plaza has unique advantages with its location and consumers. The sooner it starts business, the sooner we will make profit, and the more market share we will grab. We can't afford to delay even for a day."

He called for a meeting of the Board of Directors on this issue after the Spring Festival of 1996.

Mr. William Choi spoke up at the meeting, against the immediate opening of the Wuhan Plaza. He was a perfectionist. The Wuhan Plaza symbolized his deep love for the motherland. In his opinion, it should open with grand fanfare, with top class construction, decorations, mechanical and electrical systems in China. At present, when nothing was ready, the grand opening was out of question.

I replied, saying that if we didn't open to business, these No's would persist forever; only when we pressed on with the grand opening, could everything be turned around, thus overcoming and eliminating those No's.

Mao said, "China has its own way of development; so does Wuhan. The Wuhan Plaza shopping center must go into service before the National Day of 1996." He paused for a moment and added, "We will open anyway, even with no electricity, no water, no road."

Suddenly, he turned to me, saying, "Bingxin, this is your job."

I nodded. This way, a consensus was reached at the meeting.

2. General Manager, a Super Processor

The Board of Directors decided that the Wuhan Plaza would open on September 28, 1996. It looked into ways to speed up the project. September 28 was a lucky date in the Chinese folk tradition, meaning "long and prosperous," but for us, it was a difficult hypothesis. Our previous planning and work would be put together, adjusted, arranged and tested in real-time operation. Unpredictable and unpredicted potential risks would call for flexibility, swiftness, versatility and prompt action. Human intelligence, physical endurance, and charisma would be put to test on the razor's edge. This edge was very sharp. The result could be a Waterloo, or a Normandy.

Many signs pointed September 28 to a Waterloo. First, in addition to the exterior of the Wuhan Plaza building, the interior was disheartening as well. The central air conditioning system was not installed yet. The missing glass sheets exposed a sulky sky. Counters and shopping sections were a mess of glass and stainless steal frames. On the floor was some stinking human feces left over by temporary laborers from the countryside. Most sales assistants were still to be recruited, their experience and skills yet to be developed. We were short of hands. Even if we opened to business ignoring these problems, so many green hands might put up a fiasco. Moreover, computers that would support the entire operation had not been tested, the result yet unpredictable. Besides, we had recruited around 1,000 vendors, with more than 200,000 products — which would take up almost 30,000 cubic meters and weigh more than 80,000 tons. It would be an impossible job to ship these products in, check them, enter them into the computers, move them to the staging area and display them on the shelves nice and neat.

For every business, rolling into operation is a master event, which involves tons of hard work, as well as complex and delicate system tuning.

For us, it appeared even more formidable. It was like walking on thin ice, like standing on the edge of a bottomless water pool, like guiding thread through the pinhole, like reaching for stars and galaxies.

Key to the formidable task were the following factors: whether we could stay away from errors in sorting through the issues, big or small; whether we could proceed with precision in dealing with general and specific problems; whether we could work out conceptual and operational solutions.

Many people were skeptical, because this would call for a super processor.

I was absolutely positive, though, because we had two sets of network. One was the computer network. It was accurate and efficient. The other was a pool of well-trained staff. It was elite and capable. Computers aside, I will focus on the staff here.

The staff of the Wuhan Plaza had been hardened under extreme temperatures. In other words, they had gone through advanced training. In 1995, based on the belief that "human assets take the priority to profits," we conducted pre-job training. I went to Hong Kong and, after careful search, picked Shineway Management Training Company to provide training to Zhuang Xianming and four other senior managers. Later, two Hong Kong training companies and one Taiwan company were brought in to give training to department managers and management staff. Their training was systematic, ranging from concepts to job descriptions, from instant service to public conduct and rituals. They provided novel training methods. For example, when presenting team work, they avoided lecturing on its importance. Instead, a team leader led a blindfolded team through various barriers, accompanied by miserable music. Hand in hand, they groped in darkness, which gave them a sense of difficulty and danger, as well as a feeling that everyone shared the same fate and the appreciation of the team power.

This way, they integrated into the team, and our company obtained a core group. Although the company spent hundreds of thousands of Hong Kong dollars on training, this was not seen as an expense, but an ingenious strategy. I dare to say that no other retail business in China had spent so much money on staff training. On the other hand, no other business could boast such an enthusiastic and self-disciplined team which excelled in business.

This group was not big in number, with some 60 people.

We believed in the effect of multiplication and fission. We trusted that they would each build a capable team in the shortest possible time.

This group would become the most powerful network to support September 28.

If only they could be backed up by a super processor.

The general manager should be the super processor of the business.

That is because she gives all the instructions and collects all the information. Her work is to evaluate the information, determine its nature, dissemble, synthesize, summarize and transform it. Her office is none other than a sensitive nerve center, the CPU of a computer. There, every telephone line is an outreaching tentacle; every folder is a large hard disk; pen, ink and paper become function keys on the keyboard. Her daily work is to continuously open or shut this path or that one.

She must know these paths by heart; in the meantime, she must have enough energy to plod through them.

Out of this consideration, I was changing clothes before a mirror the morning after the Board meeting. The mirror revealed a face with some signs of exhaustion. She was not the same hospital clerk studying at the Dianshi University ten years ago, nor the same milling machine operator 20 years ago. She was more mature, wearing a skirt. I changed out of the skirt into a pair of jeans, with reluctance.

Frankly, I was no longer at the age for jeans. But I was tall and slim, and looked brisk in jeans. For more dramatic effect, I put on a shirt that tied up in the front. When I entered the office, my staff said I looked younger. I corrected them by saying that I was not younger, but more energetic.

I felt I must let my staff sense my energy and confidence. Before a major battle, every little detail about the commander would have a strong impact on the soldiers. In addition, we had always focused on details, so that everyone was tuned to them. I showed off these details on purpose. I didn't hang around for long, though, and disappeared into the General Manager's Office. Sitting down, I started to list the to-do tasks in the notebook, which included: the construction schedule, fitting-up and display, recruitment and training, computer testing, vendor notification, trucking, commodity shelving, moving inventory upstairs, meals and toilets, drinking water...

After completing the list, I called in the person in charge of property management, telling him that he must hand over a furnished department store by September 15, and watch out for the quality of electricity wiring and fire safety.

Then I made a call to the manager of the Human Resources Department and instructed him to pick the 600 people that were to be transferred from the Wuhan Department Store before the end of May, to recruit 2,000 more sales assistants, and then to put them to intensive training until mid September. We would use schools for training facilities. As for teachers, we would let the more experienced teach the less experienced.

I spent more time with the manager of the Commodity Department. I asked her to bring together all the experts. In the meeting-room we would put up a board, showing all the steps in the circulation of commodities, from notification to counter display. All the links in this cycle would be studied in detail, from the technology involved, through the timing, to load balancing between peaks and valleys.

I gave a flat order to the Computing Center that all computers must be configured and tested before May 20, so that the accounting program could be put in service on June 1.

It was already dark when all this was done. Then I realized I had missed my lunch and dinner.

But I didn't want to eat. For some reason I recalled a Soviet movie I saw when I was young. There were some discussions in the movie about a commander's position in a battle. To sum up, he should lead his soldiers in charging, cover them up in retreating, and mix up with them in marching.

"We are in a battle," I thought. My position was an issue for consideration.

I didn't dwell on the issue for long. I must have some rest now. I didn't realize it was raining till I got out of the building.

3. Look into Every Detail in Person

We fought our way through barriers and passes amid wind and rain; we quested for success under the burning sun. Here "quest" is used to describe the road to success, because success is not waiting at a certain place for easy picking, like a peach in a peach tree. Success is forever a flashing lightening, a slippery fish, an inevitable growing out of a series of the accidental, and a sum of many variables. It is either naive or mistaken to think that success could be defined by plans on paper and that thorough planning would take care of everything.

With this understanding, I followed up my orders by inspecting every site. I felt I should look into every detail in person, and catch all the potential risks by hard walking. To be frank, I envied those general managers who could sit in a command center and work out strategies that would assure victories a thousand miles away. But I didn't dare to copy them. My experience told me that the ease might be disguising numerous little mistakes and little tolls. The general law is that the more plugging and weeding, the better the crop.

For example, after we swung to action, almost 1,000 workers were immediately brought on site. Every floor was in full motion, with welding sparks showering everywhere. In these bright sparks, shelves and counters were put together, shopping sections were constructed, and the stainless steel railing in the supermarket was taking shape. But it would be wrong to assume that everything was OK. Soon after, I found that workers responsible for fireproof coating didn't know what they were doing.

According to regulations, fireproof coating should be painted thick in three layers. These workers painted thin without even knowing how many coatings they had done.

This would pose a serious threat to the Wuhan Plaza building. Once a fire broke out, the consequences would be unthinkable.

I promptly summoned the person in charge of property construction, and asked him what was going on.

He didn't say anything. It was easy to understand why he hadn't discovered the problem: he was very busy. In addition, different people saw things in different lights. One person's bomb might be another's toy.

I gave him a flat order that he must notify the vendor company in writing whenever he discovered problems, and that he should pay close attention to the fireproof coating, leaving a mark after each coating.

After this incident, I went to the main entrance of the building. Two gigantic sculptures had already been put up outside. The "Happy Horse with a Human-Head" had the bow drawn in his hand, and the "Warrior Guard" was serious-looking, amassing an explosive force under the cold expression. These two sculptures were designed by an American artist.

Now they were standing there like deserted kids, surrounded by a huge pile of debris, their heads covered with ash from floors above under construction.

If something fell from above, these treasures in both Chinese and Western styles wouldn't stand a chance.

Protective nets should be added. So should some fabrics, for safety, and also for hiding them for dramatic effects at the opening ceremony.

I once more summoned the person in charge to give my instructions and then said to myself, "You have to look into every detail in person, because you have great responsibilities on your shoulders."

Some of these undertakings were not related to my job responsibilities; rather, they grew out of my desire for perfection. As soon as I left the main entrance, I hit upon such a case. My thoughts wandered from the sculptures to the corporate image, and then to promotion events before the opening ceremony. I had already arranged for the events and asked the staff in charge to come up with a specific plan. The plan reached my desk the day before. As usual, it suggested media advertisements on newspapers, radios and TVs, very complex and colorful. This plan was smarter than a routine promotion plan for the grand opening. Generally speaking, when a business like ours started rolling, the advertisement expense was never under a million. Our budget was a little bit less than the average, proving it was based on the principle of thrift. But, it seemed there was something missing. I couldn't articulate it. It was just a gut feeling. Now, standing in front of the sculptures, I understood. The promotion plan lacked individuality.

Our business would start under extremely unusual circumstances. Description of the exterior, or even photos of the Wuhan Plaza building on newspapers, wouldn't make sense.

It was the unique operational mechanism and the special services that should be publicized, as well as the set of values of our business.

Ads were not the optimal channel to present our values. The best form would be serial reports.

For serial reports, we would have to contact the news department of the media, not the advertising department. We were missing the whole point.

I immediately took remedial measures and made calls to media reporters. While I was on the phone, it dawned on me that office work should be energized and perfected in operation. Racking brains in the office would not lead to solutions to all the issues, because it usually relied on conventions and experience. Life was always changing. Only in the ever-changing life could we find truth.

Later on, Wuhan's Changjiang Daily published more than 20 "Reports from the Wuhan Plaza" for us. The Publicity Department of the Party's Municipal Committee also gave news briefings, calling for the media to promote the Wuhan Plaza. We saved our promotion expenses, as well as the expense for the news release. The actual expense was 40% less than the original budget. Yet this was not the whole point. The serial reports generated a much bigger impact. As a result, before the Wuhan Plaza opened its doors, a sense of mystery and suspense had been created, and an overwhelming force gathered.

Of course, I could not foresee these results at the beginning. I only felt that decisions made in the office should be perfected in their execution. Driven by this idea, I went to the Human Resources Department. The staff there was swamped with recruiting new hands and bringing staff over from the Wuhan Department Store. It was no joke to put 3,000 people in place when the doors opened. They all knew that time was running out and they were facing enormous tasks.

But mistakes might occur when time was running out. For example, when I asked the Human Resources Department about bringing staff over from the Wuhan Department Store to the Wuhan Plaza, I was told it was not finalized yet.

I went to Mao at once, only to find that he was pondering over it.

I understood his hesitation. As an old enterprise, the Wushang Group had thousands of employees. Downsizing was inevitable. However, as the profit generator of the Wushang Group, the Wuhan Department Store would probably bleed and lose some profit if a large number of experienced employees were reassigned to the Wuhan Plaza.

Mao hit upon an excellent idea : pick the candidates by drawing lots.

As a result, the manager of the Human Resources Department conducted an unusual job transfer operation.

All the staff of the Wuhan Department Store were listed and numbered. Those with their number drawn were transferred. A list of 600 employees was ready in less than an hour.

Though the group was not young, 40% of whom were over 30 years old, I believed they were experienced and had great potential. I was confident that I could build an excellent team out of them. It was proved later on that they were good workers. Now most of them are leaders at various levels in the Wuhan Plaza.

When this was done, I brushed aside the lunch brought over by my secretary and went to the Training Department to look into the details in person. Our Training Department was training teachers for the upcoming general training. The teachers, numbered 20 plus, were the cream among the 60 trainees taught by overseas companies. Their task was to train staff at various levels, old and new. In this function, this training class was very much like the Huangpu Military Academy[4] to the Wuhan Plaza. I expected its trainees to lead charges in the upcoming business battles.

The training class was conducted in a disused elevator controls room of the Wuhan Department Store, about 20 square meters in size. It was a forgotten corner, with no windows. The air was hot and stuffy, thickened with the foul smell of old urine left off from who-knows-how-long-ago. Simply put, no one could stay long in such a place.

When I found the room, my blouse was wet through with sweat.

I was deeply touched when I saw the trainees. They were hardworking and self-disciplined, under the adverse conditions.

Suddenly, I felt hot and dry.

I left quietly, to return with ice bars, sweat-sour plum juice and red-tea – that was the only way I could express my appreciation for them.

When I was leaving, I heard some say, "Come on, guys! Let's double our efforts to repay Chief Hu."

I shook my head, with a smile. I took their remarks lightly, and seriously.

I took the remarks seriously because they brought up a question: Ever since the ancient times, a commander had been expected to be "kindhearted, trustworthy, intelligent, brave and strict." In order to meet these goals, should he work in the army tent like Sima Yi,[5] or should he look into all the details in person like Zhuge Liang?

Thinking and walking, I stepped into the training class of the Commodity Department before I realized it.

Because there were computers here, the conditions were better than in the "military academy." Once in the room, I could hear the clicking sounds of the keyboards. These soldiers were drilling before a battle. A large group of young people had been recruited as computer operators. We had rigorous requirements for them: professional, skilled, accurate, detail-oriented and efficient, because they were the basis of the support for the whole enterprise. Unexpectedly, these requirements later on evolved into such recruitment tests as needle threading and green bean counting competitions. These were unprecedented recruitment tests indeed. I was very emotional when I heard about them, feeling that I must show my appreciation for them, even if I were ill in bed.

I was not ill in bed of course. But to be frank, I was exhausted. My legs were so heavy that I walked as if on cotton fiber.

It was deep into the night. The street was quiet. The universe was filled with the clicking sound from computer keyboards.

I was so moved. I would never have had this feeling if I had not looked into all the details in person. I found the department leaders and asked them to send the staff home by taxi if they lived far away, and told the boys to see the girls home.

I did not go home till the last taxi drove into the night. I went to sleep with my clothes on. The last sound I heard before fading into my sleep was the tick of the clock.

4. Waterloo and Normandy

Time passed so quickly. July soon came.

Before that, we had completed a simulated test of the computer system on May 17, and put the accounting application into service on June 1.

I remember everyone in the office was nervous when the computers were tested. The office was so quiet that we could hear the sound if a needle fell to the floor. Breath became heavy and then was held back as much as we could, for fear of frightening away the good luck.

Thanks to heaven, our computer system worked perfectly. It stood up to the test. Now the people would be put to test.

Not just a few people, not just a few dozen management staff, but an army of 3,000, a thick crowd.

With the 3,000-people strong army, commanders at all levels must stand fast in their posts.

All the letters and faxes had already been sent to the vendors. All the media had received the information that we would start business on September 28. We couldn't afford any slip. Otherwise we would lose credibility with the residents in Wuhan, and with our colleagues all over China. Bold maneuvers would become big jokes, and all the profits would go down the drain.

Time was the key, which truly meant life or death. Time became our ruthless competitor, running against us with its steady steps, never letting up.

The secretary sent me some files. In those days, the red file folders remained full. My folders had 3 colors. The red ones contained urgent cases; the blue ones had to-do cases; and the yellow ones were for my information. The thick red folders indicated that emergencies were popping up everywhere. There were tons of issues to deal with.

Under the mounting pressure, I went into top gear. I would press my senior assistants, who would in turn press the department leaders. In old times, there were military pledges and life-or-death pledges. Now that the business warfare was heating up, why couldn't we set up military pledges? I asked the Office of Confidential Information to type some pledges specifying requirements and deadlines. The staff would sign the documents to give their pledge. Should they fail, they would be removed from office.

The pledges were signed in a solemn mood. The whole building fell deadly silent as managers at all levels were signing up.

"The wind is whistling and the Yi River chilly; the hero is setting out, never to return."[6] When the ancient hero Jing Ke crossed the Yi River, the occasion couldn't have been more dramatic than this. Most importantly, we had numerous heroes like Jing Ke, who emerged in the difficult times for our enterprise, and stood up to the moment of life or death.

This occasion had a tragic splendor and soul-shocking force. In order to make the best of it, a pep meeting for the opening of the Wuhan Plaza Management Co. Ltd. was called on August 13, 1996. I gave the keynote speech.

It was like a sports meet. Each department entered the meeting-hall with a sign-board and then stood solemnly. It was not a sports meet, though, when all raised their right arm, and a forest of arms filled the meeting-hall.

Is oath-taking necessary for grand openings? Yes, because business operations are also a war. Our actions were part of the Chinese battle for its place in the world at the junction of the two centuries.

Oath-taking is nothing but a promise from the heart, a heart-felt obligation. And the heart is empowered and becomes overpowering from this very moment.

After August 13, 1996, the battle for the opening of the Wuhan Plaza was launched on all fronts. We still faced two prospects, Waterloo or Normandy, but it was more like Normandy. By the way, the Japanese invaded Shanghai on August 13 sixty years before, which was called the "August 13 Incident" in history books. Is August 13 a date for actions?

The billowing dust of the battle and the bustling army at war filled the Wuhan Plaza, which gave out a roaring clamor.

I remember that twenty yellow buses, full of the Wuhan Plaza employees, headed for the Armed Police Training Base in the suburbs of Hankou every morning.

Fifty classrooms were rented from the Wuhan Geology College and were filled with our employees everyday.

Guided by a flag, a large contingent jogged on. It was a twenty kilometer forced march to the second Yangtze bridge by the Wuhan Plaza management team. It was a march to train the stamina of the staff, a rare case in the Chinese retail business after the Cultural Revolution.

Was the Wuhan Plaza crazy? No. The Wuhan Plaza was forging people, to shape characters required for breaking new grounds.

At that time, I was cold as iron, busy as a whirling top, and tired as a withered radish.

My biggest wish was to have a good sleep, or to crack a handful of melon seeds while watching the television.

It is said that melon seeds are one of women's favorites. I agree. My daughter likes to crack melon seeds, too. But to my sadness, her paperwork was ready then and she had to leave for her studies abroad. I saw her fly away with tears in my eyes.

Who knows the sadness of bidding farewell? A poet said that a mother who lost her child was like an emptied bag, with no happiness and faith within. I felt like an emptied bag, too, the only difference being that perhaps I would no longer have happiness, but I still had faith.

I remember that after I saw my daughter off at the airport, I went back by car in silence. Summer tree leaves swept by in lines, which brought me back to my hometown Nantong. It had quiet lanes, and an abundance of green pagoda tree leaves. In summer, the fragrance of flowers on pagoda trees filled the air morning and night.

Nantong as a city was established by Cai Rong in 958 AD. It was then named Tongzhou, also called Congchuan and Zilang. I liked Zilang the most... Suddenly, the car stopped and I was back at the Wuhan Plaza.

I combed my hair with my fingers, and rose rapidly to open the car door.

The Wuhan Plaza welcomed me with its noise of internal fitting up. I became Hu Bingxin again, or, as I was often called, General Manager Hu.

The issue for me now was how to keep calm in the noise. When 3,000 people were activated, I should follow instructions from *The Art of War* by Sunzi: never wince even as Mount Tai crashed down on you, and never move the eyes even when a deer dashed across.

To adjust my emotion and mind, I started with the yellow folders for several days when I browsed business files.

The yellow folders opened another perspective. In these folders, I found a suggestion on how to clean up the business floors before the grand opening, an idea on how to simplify the opening ceremony, and letters from some vendors informing the possible delay in the supply of some commodities.

Cleaning up was important! I brought in the Wuhan Sanitation Co. immediately. This company was known for cleaning up construction sites.

Cleaning up the construction site was not enough, though. It had to prove itself in regular clean-up later on, too. I signed a strange contract with them. The body of the document had only 2 pieces of paper, but the attachment was thick. It listed in detail all the requirements for the cleaning work, rewards, penalties, and even the frequency and methods for floor cleaning. The sanitation company said they had never signed such a demanding contract. I replied that I couldn't trust the well-being of the company to careless vendors.

After completing the contract, I brought in the team in charge of planning for the opening ceremony. We discussed ways for a simple ceremony. Since the front entrance was so messy that no singing or dancing could be performed there, and no ribbon could be put up for cutting, we would just make two big sets of wooden locks and keys, paint them gold, and use them as symbols at the opening ceremony.

This decision was reached in two minutes. Next, I looked into the seasoning of goods and their peak volume. Vendor letters in the yellow folders reminded me in time of the need to calculate the logistics of the commodities: how to circulate the commodities with the highest efficiency in the shortest time.

The issue of commodity flow pointed me to a report in a red folder submitted by the Commodity Department. It stated that because the elevators were not working, the processes for staging commodities could not run. I thought for a while, opened the red folder, and scratched the staging area.

Red folders, yellow folders. They were finally mixed up altogether. Outside, a strong wind descended out of the blue.

A welcome wind! It sent dust and sand flying across the air. Revolting against the stuffy August and promising a fresh new world, the wind whirled on, crushing dry weeds and smashing rotten branches, in the spirit of the "monarch's overpowering gale" in Song Yu's[7] "Ode to Wind."

At the same time, an even stronger wind of training was blowing among the Wuhan Plaza's staff.

Intensive simulated training was being conducted in the classrooms of the Wuhan Geology Management College.

Dozens of people sat in the back rows, watching two trainees playing the roles of a customer and an assistant in transaction. The new trainees just starting out were as timid as trembling leaves in the wind.

At the Armed Police Training Base, a row of students were standing at attention, with a card between their legs, another between their left hand and left leg, and one more between their right hand and right leg. They were told to remain in that posture, rain or shine.

This was to train the trainees' stamina for standing, because they would stand eight hours at work everyday.

This training had already been conducted under the burning sun several times. The only difference today was the strong wind, which replaced the burning sun.

The wind blew sand into eyes, but the trainees were not allowed to waver. The wind blew so hard and they almost swayed, yet they couldn't move.

The coach gave the countdown in a loud voice ... five minutes... three minutes ... one minute.

The half-hour training session finally ran out. The trainees dropped to the ground like crops cut down. Some of them pinched their cramping legs, some started to cry – they were the only child in the family.

They felt sorry for themselves, and I felt sorry for them, too. But I didn't show my feelings. I believed in "more sweat during peace time, less blood at war," and also, "only after you have gone through the hardest of hardships, can you rise high above others."

5. Group Assault Before Dawn

By early September, training at the Wuhan Plaza was mostly completed. The remaining task became complex yet simple, that is, to mobilize the 3,000 troops for a final assault.

At the center of the action was the processing of commodities. Providing support for this center was our systems engineering.

According to our principle of separation of purchasing from sales, our commodities must move through these links: notifying vendors, shipping goods from them, receiving goods at our end, inspection, assigning serial numbers and bar codes, computer entry, receiving and moving the goods to the counter by the sales teams, and counter display.

A huge volume of goods moved through each link. Accuracy, speed and extreme care were required at each link, with zero tolerance for errors. In addition, these links had to be joined.

All the problems piled up on my desk, and I suddenly felt overwhelmed. I went for inspection. The shopping area was yet to be finished. Although the cleaning company had done their work, paint stains from construction could be seen everywhere on the floor. I went to the main entrance. The debris had not been cleared; the ground not yet paved, showing black and yellow earth, much like spots of mange. Without bricks, the square looked miserable; without frontal decoration, the Plaza appeared weird.

There were only 10 days left. My heart sank.

But I was not scared. When the media called to ask whether we could start in time, I assured them categorically that we could.

I had my reason to be confident: the initial problem regarding the commodities had been cleared, because we had taken precautions in advance.

The most important reason was that teams of the Wuhan Plaza had been trained and supplied, eager for the assault.

I might as well explain briefly the problem we had cleared. There were several steps involved: notifying vendors, shipping goods from them, storing them in the warehouse, and moving them into the staging area.

When the managers of the Merchandise Department were discussing the issue, I had told them to notify the vendors by mail in advance to firmly lay out the schedule, in order to balance out the peak time. As a result, official letters were sent out, which clearly defined the exact date for the arrival of goods. We even gave training classes to the major vendors from Wuhan and from outside, suggesting they set up offices in Wuhan to monitor the flow of their goods. This simplified the issue of supply of goods: the vendors just followed our timetable.

As for the warehouse and the staging area, we decided not to set up the latter for the time being. The warehouse had already been rented, and ten trucks had been borrowed for moving the merchandise. Staff had been trained for different posts in this process and simulations had been carried out. The final assault would turn out to be a precarious victory as well as a solved puzzle.

By "solved," I mean the channels were open, the workflow was simplified and the posts were staffed.

By "precarious," I mean we were under extreme pressure of time. People were not made of iron and steel. There were tons of work to complete in a short time. I wondered whether they could mount the charge.

Besides, I had to watch out for the unpredictable.

Finally, I needed to find a way to keep people in high spirits.

I had been away from home for 3 days. I just bought my underwear from a nearby shop.

I was so tired that I could fall asleep right after I sat down. But when I closed my eyes, I felt pain in my temples and all kinds of strange images and ideas were turning in my head like whirlwind. They stopped me from sleeping.

I don't know why, but what appeared most often in my mind at the time was the massive pagoda tree flowers in Zilang. They were swaying gently in the breeze and sending out waves of fragrance. In the fragrance, my daughter, who was studying abroad, ran up while shouting "Mom, mom!"

But the most lingering thought was how to transform a general manager's will into the rank and file's action.

I believe that manipulating power is useless. In the same position, one manager could do well; another might fail. I never favor the views in some present-day books which talk about gimmicks and calculations for power manipulation. They smell of street peddlers. We are general managers of large modern enterprises. A general manager's success depends on two factors: her IQ and EQ. The IQ leads to intelligent calculations, while the EQ, a natural gift, will show up in the enterprise culture.

Emotion is a necessity. Isn't the "theory of relationships" a hot topic now? Isn't relationship considered a kind of productive force these days? Relationship is based on emotion. Can we say, then, that emotion is also a kind of productive force?

Because of emotion, we human beings marry and reproduce, unite and stay close. Emotion is the driving force of human reproduction. Can we also say that it is the driving force of human production?

In ancient times, General Wu Qi sucked pus out and bandaged the wounds for his soldiers. In return, the soldiers were more than willing to give their lives for him. Wasn't it the power of emotion?

Emotion. I woke up and opened my eyes. Someone was whispering nearby.

On a simple problem – the toilet. Toilets in our building were not finished yet, but people needed to use them. Thousands of employees had come on-site the day before, rushing into the gate like mighty torrents and flowing everywhere like rivulets. Their first job was the to scrape off paint stains on the floor. The work was much tougher than it looked. With numerous paint dots clung tightly to the floor, it would take time and a strong will to scrape them clean. A great number of people had worked for thirty-eight hours, during the hot summer day and over the mosquito-infested night. At the stuffy noon time when the central-air was still not operational, they had only fast food, with a couple of bottles of spring water from the company. People might carry on with less food and water, but they must answer the call of nature and use the toilet.

They went to the Wuhan Department Store to relieve themselves. With the sudden influx of thousands, toilets there immediately went into short supply.

The simplest solution by the Wuhan Department Store was to keep the Wuhan Plaza staff from using their toilets, which led to the whisper I heard when I was dozing off.

The whisper was soft, but echoed like a thunderbolt in my mind.

I felt bad for my troops. They hadn't slept for 38 hours. Their voices were all husky. A manager named Li Li was working barefoot. When asked why she didn't have her shoes on, she replied that her feet were swollen.

They all had swollen feet, and couldn't wear their shoes. Yet, people might walk on bare feet, but they must use the toilet.

My heart sank. I rushed to the Wuhan Department Store immediately.

I felt grateful to Chief Mao again. He talked it over with Wan Laihong, Secretary of the Party Committee, who then persuaded all the middle-level managers at the Wuhan Department Store. That ended the toilet issue.

There was one more thing that I should thank Chief Mao for: he told his men, "Get a pair of cloth shoes for Bingxin."

Cloth shoes sold out at the Wuhan Department Store in no time. The Wuhan Plaza staff helped break the record in selling cloth shoes at the Wuhan Department Store.

The swollen bare feet in cloth shoes, the drooping eyelids fighting sleepiness, my laudable troops continued their assault into the 48th hour.

Without elevators, the merchandise with a volume of 30,000 cubic meters was carried from the first floor to the eighth floor on human hands and shoulders.

The narrow emergency staircase was not designed for this unexpected heroic undertaking. With the commodity flow and human flow, it became very crowded. Looking up, I saw columns of human back all wet-through; looking down, I saw lines of human faces breathing hard. Grey was the color swarming around, and sweat was the characteristic smell.

"Stop!" was on the tip of my tongue, but what I did instead was adjust the commodity flow and human flow.

I shouted with my husky voice to direct the flow on different floors, to turn disorder into order. Finally I found that my vocal cords felt painful.

This was the sixth sleepless night. My staff tried to send me home, with their husky voices, but how could I leave?

Many of our staff were the only child of the family, and they had worked on site for several days and nights; many of the sales assistants were not much older than kids, yet they refused to leave when their parents came to pick them up. Many slept on card boards on the floor when tired. How could I leave?

I had to make hotel reservations for the old and weak, to arrange for taxis to take some of the exhausted home, and to check the commodity on display for the last time.

I had many, many things to do. It was already September 25. This was our battlefield of life and death. I just could not leave.

The night of September 25 was the most monumental time in the history of the Wuhan Plaza. If one day I could erect a memorial for the Wuhan Plaza, I would engrave this date on it.

I would also engrave the names of those who had worked day and night, with their not-so-splendid but great achievements.

At 3 a.m., the achievement showed as a large number of people fast asleep on the floor, lying about in disarray in all postures, like a battlefield after fierce fighting.

When the day started to break, they woke up, full of vigor again. They hurried to wash up and prepare for the last program: sales simulation.

The purpose of this simulation was to test our readiness for the last time — everything must be perfect.

The invited staff from the Wuhan Department Store entered as customers. They pretended to purchase, to return merchandise, to exchange goods, to raise a dispute. Every possible situation in the business was simulated.

Our young staff were a little bit nervous at first, but got over it gradually and became very professional.

This meant they had grown mature fast, in just a few days, although they walked as if they were stepping on wool...

6. Choose Career Over Peace

6,000 swollen feet backed up the opening ceremony of the Wuhan Plaza, and the Wuhan Plaza itself.

On September 27, 1996, I washed my face carefully, made up lightly and changed into a clean dress, to attend the news conference with Chief Mao and announce to the public that the Wuhan Plaza would open on time.

At the conference, Chief Mao appeared in high spirits, and I was calm and relaxed. We walked among wine glasses, under camera flashes, but who would realize the pain under the disguise of my calm expression! I was so tired that I could barely stand. And I was worried about the worsening health of my mother, who fell to Parkinson's disease 10 years ago.

I would very much like to sit before her bed for a couple of hours. The scenes of her bringing me up often flashed through my mind, but I could only make her a promise: I would visit her when I had time after the opening ceremony. I had to direct the opening of the enterprise now.

I must say that our opening ceremony was extremely simple, yet highly successful. The ground in front of the building was hurriedly paved the night before. There was no singing or dancing, or ribbon cutting. Three hundred sales assistants lined up outside the eastern and western gates, to witness the leadership opening a symbolic lock with a symbolic key. But our start was a big event indeed. As soon as the gates opened, customers stormed in like gushing torrents. Our public relations work was successful; our system was up and running; our commodities were fully stocked. Heaven repaid the Wuhan Plaza staff for their relentless work.

300,000 people swirled in the Wuhan Plaza.

A 500-meter queue formed before Gate 5, where televisions were sold, and zigzagged to the main entrance.

Crowds lined up at the cash registers. General Manager William Choi, who had arrived from Hong Kong for the occasion, walked up and down in excitement.

Sales rose sharply, 1 million…2 million…2.5 million — this was the volume of only a half day. Judging from the momentum, daily sales could reach 5 million.

The hard labor in the past few months did not go down the drain. The Wuhan Plaza emerged as the winner of its Normandy! I sat in front of the screen in the computer control center, watching the vigorous numbers. I was so excited, but I reminded myself to watch over any possible accidents. Diagram of curves indicated that we were breaking records. This, as expected, would send shock waves through the retail business in Wuhan and in China. Great! I couldn't help cheering, like a football fan watching a most beautiful shot. But right at the time, the secretary hurried in and whispered to me that the Fire Brigade was summoning me.

Why did the Fire Brigade summon me for the grand opening of the Wuhan Plaza?

Why at this moment, after the all-out assault by 3,000 people?

The Wuhan Plaza was a new-born baby, in need of care. Summoning me would put the new-born baby in danger.

A sense of displeasure took hold of me, but I brushed my dress without making any fuss, and picked up the telephone.

Over the phone, I found out that I was summoned because our fire-safety facilities hadn't been inspected. I immediately told the Fire Brigade that they got the wrong people, because the fire-safety facilities fell under the responsibility of the developer. I had pressured the developer a few months back. I had someone contact the developer, but his cell phone was turned off; nor did he answer paging messages. He was not at home or in his office.

The Fire Brigade was pressing hard; the developer was nowhere to be located. On the very first day of our business, I felt that there was an invisible hand pulling me down at the critical moment.

I couldn't tell what hand it was. The Fire Brigade stepped up their demand, asking me to go to their office.

How could I go? So many customers, so much pressure. Anything could happen at the time. I must stay where I was to deal with all kinds of problems. Besides, groups of leaders from the central, provincial and municipal governments were inspecting the Wuhan Plaza.

But officials from the Fire Brigade came over. I had to go to their office immediately. If not, they would take me to their office by force.

I hurried over. When I walked across the bustling halls, I felt bitter.

A leading officer at the Fire Brigade bombarded me for 2 hours. He had his own reason. The Wuhan Plaza was a huge shopping center. It must pass fire inspection before opening to the public. But where was the developer responsible for this job?

I was tired to the point of breakdown. My personal feelings, the issue of economic development, the well-being of the company: these were all irrelevant. Their hidden motives dawned on me, from which I saw another side of the world.

I remember that tears rolled down my face when I came back to the Wuhan Plaza two hours later.

I had been stretched too thin; I am a woman. With a body and mind that had barely rested in a month, how could I pull myself together to deal with the complex hidden motives?

And, I could hardly imagine that the developer could be so irresponsible.

These were our economic environment and cultural environment? I felt hurt, and indignant.

And here, I would like to express my heart-felt thankfulness to Dong Shaojian, Vice Mayor in charge of commerce. Since the Wuhan Plaza hadn't conducted any fire-safety inspection, the Fire Brigade sent over an official document, ordering us to close our doors. It was Dong who gave his opinions on the document as follows: The Wuhan Plaza was the pioneer of modern retail business in Wuhan. It had had a tough time. Now that it had already started operation, let it stay open. But the Wuhan Plaza must complete fire-safety inspection immediately.

This way, with the support from all sides, the business soared, to the point of a miracle. Daily sales reached 5 million for 3 consecutive days. In a weak market, it was the best record in China. It also meant that we would spare no efforts to maintain the momentum.

We can't have the best of all worlds. Gain and loss always go side by side.

I was pondering over this issue, when a loud noise came from downstairs.

My intuition told me something had gone wrong. I was right. My secretary showed up, telling me that a group of veteran staff originally from the Wuhan Department Store staged a sit-in in front of our building. This happened in less than 10 days after our grand opening.

I jumped to my feet.

I went down and found out the reason of this sit-in protest.

When dozens of the veteran staff originally from the Wuhan Department Store got their pay on October 5, they discovered that it

Bingxin Hu: A Short Profile

1975:   Section Chief and Deputy Director, The Commerce Workers Hospital,
        Wuhan, Hubei Province
1984:   Section Chief, Organization Division of the Communist Party's Commerce
        Committee, Wuhan, Hubei Province
1988:   Deputy General Manager, the Wuhan Department Store Group Co., Ltd.
1994:   Executive General Manager, the Wuhan Plaza Management Co., Ltd.
1999:   General Manager, the Wushang Group, Wuhan
2000—: Executive President for Greater China of the Hong Kong Goldlion Group,
        and General Manager of Goldlion (China) Co., Ltd.

From 1994 to 1999, Hu was Executive General Manager of the Wuhan Plaza Management Co., Ltd. Under her management, the shopping center ranked number one in revenue and profitability in China's retail for two years in a row.

Inspecting worksite at the Wuhan Plaza Management Co., Ltd. The management principle of the Wuhan Plaza was "Rules are higher than the General Manager."

In the summer of 1998, Wuhan was stricken by a terrible flood. Duan Lunyi (with loud-speaker), Deputy Mayor of Wuhan, visited the Wuhan Plaza, encouraging the workers to fight against the flood. Bingxin Hu is the third from the right.

With visiting provincial and municipal officials: Jia Zhijie (first left), Party Secretary of Hubei Province; Jiang Zhuping (third from right), Governor of Hubei Province, and Qian Yunlu (first right), Party Secretary of Wuhan.

Showing the Wuhan Plaza to Wang Hanbin (third right), Vice Chairman of the National People's Congress, along with Mao Dongsheng (far left), Chairman of the Wushang Group.

Welcoming Mu Qing (third left), former president of the Xinhua News Agency, to the Wuhan Plaza.

With Dr. Zeng Xianzi, Chairman of the Goldlion Group, Hong Kong

Signing copies of the Chinese edition of *Breaking Grounds* in Wuhan.

Promoting the Wuhan Plaza management model and the Hong Kong edition of her book in the former British colony.

The audience.

And the fans.

With daughter Xuan Wang. Left: Having fun in Mom's office in Wuhan. Right: Attending daughter's Commencement at Boston University.

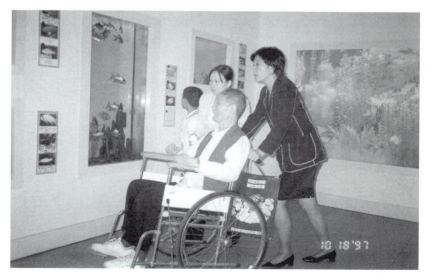

Visiting a museum with her eighty-year-old father.

Keeping smiling

Keeping fit

In Sydney, Australia

was below their expectation. Moreover, some new, young sales assistants received similar salary. So they went to the Wuhan Department Store for an explanation, like married daughters returning to their own home, hoping to find some consolation. But unexpectedly, the answer given by the management there was not satisfactory. They sat in the conference room on the 8th floor for 40 minutes, but nobody bothered about them. That started the sit-in.

This issue could have been solved like a breeze. But now it snowballed into an event, with dozens of people sitting in front of the main entrance, after they had shed sweat and blood for the success of the company.

I felt pain in my heart, for the Wuhan Plaza, and for them, too.

Sit-in at the main entrance would not be permitted for any reason. My first job was to gather the new floor managers, to persuade the strikers to find a good place for exchange of opinions.

The strikers were reasonable. We went to the conference room on the 8th floor of the Wuhan Department Store.

But once in the conference room, the atmosphere reverted. They became irritable, their attitude extreme. I asked the floor managers of the Wuhan Plaza to step forward, but they were blocked. In talking with the strikers, I felt the pressing need of communication.

During the days when the Wuhan Plaza went into operation, word got around that the management style would be tough. Perhaps they thought we were mistreating them.

I walked out of the conference room right away and dialed the phone number of Chief Mao.

I briefed him on the incident, and added, "If they can go back to the Wuhan Department Store, I will head back to the Wuhan Plaza with my floor managers; if not, could I take charge of the dialog?"

I cut to the point: this sit-in protest was in fact the collision between two systems. At the critical moment, Chief Mao took the top managers of the Wuhan Department Store out of a meeting they were chairing, and I started the dialog.

Facing dozens of my workers who had, with their red eyes and swollen feet, shared the hardship with me, my eyes were moist with tears. I wanted to speak out loudly, "You built the Wuhan Plaza with your own hands. Care for it as you do for your eyes." I also wanted to cry out, "We got through those difficult days. What's all this about?" But I didn't raise my voice. Instead, I just began to talk straight, about the startup of our company, about the primitive accumulation for our company, about our exploration in management, about our benefit plans to be implemented.

Most of the people were reasonable, and the conference room started to quiet down.

That ended the crisis, which never re-surfaced afterwards.

Later, whenever I walked in the imposing Wuhan Plaza and interacted with the bustling customers, I would remind myself, "This is a wonderful place. Do whatever you can for it."

I knew that I would say good-bye to a peaceful life. In this boiling world, where could I find idyllic peace?

7. Get Used to Being Misunderstood

My kindhearted mother would not see me worried about her illness. When I occasionally dropped in at her hospital, she would tell me from her bed, with difficulty and a blurry voice, "Go and do whatever you are supposed to do. The business is more important. We can't risk any delay."

It was true. We couldn't risk any delay. We started our business with swollen feet. It was a hurried start after all. Now we must attend to the details and start systematic operations.

The most pressing issue was to implement the new system. But being new meant being strange, which in turn brought about conflicts and complaints.

I just ignored the complaints before they transformed into an obstructive force. I had always acted that way.

For example, I was said to be "arrogant" and "power-hungry." I became "unapproachable." To see me would "require an appointment." I brushed aside all these remarks with a smile. Since China took on the reform policy, each and every successful entrepreneur had been labeled as "arrogant" and "power-hungry." I wouldn't waste my thought on that. The company did make a rule that appointments be made for face-to-face meetings, but its purpose was to introduce accuracy, order and scientific management. We had studied the conventions of big foreign companies for their top officials to meet visitors. It was also for the safety of the cash box in my open-style office.

Busy people never mind gossips. My mind was occupied with how to implement the new system, and how to avoid falling into old traps. It was not easy to implement the new system. Everyone had inertia. They knew the principles and had memorized all the rules, but by and by, the old habits started to take over. This was an example of the subconscious. It was based upon "the collective subconscious," which I had read about, i.e., the historical inertia shaped by many people over quite a few years.

I realized that by going after the individual cases of rule breaking, I was in fact fighting the historical inertia that had shaped their behavior. This fight compelled me to take a hard line. For instance, several people's contracts were terminated because they were found smoking in the toilet.

The aim of the new system was to streamline the operation. I remember that sales promotions were planned one after another based on the calendar. After the opening ceremony was the National Day, then Christmas, then the New Year, followed by the Spring Festival. We must push for tides of sales continuously, one after another, never letting up. I considered sales promotion as one of the most powerful means in the market economy. To my regret, our promotion could not be conducted in front of our main entrance, because the upper levels of the building were still under construction. Objects kept falling down. We had to watch out for this possibility.

If anything fell down out of the blue, everything would be messed up.

In fact, things often fell down, which worried me and resulted in some damage to our business.

We paid full rent, but the real estate properties we were using were not fully functional.

By the law of the market economy, the rent should be discounted.

I raised the request to the Board of Directors for a discount in rent for two months.

Mao didn't show his position upon hearing the request.

Since there was no reaction, I raised the issue on another occasion. I submitted a written request this time, to make it official.

Unexpectedly, this touched off an uproar.

Thinking back on it, I realize that the hell broke loose because conflicting concepts were involved. I believed I did the right thing, but others disagreed. It revealed different ways of thinking. Later on I learned that all sorts of comments started flying the first time I mentioned a rent discount.

"You are the Chinese deputy general manager in a joint-venture. Are you acting in the interests of the overseas investors by requesting a rent discount?"

The justification for the request was not considered. Instead, the identity of the person raising the request was examined. This was the traditional mode of thinking that looked at the relationship instead of the fact.

"You were appointed by the Board of Directors. Now you are bargaining with the Board. Aren't you ungrateful?"

The legal status of my position was ignored. Relationships became the dominant consideration. Another case of the traditional mode of thinking that looked at the relationship instead of the fact.

There were other subtle cases of conflicts between principles/regulations and imagination/relationships. Past gossips describing me as "conceited" and "power-hungry" also slipped in, worsening the misunderstanding. It so happened that in the meantime, I presented my views on improving business management at the Wuhan Department Store, not knowing what was in store for me. Now I found myself in the center of a hurricane. "Hu Bingxin is unbearable. She is grabbing power from the Wuhan Department Store, and acting in the interests of foreign investors. She is losing her senses!"

Was I losing my senses? I respected everyone, never pushing them around. Sometimes I raised my voice, but it was all for the sake of business. I never took it to heart, neither did others. Nothing personal. All work-related.

Was I acting in the interests of foreign investors? The Wuhan Department Store was the holding company of the Wuhan Plaza. When the Wuhan Plaza contributed more profits with a rent discount, the Wuhan Department Store Group would collect the lion's share. Why was I acting in the interests of foreign investors?

Was I grabbing power from the Wuhan Department Store? I was the Deputy General Manager of the Wuhan Department Store Group. It was my responsibility to offer suggestions.

But rumors spread like wild fire. The Wuhan Plaza was still a new-born baby. We worked day and night for its growth, more than 10 hours everyday. In the midst of the vicious rumors, I felt burned out.

When I returned home, I didn't look well. My husband was shocked, wondering what had happened. Without answering, I sat down, with my hands on my chest, and asked for a cup of water. He sensed something wrong and took me to the hospital immediately. A checkup showed that my left ventricle was not supplied with sufficient blood.

It was not difficult to imagine how angry my husband was when he said, "It is a crazy world! Empty-talkers are doing better than real workers; on-lookers are doing better than talkers; and time-killers are doing better than on-lookers."

He added, "It's all because of your new system. They dare not challenge the new system, so they are going after its supporters."

I still felt great pain in the chest. I felt those rumors were like broken glass, clear and invisible, but cutting at my heart.

I was sorrowful for the broken glass and traced back, to see when and how the glass was broken.

I couldn't help giving out a sigh. So shameful was the traditional thinking that "I am no good, but I wouldn't allow anyone to do better than me." So disgusting was our national love for gossiping and internal fight. No wonder it was said that to get anything done in China, 30% of your time was spent on work and 70% in dealing with people.

It was totally out of proportion.

I was terrified. If this were true, why should I waste my time?

But, the bustling Wuhan Plaza and the enthusiastic people stopped me from slipping back.

I began to consider whether I could change this disgusting tradition and fight my way out.

Could I stay out of the fight? I asked myself.

Kind of difficult. I have emotions. I am a human being, too.

But a voice reminded me: there are professionals, as well as the natural person.

Professionals... I suddenly woke up.

I discovered, to my surprise, that after all, the root of the problem was in me.

When I complained about others burdened with tradition, I fell into the pitfall of tradition myself. I expected others to focus on facts instead of relationships, and see me as a professional; yet I was acting like a natural person without realizing it. A professional versus a natural person — these contradictory traits should reside in the same person, forming the new character badly needed by the market economy. The process to create this new character seemed to be a tough one.

The traditional force was the major obstacle in this process.

Therefore, let's fight against the tradition. I would meet the challenge and push on.

Only when I pushed on could I ask my staff to be professional, to treat customers professionally, and to act professionally even when they were wronged.

As a professional, I had to get used to being misunderstood and wronged. Following this train of thought, I felt my anger subsiding, and my heart less painful.

The next morning, I went to the office and made a call to Mao.

My voice was calm, so was his in the telephone. We were very professional. We were handling our daily business, not a dispute.

"It is good to be professional," I thought when I put down the telephone. If everyone was professional, life would be much easier, and there would be fewer disputes. There would be fewer glitches in work and the chances to get wronged would be few.

This was not daydreaming, but the way to go. To prove it, I had a successful talk with Mao later on, about the reasons, advantages and disadvantages of a rent discount, and about the rationality of my suggestions to the Wuhan Department Store.

As a result of this talk, Mao commented on my merits at a meeting later on. According to him, my contributions far outweighed my shortcomings. He even counted my seven strong points.

As for me, I did my work as usual, before and after the talk.

The storm passed. We all handled the incident professionally.

Its impact on the Wuhan Plaza was a new emphasis on professionalism by all the staff.

8. Constant Vigilance by Staying Alert

Promotions brought in business. The Wuhan Plaza was doing better and better. Before our doors opened in the morning, crowds would gather outside, waiting to be welcomed in. Boots and leather shoes were stepping impatiently on the pavement covered by snow, stirring up clouds of steam. When the orange sun rose above the crowd and melted the snow, the doors of the Wuhan Plaza opened to the excitement of the people. The crowds spilled onto every shopping floor, bringing bustle and excitement along.

Every morning began like this. The Wuhan Plaza seemed immune to the fluctuation on the market. The trick of staying hot was new merchandise with promotions. People tended to follow the crowd, but they also liked to seek out new things. If you kept introducing new merchandise, and carefully planned for every introduction, waves after waves of hot sales could be pushed even in a very weak market. The Wuhan Plaza didn't have to worry about lack of new merchandise anymore. The difficult days of bringing in vendors were now history. With the reputation of the Wuhan Plaza spreading far and wide, vendors would feel honored to sell their products in our shopping center.

This treasure land became the intersection where the merchandise flow and human flow met, the focal point of good fortune and crisis. This issue was my greatest concern at that time. All kinds of characters were mixed up in the crowds, a very complex situation. Accidents could strike any moment. The abundance of merchandise attracted crowds of admirers as well as thieves and robbers. In order to prevent accidents, we compiled the internal newsletter *Reports from the Frontline*, which was broadcast on TV screens on the shopping floors to keep the staff on guard.

But this was not enough. Our shopping center was the epitome of the society. The society was so large; there was no lack of strange things. These strange things might strike the Wuhan Plaza some day. What should we do? I believed that there should be an emergency system in our mind and in our computers. Although we couldn't store thousands of countermeasures as in the Patriot missile system, we could set up a Red Channel to fight against the unexpected. I issued an order to my staff: in case of a crisis, if the counter team couldn't handle it, pass it on to the supervisor; if the supervisor couldn't handle it, pass it on to the floor manager; if the floor manager couldn't handle it, pass it on to the senior manager; if the senior manager couldn't handle it, pass it on to me.

It turned out that our Red Channel responded rapidly, usually in less than 3 minutes.

I did not stop. I warned all the departments, especially the Supervising Department, that we must be extra-cautious, snipping the crisis before it broke out.

The most effective way to handle the crisis is through anticipation and prevention. The success of our business hangs on them.

Realistically, we can prevent most of the accidents, but not 100%. Accidents do happen once in a while, putting me and the company at risk.

In the fall of 1997, an unexpected accident struck us before the Teachers' Day. Having discovered our land of fortune, a brewery in Hubei Province contacted us after completing all the paperwork for security and use of public passageways. They planned to conduct sales promotion right in front of our main entrance. Their promotion was an old trick. They placed an ad in the newspaper, giving thanks to teachers. Anyone presenting the newspaper could get two bottles free. The intention was to build a customer base and promote the brand name.

Our managers gave their approval. But nobody ever anticipated the size of crowds two free bottles of alcoholic beverage would bring. To maximize the effect, the brewery purposefully held back on giving out the free beverage.

People stood in queue at first. Then the queues disbanded. The team from the brewery could no longer control the crowds.

The crowds pushing for the free beverage milled around. Our security guards failed to maintain order.

People pushed against each other. Human waves started to take shape. The crowds were getting out of hand.

Forced by the traffic in the street, the human wave began to push back, towards the windows of the Wuhan Plaza — glass sheets more than 10 meters high and 10 centimeters thick. The glass was under enormous pressure, and our shopping center was thrown into a crisis.

If the glass gave way, there would be casualties.

Moreover, a shopping center without a glass wall was like a bank without any protective barriers. We were exposed to possible plundering.

The Red Channel was activated. I showed up on the scene in less than one minute.

I gave the order to bring over all the security guards, all the management personnel, and all the policemen from nearby stations, in an effort to stop the tide.

We failed. The crowds were beyond control. They had lost their senses.

The team from the brewery panicked. They offered to give out the free gifts, to defuse the situation. I was outraged – doing so would worsen the chaos. No gifts were to be handed out.

I just called for the riot police.

Riot police of the Wuhan Public Security Bureau, a symbol of power and authority, with their batons and epaulets.

The agitation was put down. The incident tested our capabilities in dealing with emergencies, as well as our Red Channel.

Later, I took stern disciplinary actions against the brewery and our Planning Department, and demanded an emergency plan for every public event.

Crisis control was built in our training plan. The impossible sometimes happen in our life. Ways to control them should be part of the emergency system.

Talking about control, I remember a story from a friend of mine. He said he was at a cocktail party offered by a foreign company, when he found water dripping from the ceiling. A manager of the company immediately took up a glass of drinks, to go and stand under the dripping water, talking with others until the end of the party. His suit was wet through.

I admire this manager's ability to react to and control emergencies. He avoided alerting the guests, and in the meantime saved the company's image. We should also be equipped with the ability to control unexpected events. It might be the best way to deal with a crisis should one arise.

An event left me pondering. A security guard from the Huaxin Management Co., which was in charge of property management of the Wuhan Plaza, hit a tricycle worker in a dispute. The incident had nothing to do with us, but since we rented eight floors of the building, many tricycles flocked to our shopping center like locusts in a short while. Everyone was pushing their way in, fuming with anger.

The Red Channel at each level tried to stop the riot but failed. The incident was brought to my attention.

I went to the scene immediately. I couldn't allow the young Wuhan Plaza to get hurt.

The uproar swept me like ocean waves and gusting winds. I realized that the angry workers would tear me up if I referred them to the Huaxin Management Co. for the solution.

Standing in front of the crowd, I asked in a low but firm voice, "Do you want to make trouble or solve the problem?"

The push of the mob was checked for a moment. No one would dare to say they wanted to make trouble. So they stated, "We want to solve the problem."

Solving the problem was easy. I apologized to the tricycle worker on behalf of the Huaxin Management Co., and paid him RMB 2,000 for medical treatment.

RMB 2,000 was no small money for a tricycle worker. More persuasive was my positive attitude to the solution of the problem. The crowd dispersed.

Another crisis was prevented. Through the event, I saw the value of being "positive." A positive attitude would be the key to crisis control.

I would like to mention here a case of pro-active crisis control. It happened in the summer of 1998, before the big flood began to threaten Wuhan. At the time, the flood had not really come. Only the satellite cloud charts and the weather forecast on the television were giving out the warning. But I felt that we must prepare for the rainy day — we had two ramps leading to the underground parking lot. We must be pro-active.

We started 24-hour flood watch, stored sandbags, boards and clay in a corner of the parking lot and gave training to all the security guards. Once the flood came, emergency measures would be activated.

Not long after we had everything in place, Wuhan was struck by a heavy downpour. The rain kept pouring down, like an overturned kitchen sink. At 7:15 the next morning, the senior manager of the Property Management Department called me.

His neighborhood was flooded in deep water. He couldn't make it to the company.

I shouted at him, "You must! Swim over if you have to."

I left home against the rain. By that time, Wuhan's streets were flooded and littered with all kinds of dead vehicles. Traffic was completely stopped.

I worried about the Wuhan Plaza, and plodded in its direction in the water that reached my thigh. It took me an hour to walk the distance, 40 minutes more than in normal weather. My eyes were moist when I entered the Wuhan Plaza. Our pro-active measures proved effective. Directed by the supervisor on duty that night, the security guards sealed off the main entrance and the ramps to the underground parking lot with clay and boards. I was so thankful to these well-trained staff who kept water out of our shopping center. In the department store next door, the basement and the first floor were soaked with water. Excited by our success, our insurance company rewarded us with bonus, not insurance compensation.

The bonus was an approval of our emergency system.

Holding the bonus, I told the staff that the emergency system was in fact a system engineering project involving our emergency awareness and our capabilities in dealing with emergencies, as well as our emergency plans and measures.

What I meant was this: key to the emergency system were our emergency awareness and capabilities. These, in turn, came from our sense of love and responsibility.

9. Bring Flexibility to the Business

It is exhausting to manage a company. After the Wuhan Plaza opened to business, I often felt the daily work was more and more overwhelming. Only then did I understand why "it is difficult to make a fortune, but it is even more difficult to keep it." For sure, it is difficult to build a business. But in a way it is easy, because you are presenting a totally unknown company to the public. You are not held up by social conventions or traditions. It is a different story to manage a business. You have to keep and develop the image you originally presented to the public. You must continuously improve. Going backwards is out of the question. This is very tiring.

In those days, while trying to take every precaution against any crisis, I also had to carefully watch out for unexpected events. Unexpected events are different from crises. While crises are destructive, unexpected events only have certain impact. But who would say that impact can be ignored? Many companies manage to struggle out of crises unharmed, only to fall under the build-up of numerous small events. "An ant-hole may collapse a thousand-*li* dike." As a new business, we had many parts to fit together. All types of little things could happen any time. For these little things, the only choice was to follow up on them, at the cost of getting tired out.

Honestly, our little events differed from those in other companies. Their little events often resulted from loose management, while ours came from stringency. Why does stringency lead to little events? Stringency sometimes leaves those even more passive who are lazy with their brains. Stringency brings about rigidity, which sometimes overrides flexibility.

In that case, why should we insist on stringency? I believed stringency was necessary in spite of the side effects. Over the years, our businesses had never been over-stringent; rather, they were too loose and free. The main problem with management was looseness, laziness and disorder. I would rather overact to correct the problem. Our means of over-action was sending out the Fault Notice. Anyone breaking the rules and regulations would be issued an alerting Fault Notice. It was not the usual kind of criticism, but a written verdict directly threatening the pay, the bonus and the job. We had three kinds of Fault Notices: light, heavy, and serious. They were similar to the red and yellow cards on the football field. One red card would send the player out of the game. Several yellow cards would void the contract.

The Fault Notice was merciless, feared by every employee. Its power could be observed when the employees arrived at work in the morning: At 8:30 a.m. sharp, thousands emerged from the underground passage, leaving no one behind. Looking serious, they walked on briskly in silence. With so many people marching on the narrow stairs, the human flow formed a disciplined army, and passed group by group. It was like the scene described in an ancient novel. "No military order was heard; there were only the continuous footsteps." Ten minutes later, the army passed, leaving behind an empty silence and lingering thought.

What was the thought about? I believed that in a situation like this, I wouldn't worry about discipline — discipline had already been built into the character.

What we should think about now was the opposite: How could we introduce some flexibility into stringency?

Insisting on discipline while remaining flexible. That was the challenge.

This challenge had to be met. Otherwise, small events would keep bothering us.

I still remember one such event, which had to do with painting the shopping area. A request was submitted to me as required by the regulations. I signed it. The procedure was flawless, but there came a problem. When I walked around the shopping center soon after-wards, I found something dripping from above. Looking up, I dis-covered it was white paint. The report didn't say anything about ceiling painting, and I was too busy to notice it. As a result, the paint was dripping down on the escalators. It might stain our cus-tomers' clothing and tarnish our company's image.

I was mad and summoned the responsible person over. "Who allowed you to paint the ceiling?"

He said, "You did. You signed the report."

I was surprised, feeling annoyed and amused at the same time. I had agreed to painting the wall, not to dropping paint from the ceil-ing.

Painting the wall was more general than painting the ceiling. While painting the wall was OK in general, painting the ceiling needed special arrangements. He was not using his brain.

But I understood that it was not all his fault. We had a rule in the company not to disobey the superiors. The purpose of the rule was to make sure that instructions from the superiors were carried out faithfully. If he had disobeyed my signed instructions, he would have received a Fault Notice. There were no blunders made. His problem was that he overlooked the specific details in following the instructions. The overall planning, including rules and regula-tions, was based on normal operations. It might touch upon special cases and alternations, but couldn't include all the details for these situations.

The paint was dripping because there was no flexibility on spe-cial cases.

I demanded a change in the painting schedule. Ceiling painting should be done after business hours.

From this instance, I felt flexibility was the required quality of a person, and of an enterprise.

I brought this case to a meeting. My conclusion was that without flexibility, a drop of paint could tarnish the whole company.

To bring in flexibility, I usually trained the staff through live demonstrations.

When I was inspecting the shopping center in the afternoon on the National Day in 1998, I heard the unnerving sound of electric drills. At the time, the shopping center was packed with shoppers busy with holiday shopping, with nearly 400,000 people passing through. I felt alerted: the discordant noise disrupted the atmosphere at the Wuhan Plaza and the pleasure of shopping by the customers.

I hurried to the scene, and found several workers putting locks on safes. Upon asking, I was told that the Tax Administration Agency required the use of a new type of invoice. The deadline fell on October 5, which was just around the corner. 580 locks had to be installed in the meantime. It was obvious that time was running out. The Property Management Department issued a Work Order, in spite of the ban on repair work during business hours.

I sent for the head of the Property Management Department and reprimanded him, so that he would remember the lesson.

He was not angry, just feeling somewhat hurt. He kept shaking his head, "I did my calculations. I can't have 580 locks installed in the evening. What can I do?"

I thought I would point him to alternatives. "I don't care. You are not allowed to do the installation during business hours, and you must finish the work in time."

"Then," He said, "I'll have to bring in more workers."

We laughed together.

At last he was brought around: The abnormal should not be a problem as long as we used flexibility.

The head on our shoulders is there for solving problems.

Of course, problem solving sometimes implies taking on responsibilities.

One event served as a wake-up call for me. It was not a case of inability to be flexible, but a case of not having the courage to be flexible. It almost led to a joke of immense absurdity.

It all happened in the employee canteen soon after our grand opening. It was the last day of the month, 31st. Hundreds of employees found that their dining cards were rejected by the computer. The cause was very simple. By design, the computer application included 26 workdays, overlooking the 31st of some months. Without the

31st day in the computer, no one could have the meal. People wanted to eat, but the computer wouldn't let them. Humans found themselves at the mercy of the lifeless machine.

This was a new problem to us, but not an unfamiliar one in the information age. The conflict between humans and machines is widespread in the information age. On the one hand, machines extend human hands and brains; on the other, humans are controlled by machines. The only way to solve the conflict is continuous coordination between humans and machines, with humans coding more comprehensive strategies into computers, and computers providing more information and services to humans. However, from a philosophical perspective, coordination and balance are always relative, while non-coordination and imbalance are always absolute. In this consideration, computers will never replace human brains.

For example, when the computer rejected dining cards that day, the human brain had to take over.

The employees sought help from the human brain — the manager on duty, but he didn't show his position.

The reason was simple. It was against the company rule to dine in the canteen without passing the card through the computer. Moreover, it was against the company rule to let the employees dine out during the half-hour break. The manager on duty went to the Computing Center, and the Computing Center went on to look for the cause. In the meanwhile, time was running out.

Deterred by the system and a potential Fault Notice, he backed down and lost his common sense.

In fact, there was an easy solution to this problem for people with a sense of responsibility and an open mind.

Flexibility was key in this case. To achieve flexibility would require a greater sense of responsibility.

Continuous uproar and disturbance... At last, Xiao Zhouyun, a senior manager and president of the labor union, stood out and announced her decision. "Register your name and go eat. I will take the punishment later on if any."

When the incident was reported to me, I didn't punish Xiao. Instead, I thanked her at a meeting. It inspired me to start a discussion, focusing on the kind of company we should be, the kind of manager we should be, and the kind of improvement needed for our work.

The conclusion? We must insist on stringency, but we should also allow for flexibility, seeking for its justification and limits.

We live in a contradictory world. On the one hand, contradictions exist everywhere; on the other, each contradiction appears in a particular form. This is why "there are no two identical leaves in the world" and "one can't cross the same river twice."

I thought I must inject the spirit of flexibility into the new-born Wuhan Plaza, to prepare it for the commercial wars which had no set rules, and for our customers, each having their own individuality.

10. Public Awareness and Zero Defect

With public awareness built in, flexibility is not difficult to achieve.

I am impressed by the story of a friend who was late when he arrived in Hong Kong because his flight was delayed. The hotel room he had reserved was taken by somebody else, but a service representative at the hotel was very considerate and drove him to another hotel.

I also like the story of Gordon Bethune, CEO of the U.S. Continental Airlines. Once, an airliner was short of five meal trays. The flight would be delayed if the food were to be taken from the airport. He decided to let the flight attendants on the plane handle the situation. It turned out that they were very flexible. By looking for passengers who didn't want meals, they managed to solve the problem.

In the above cases, public awareness became the motivation for flexibility, and active minds facilitated it.

I experienced a similar event. That was a winter day. Before our business hours, many people had already gathered at the main entrance, waiting for shopping. Because of the cold, they hunched their back, stamped their feet and asked the security guards whether they could come into the hallway to stay out of the cold. The security guards wouldn't let them in, because it was not the opening hour yet.

The security guards were justified in keeping the doors closed, but they made a mistake not to pass the customers' request on.

Their fault was their indifference to public needs.

I arrived in time, and told the security guards to open the doors and let the customers in, out of the bitter cold.

The doors opened. It struck me that we were opening more than just glass doors.

That was a door of convenience for customers.

Year after year, we had been advocating convenience for people, as well as top-quality service. We had commended numerous model service workers. When the Wuhan Plaza went into operation, our priority became how to meet people's needs for convenience in the new age.

To meet people's needs in the 1990s, we should not stop at individual cases. Instead, this issue should be put on the agenda of the management. Adopting a new approach, we would transform our system to provide top-quality service.

Large retail businesses are exposed to the public everyday when they open their doors, engaging business activities in the public arena. The biggest convenience for the customers is a pleasant, modern ambience for them to enjoy whenever they step in the shopping center. They would feel welcomed and pleased, trusting and assured, with detail-oriented perfection in service.

To achieve this, we would need zero defect.

To achieve zero defect, we would need to be perfect in every little detail.

To handle every detail flawlessly, we would need to extend the management of our service to every corner of the company.

Finally, to reach this level of management, we would need to develop four major concepts: big market, intensive management, all-around service and extensive training.

The logic was clear. From any perspective, management was the key. Management was just the means, though, not the goal. The goal was to satisfy the customers, who could enjoy modern and personalized service at the Wuhan Plaza. They would leave with smiles and good feelings, as well as the merchandise.

We set to work systematically towards that goal.

We worked out many details. For example, if you make a call to the Wuhan Plaza, the first greeting you hear would be a gentle self-introduction, "Hello. Wuhan Plaza."

At the main entrance of the Wuhan Plaza, there is a big poster "No Admission for Those with Indecent Clothing or in Slippers."

At the end of each escalator on every floor, there is a noticeable yet warm sign, which says, "Please Watch Your Steps on the Escalator."

When it rains, the security guards and sales assistants will wait at the main entrance, handing out a free plastic bag to every customer and helping them to put away the umbrellas.

For those with kids, the Kids' Paradise upstairs will be a great help. The assistants there will play with the kids, so that the customers can shop care-free.

Once the child of a customer peed outside a counter. Before the customer could apologize, the shop assistant had come out and kneed down to mop the floor clean.

These are little things, but they convey to the customers our values in humanized service.

Many behavior scientists looked into factors that prevent human interaction. The conclusion is "separation."

A door, a counter, a piece of glass, these can make people feel separated, as if they were outsiders. To provide humanized service, we will need to pull down these barriers.

Our solution was "zero distance." Customers could feel the commodities they were interested in with their own hands, or pick clothes as if in their own home wardrobe. Ninety percent of our commodities were exhibited on open shelves, with the exception of jewelry, brand watches and cosmetics.

Rows of shelves, grids of lights and a superb collection of beautiful commodities. When you roamed leisurely among them, you would feel light-hearted, romantic and fascinated.

But our open display was different from shelves in a thrifty shop. The basic difference was the commodity, and the graceful atmosphere created elaborately. Over fifty-five percent of the products we carried were famous brand names which could not be found in other stores in Wuhan. We had the biggest shoe collection, the biggest clothing collection, the biggest telecommunications department and the biggest food court in Wuhan. We were just like a magic box, a big box with countless exciting small boxes in it. In the small boxes were numerous beautiful items. Between the boxes, we filled the transition seamlessly with stainless steel, color lights, oil painting and indoor plants. As for the boxes themselves, they each came equipped with unique characteristics.

To define these spaces, I made several trips to Hong Kong, Singapore, Malaysia and Thailand. In January, 1994, when planning for the opening, I went with Mao to the United States, and later on, to Australia. I dare to say that our display was fashionable, exotic and modern.

Yet this was not the key point. The key point was that we took up responsibility for all these boxes, big and small; we made our promise on their behalf.

We told the public that all the shop assistants in the Wuhan Plaza, whether our employees or vendor staff, could be brought to our attention if they were unhappy with them.

We would provide post-sales service for all the commodities in the Wuhan Plaza, no matter who sold them.

I felt we must take the responsibility. I liked "Sam's Pledge" of Wal-Mart. At the grand opening of each store in the chain, President Walton would fly over in person, and make the pledge with the staff. The pledge went like this: "I want you to promise that whenever you come within 10 feet of a customer, you will look him in the eye, greet him and ask if you can help him."

I was also enlightened by Henry Ford's remarks. The father of the automobile industry said that only the public could bring business with them. Enterprises were built on public support. In turn, they should offer service to the public. These remarks were very insightful. Without public support, businesses would stand no chance. We must honor the public, for the sake of our business.

I believed that I should crystallize this public awareness into concrete measures and goals. Our measures and goals could be summarized as Three Zeros: "zero distance in sales," "zero mistakes in checking out," and "zero complaints about our service." Among these Three Zeros, "zero complaints" was the highest order. To keep track of complaints, I would check the records personally every month. Following is a random list:

October 1 to October 15 — 147 thank-you letters, 5 complaints. Complaints accounted for 3.2% of the total written feedback.

September 16 to September 30 — 291 thank-you letters, 10 complaints. Complaints accounted for 2.6% of the total written feedback.

Honestly, for a shopping center with daily customer visits reaching 300,000, the number of complaints in a half-month period was next to zero.

But I was not happy. I told the staff that they must improve on the quality of service and merchandise.

Our pledge of service quality was tested in an incident, when a misbehaving customer threw the shoes he was buying to the floor three times. The floor supervisor picked them up three times, finally turning the customer around.

Our pledge of merchandise quality was tested in the following case. A bunch of people bought a box of red Marbolo cigarettes. Two weeks later they came back, complaining that half of the cigarettes in the box were white Marbolo. We could have rejected their demand for return, based on the policy that food and similar merchandise could not be returned, but we accepted the return after the cigarettes were inspected by the Merchandise Inspection Department.

We sometimes felt abused trying to keep our pledges. For example, a customer spent RMB 18,000 on a diamond ring for her daughter, but her daughter didn't quite like the ring. So she found an excuse and wanted a return. In the process, she insulted the floor supervisor, who couldn't help talking back. In the end, we managed to send the big male supervisor to her home to apologize to her, accepted her return and reduced the supervisor's salary.

We sometimes felt exhausted trying to keep our pledges. For example, a customer bought a pair of shoes. One year later, he asked us to repair them, which we did. Then he demanded that we compensate for them; again we agreed. A pair of shoes haunted us for five months. (We had to talk it over with the vendor.) The expense was far greater than the price of the shoes.

But we did not complain. These were our responsibilities. We were an enterprise serving the public. We must reach the goal of "zero defects."

I sometimes reminded myself that we were part of the first publicly traded company in the retail business. From a broader perspective, we should strive for zero defects for the sake of millions of our share holders.

The public were our share holders, our support, and our customers. Entrusted with their wishes, we were responsible more than just for ourselves.

Most importantly, the public were evolving. They were improving rapidly. We were compelled to keep up with the times, searching for the infinite.

(Endnotes)

[1] The place where a famous battle took place in ancient China, between rulers of three different kingdoms. Zhou Yu, a general from the Wu Kingdom, defeated the army of the Wei Kingdom by setting fire to their ships. Wind was a key factor in the battle.

[2] This is a line from an ancient Chinese poem. Yumen was the passageway to the western deserts on China's northwestern part.

[3] This is a metaphor taken from ancient Chinese writing.

[4] The Huangpu Academy was the best-known Chinese military academy in the early 20th century.

[5] Sima Yi and Zhuge Liang were two rivaling top strategists in the Three Kingdoms period in ancient China.

[6] This was an ancient line describing the scene when Jing Ke, an ancient hero, set out to assassinate the First Emperor of the Qin Dynasty.

[7] Song Yu was an ancient Chinese writer who lived more than 2,000 years ago.

4

Strive for Excellence

> The soldier who doesn't have the ambition to become a general is not a good soldier.
>
> The general manager who doesn't have the ambition to create a top-class enterprise is not a good manager.
>
> — Author

1. The Wheel of Fortune

In the infinite time, a strong position can only be relative. When I started the business of the Wuhan Plaza with extreme caution, I saw that the Chinese retail trade was undergoing dynamic changes. Different forces were wrestling, some popping up, others sinking to the bottom. In this turmoil, the aggressive tactics from foreign retail businesses appeared most threatening. In contrast, the domestic retail businesses were struggling for survival. What a sad picture!

When did foreign retail trade businesses start to make their inroads into China? According to the data, they entered in the early 1990s, when China was opening up to the outside. The background was the tendency of global economic integration, as well as reorganization in production and sales introduced by the information revolution. In July, 1992, the Lufthansa Friendship Shopping Center backed by foreign investment opened in Beijing, which marked the beginning of foreign investors' intrusion into the Chinese market. I remember that no one was sure about its success at first. The General Manager of Lufthansa told reporters before the grand opening that he was not certain whether the Chinese people could afford the expensive merchandise there, or whether they would feel at ease in the luxurious shopping center. He was ready to incur loss for two years. But loss didn't occur. Lufthansa was born in time for the migration to higher-grade merchandise in China, to meet the needs of the newly formed middle class. As a result, water beds priced at RMB 20,000 and brand-name watches as expensive as RMB 320,000 found their buyers. The business was exceptionally good. The success opened a fanatic influx of foreign investment. Soon, famous and not-so-famous foreign retail groups stormed China.

The Wing On Department Store and Sincere Department Store landed from Hong Kong.

Paris Spring, Lafayette, and Carifour from France.

Yaohan, Ito Yokado, and Jusco from Japan.

Makro from Holland.

Metro from Germany.

Retail companies from Singapore, Malaysia and Thailand.

PriceSmart from the U.S.

Last, but not least, was Wal-Mart from the U.S., boasting its top sales revenue in the world and the gigantic image of the largest chain store in the world.

The Chinese cried in alarm, "The wolf has come!"

Judging from the image, momentum, scale, and speed, the wolf was really here. In less than six years, joint ventures and various kinds of enterprises with foreign investment numbered more than 200. The gigantic foreign retail army was carving up the Chinese market. Foreign stores dominated the Chinese retail. Colorful flags from many nations decorated the landscape of Chinese cities. Dark clouds hung over the Chinese retail businesses. The overwhelming and devouring force was rolling in. People cried out that "the Chinese nation is facing the most critical moment",[1] with many signs pointing to the demise of the Chinese retail businesses.

A Hong Kong friend of mine, Ms. Choi Kwai Cheung gave me her advice.

She said that in the 1970s, Chinese businesses dominated the retail market in Hong Kong. In the 1980s, foreign investment began to make its way into Hong Kong, such as the British Swire, the well-known Martha Department Store, the Japanese Yaohan and Sogo Department Stores.

Gradually, the wind changed. The market took a sharp turn in the 1990s. Businesses with foreign investment took the lion's share. Foreign department stores dominated the Hong Kong landscape.

Her voice had a sad tone. As Chinese, though not narrow-minded nationalists, we were worried about our retail trade.

Our retail trade was indeed hard pressed like never before. It was a giant before the 1980s. In the 1990s, however, it started to stumble. This was the direct consequence of high-level misplanning. Too many department stores opened up and rivaled to put each other down. There was actually a deeper reason: the original basis that supported the good old times had evaporated. The shortage economy was gone forever, and the planned economy was being transformed. All the business models, business forms, business orientations and business concepts derived from the planned economy were declining to a slow death. Quite a few businesses in China failed to see this trend. They held on to the old system, refusing to change, while complaining about the weak market and the influx of foreign investment. The pride and arrogance in the good old days turned into depression and loss of direction. The negative attitude impeded normal business reasoning. Former retail giants were steadily deteriorating, which in turn resulted in general panic. It was a time when "the Chinese nation is facing the most critical moment." The danger did not come from the competition of foreign investment, though. It lay in our own slip – the failure to see that Chinese retail trade was at a turning-point, when the business model, business form and management style would have to be re-developed. China needed to conduct its own experiment, with a fearless, aggressive self-confidence.

"Am I fearless?" I asked myself.

I must be fearless, and I could be.

During my visits to other countries, I met with all kinds of top managers in the retail business. They had two eyes and one nose just like us. Some of them were thin, others heavy, but not as strongly built as we had imagined. Nor did they have three heads or six arms. Some of them had been in the business for five or six years. Some were just out of the university.

I also met with many businessmen of Chinese origin, whose ancestors were slaves sold to the Southeastern Asia regions, just like what *The Book of Songs*[2] described, "ragged beggars who cut a way through forest." But through the hard work of several generations, they became well-known successful people. In my conversation with them, I sensed that foreign businessmen had great respect for Chinese entrepreneurs. Wherever the Chinese went, villages grew into towns, and towns into cities. They dominated the economy in Singapore, Malaysia and Thailand, and were an active force in the world economy. Experts labeled this as "the Chinese phenomenon" or "the Chinese economy." When I read *Future Shock* by the American futurologist Alvin Toffler, I found that he spoke highly of the "Chinese economy." In his opinion, there were two most energetic economic forces in the world. One was "the Chinese economy," the other, "the Jewish economy." As a Chinese, I shouldn't belittle myself. My ancestors and compatriots had accomplished great economic successes in the world. We must and could fly even higher.

We were not short of intelligence; we were not afraid of hardships; we were not missing enterprise. In other words, we were equipped with excellent qualities for economic success.

Through investigation, thinking, and comparison, I discovered that the sharp weapons of foreign businesses included high technology and science — the product of the information revolution, the experience in market economy for hundreds of years, and a cultural background totally different from ours but with some advantages of its own.

Our disadvantages included insufficient knowledge of the information revolution and its products. We knew farming, but not capital operations; we had a tradition of planned economy, but no experience in market economy; our new operations were not integrated systematically in this changed world. In short, our shortcomings resulted from our slightly outdated cultural background.

The collision of two cultures manifested itself as rivaling forces.

The cultural problem could only be solved through reform and opening up.

I felt fortunate, because when I started working on the Wuhan Plaza project, reform in China had already passed the point of no return, though still running into disputes and controversies from time to time.

We were facing an unusual opportunity in history, an unusual opportunity in our trade. We had a lot to accomplish.

Our times were calling for heroes. Our times would create heroes. The question now was whether I dared to confront the situation.

When I was a little child, my grandfather often read *pingtan*[3] lines to me, "Draw a full bow when shooting the arrow; be a strong person when growing up; shoot the horse before shooting the rider; catch the chief before rounding up bandits."

I wanted to be outstanding. I honestly believed that those who didn't want to become generals would not make good soldiers, and those who didn't aim at first-class businesses were not competent managers.

Archimedes said that he would pry up the Earth if given a fulcrum.

I appreciated his intelligence, and admired his spiritual force.

With a closer look at the Chinese retail trade, I found that amid the cries "the wolf is here," foreign businesses gradually turned into lame wolves and sick wolves. A shopping center they built in Shanghai modeled on foreign community shopping centers located in suburban areas. It was out of reach for Chinese customers and the business was slow. The shopping centers they built in Beijing were also having a difficult time because they were disconnected from the Chinese reality, leading to incompetent and inefficient management. The old saying that "monks from outside chant better scriptures" was not an absolute truth. The chanter might be disrupted for lack of communication. In Chinese shopping centers, the enthusiasm to introduce foreign managers died down after the idea was attempted several times without much success.

The forces were rivaling against each other, with aggressive foreign businesses losing steam, and powerful domestic businesses going weak.

I understood that another opportunity had come; with efforts, we could strengthen our position.

I am very Chinese. A woman, too. I don't have any magic power, but we had a very good fulcrum – the Wuhan Plaza with an area of 76,000 square meters and with a registered capital of 25 million U.S. dollars.

With this fulcrum, could we prop up the Chinese retail plate that was sliding down? In my opinion, before doing anything, one must first dare to think!

2. Strike Power Gongs and Drums

It is said that imagination is one of the highly valued qualities for professionals in foreign countries. Imagination is the starting point of the career. With imagination, hard work and the right approach, the cliche "a dream coming true" does not sound that far-fetched. Our own imagination was realized to some extent later on.

September 28, 1997 was the first anniversary of the Wuhan Plaza. In order to celebrate it, like parents celebrating the baby's first birthday, we had a grand ceremony. I felt a little pain when recalling the simplicity of our "grand opening." Now that the whole Wuhan Plaza building was completed, with the gigantic glass walls glistening in the sun, and the colorful neon lights brightening up the night sky, we should make up for the missed grandeur. Besides, after the whole year of hardship, exploration and harvest, we were entitled to celebrating our work, showing our gratitude to those who provided support, and, in the meantime, promoting for the next round of business activities.

For this celebration, a stage was set up on the spacious square in front of the Wuhan Plaza building. Singing and dancing, balloons floating into the sky… The climax came with the Power Gongs and

Drums.[4] The planning team had offered many choices for the celebration: marching bands, an orchestra, or group singing and dancing. But, it was finally decided that, for the celebration, we were going for Power Gongs and Drums. It had a strong Chinese flavor; meanwhile, its grandeur, its power and its passion went far beyond any and all of the Western musical instruments.

When gongs and drums started, it was really overwhelming. A powerful vibration seized the moment, as if water from the Yellow River had poured down from the sky and flooded the Earth, filling streets and people's hearts. The heart was swept along: the drum beats resonated in the human chest, speeding up the pulse rate.

I was very emotional at the time. All the bitterness and pains from the past evaporated.

I was very proud, too. The traditional roughness and modernity were in full display side by side.

In the integration of the traditional with the modern, the Wuhan Plaza made its way to the celebration: it ranked first in profit in China's retail business, a gold medal achievement.

We had realized our dream — to create a top-class shopping center in China.

A pop song had this cliche, "there is a word I dare not say." It was a love song, and what followed was that it was a very important word, and that once said, people would be tormented by life and death, would feel dauntless, and would stay together till the seas ran dry and rocks turned into dust. On hearing this song, I often smiled knowingly. I understood that the word was perhaps about love. I thought it was kind of incredible: would love go so far?

But in my career, I experienced the mood expressed by the line in the song. Yes, there were some solemn, sacred and important words that we wouldn't dare to speak out easily. They symbolized enormous emotion and endless pursuit. For example, "Build a top-class business in China" had been on my mind everyday in the past ten years, ever since I gave up the Party position, but I didn't dare to speak it out. The sentence was so inclusive that it embodied many concepts, decisions, systems, measures and efforts; it was so heavy because it implied sweat, pains and emotional involvement.

I remember that I wanted to say this sentence to my daughter while reading the first letter from her, who was on the other side of the ocean. I wanted to have her understanding. I wanted her to know why I was so busy, and why I didn't take a good care of her. Her letter went like this: "The silver wings of the airliner cut through the blue sky, like fingers gliding across the skin of young girls… I saw buildings I knew changing into small boxes, streets and roads changing into straight lines or curves. My mind could no longer block my heart. I cried…" When reading the letter I wanted to cry, too. And I wanted very much to say this sentence, but I didn't.

I wouldn't let her think that I was very romantic. In the same way, I wouldn't let my friends think I was too ambitious. Soon after the grand opening of the Wuhan Plaza, we called the first vendor meeting. My mother happened to be critically ill at the time. Her heart stopped, only to be revived with electrical shocks. She was staying in the Intensive Care Unit of the Concord Hospital. I wanted very much to stay at her bedside, but, thinking that hundreds of vendors were waiting for me, I went to the meeting with a heavy heart. I talked about our business at the meeting without showing signs of agony. Then I said, "I'm sorry I can't have lunch with you. I have some personal business to attend to. Please excuse me." When my friends and colleagues knew about my "personal business" later on, they asked why I had not told them about it. I smiled in pain. What could I have said?

But today, after the Power Gongs and Drums, I went to the podium and spoke out my mind.

After I said it, I felt so happy and relieved. I had been in the Wuhan Department Store Group for ten years. "It takes ten years to forge a sword."

This comment was not made out of pretension, not even out of pride. It was a fair evaluation of the Wuhan Plaza's exploration.

Many people gave their endorsement to our business. Chen Bangzhu, former Minister of Domestic Trade, said when he entered the Wuhan Plaza, "It is a pleasant surprise that the Wuhan Plaza is managed so well. It is as good as any shopping center abroad." He wrote on the autograph album: "A Paradise for Shopping." Wan Dianwu, Senior Research Fellow at the Domestic Trade Bureau, wrote a report after his investigation at the Wuhan Plaza, speaking highly of the software and hardware of our company, believing that the Wuhan Plaza had reached the highest level in the domestic retail business. Mu Qing, Director of the Xinhua News Agency, the *Global Economic Report* and other news media, gave similar enthusiastic and exciting endorsement. The leadership of Hubei Province and Wuhan City applauded the Wuhan Plaza on many occasions. According to my record, comments from all sides could be summarized as follows:

— A modern shopping center in line with international standards.

— The top retail business in China.

— A modern shopping center with first-class concepts, first-class management, first-class operation, and first-class service.

— One of the largest tax-payers in Hubei. A new growth point in Wuhan's economy.

I asked the Document Department to collect these comments and archive them. I told them to list the comments in the section of Major Events for the company, as milestones. I cautioned the staff not to feel complacent. Our strength was relative and subject to change. In order to keep our strong position, we should always look forward.

We had to keep a cool mind.

If there was any secret in our success, it was the insistence on rational management.

Historical experience and lessons proved that rational people would succeed, while irrational thinking would lead to failure. Rebellions led by Huang Chao and by Li Zicheng[5] both bore this out.

We should turn away from the short-sightedness of an agricultural society. Amid the deafening Power Gongs and Drums, what we needed was summarizing and consolidating our experience with a cool mind.

3. Survive the Network

What filtered through the Chinese retail trade in the middle of the 1990s? Two networks, in my opinion.

One network was the traditional retail network represented by state-owned businesses. It was riddled with worrying problems. The other was a new retail network represented by foreign investment. It was threatening and full of energy, yet inviting volatility.

We existed in the entanglement of these two networks. It was difficult to bring great changes in this position. We needed to find a new way of existence. We needed to break loose.

What kind of existence? Looking closely at the current status, I discovered that a new business model was taking shape with reference to the old and the new networks. Worry and volatility were leading to rational thinking. The business status and psychological status called for rational business management.

It looked that rational business management would be the way to go. Accordingly, we should clean up the outdated elements in the traditional retail business, as well as elements in the foreign retail business that proved unfeasible in China. Our rationalization should be built on some sort of cross-breeding. Our efforts finally led to the shopping center + department store model for the Wuhan Plaza.

With the model set up, I realized that this model alone was no guarantee for success. The model had to be supported by a rational management system. Rational management, which was on the lips of everybody, had to be realized as concrete management activities. After a great deal of reading, I discovered that rational management was based on logic, science and facts. Rationalization was not limited to the planning phase only. It should be applied to the entire process of management, including mental activities such as planning, orientation and decision-making, as well as physical activities such as action, implementation and supervision. It ruled out any irrationality or impulsive behavior during any stage in the process. It should be a very clear concept, and a very comprehensive system in the meantime. The crucial point in rational management was a standardized and scientific system.

What kind of system would it be? Or, in other words, what kind of base and form would it need?

When I was reading through some Harvard management books, a big book of Harvard management forms caught my attention.

Forms were boring, dull, cold. Ordinary people would stay away from them or even detest them. Why did Harvard take the trouble to compile them?

I recalled a story.

Before the Wuhan Plaza's grand opening, I went to Hong Kong on a fact-finding trip and visited the office of Wing On, a department store. They took out bundles of rules and regulations, dating back to the 1950s, which impressed me deeply. I asked the General Manager why he documented all the management system, at the risk of falling to red tape. He didn't answer. On the way back, it occurred to me that this documentation was related to numbers, and numbers were the basis for computers.

The mathematical model! I was suddenly enlightened.

The mathematical model was realized as forms resembling red tape, and the forms were supported by computers as measures for rational business management.

The implied method was to implement rational management in standardized and scientific operations.

I felt I was closing in on the truth of a rational business and on the core of modern management.

The idea of a mathematical model originated from long ago. When we talked about "making a calculation," it included elements of a mathematical model. Our ancestors used numbers to describe the universe a long time ago. For example, there were nine layers in the sky, three domains in the underworld, four seasons in a year, mountains thousands of *chi*[6] high, and rivers tens of thousands of *li*[7] long. When studying at the Dianshi University, I wrote down a paragraph by Democritus, a Greek philosopher. He thought that the world was based on numbers, and that everything in the world could be measured by numbers. The largest retail enterprise in the world Wal-Mart was so particular about numbers that they calculated profit by square foot.

But the mathematical model was a young concept, too. Its comprehensive application to business took place in the 1990s. The driving force for its popularity in the 1990s was the popular use of personal computers. Capable of handling numbers rapidly, accurately and extensively, computers brought numbers to the most dominant position in the world. In crunching numbers, humans developed their abilities to describe differences and relations, and their abilities to observe and control. Based on computers, mathematical models became a revolutionary force in management.

We had a great number of computers, and we decided to let them manage the Wuhan Plaza with forms and mathematical models.

We set up a network and system of numbers. We would exist in this network.

We would exist with rationalization, develop with revolution, challenge traditional management, and catch up with the advance of the world.

We would derive simplicity, accuracy, objectivity and profit from numbers. We would cultivate brand-new styles out of numbers.

There was a computer on my desk, connected to the Computer Center, which in turn extended its tentacles to every corner of the Wuhan Plaza through over one hundred computers. When keys were pressed and lights blinked on the screen, I was not only stricken with a feeling of modernization, but also sensed a force. This force enabled me to learn all the important events in the Wuhan Plaza within seconds, through the scrolling forms and statistics on the screen. I could also give my instructions to the teams, on everything ranging from their language to their behavior.

All this was possible because we had integrated numbers into the company system from the very beginning. I felt we must perform this integration. By doing so, we could extend the cool mind and intelligence represented by numbers through our management, and achieve standardization and scientific modernization. The system based on numbers at the Wuhan Plaza manifested itself in many fashions, not only as various kinds of forms, but also as all sorts of rules and regulations. To take a few examples:

— Three minutes late for work would count as a slip; three slips a month would count as a major fault.

— At least 98% of the lights must be on.

— Work reports must be supported by forms and statistics; otherwise, the report writer had to be re-trained.

— All planning activities must produce feasibility studies with quantitative descriptions; otherwise, the work would be rejected.

— All the work would be graded based on the attitude, quality and result, with the employee rewarded or punished accordingly; promotion would be made based on the grades.

— When merchandise arrived at the Wuhan Plaza, they would be encoded with numbers and bear barcode labels; otherwise, the merchandise would have a status of "unregistered" and barred from sales.

— Sales numbers were entered into the counter computer, which was networked with the Merchandise Department, the Accounting Department and the Computer Center. Business operations and sales were tracked by the computers.

— Digital management was applied to all the specialty booths and vendors. Selection and elimination was performed among these vendors depending on their sales revenue and profit margin.

This digital network, as proved in our business operations, constituted a complete framework for a rational system, which in turn supported rational management to some extent. Numbers were emotionless and computers unmerciful. They allowed for no exceptions. In this way, many mistakes were stopped in the early stage. Of course, "to some extent" did not mean "completely." The traditional inertia was the cause of this difference.

As a revolutionary factor in management, mathematical modeling was often colliding with the traditional force. I remember several little events with regard to management. In all these events, the inertia was fighting against rationalization. For example, in May, 1998 we interviewed a candidate for the supermarket manager position. As usual, she was to present her plan for the position, and we had specifically arranged for a supermarket management analysis meeting. But to our regret, her speech lasted less than five minutes. And she remained non-committal to numbers that she should have discussed.

The Wuhan Plaza always insisted on reports supported by statistics. It was made clear that vague terms such as "perhaps," "maybe" and "possible" should be banned from use. I put an end to the meeting right away.

Another little event happened during a business discussion. The Marketing Department of the Central-Southern Region of the Guangzhou P&G requested more floor space for their products in our supermarket. Their manager submitted a special report to us. In the report, he listed the floor space and sales revenue of their products at the Wuhan Plaza, and compared them with the data of similar products from other companies. He pointed out that the market position of a product was indicated by its sales revenue and profit. This report combined statistics with analysis. It was straightforward, convincing me right on the spot. As a result, P&G's request to expand their floor space was approved. The Marketing Manager succeeded with his rationalization.

This was the power of rationalization, the power of professionalism.

It was easy to talk about rational management, and it was not difficult either to test it out for some time. The difficult part was deploying a closely-knit network. Even more difficult was continuously eliminating "viruses" from the network. Internally, "viruses" showed up as lack of professionalism among the employees and weak rules and regulations. Externally, "viruses" included inefficiency resulted from underdeveloped market economy integration, conventions in small-scale production formed over the past thousands of years, and interference from traditional dependence on self experience and lack of planning.

These "viruses" often made me feel frustrated when I was driving the reform of business management.

The reform would certainly meet with some resistance. We had to stay cool-minded on this.

Because of our cool mind, the Wuhan Plaza finally broke loose from the entanglement of the old and new networks.

Was this breakaway the secret of the success of the Wuhan Plaza? Certainly. But this was just the main theme of our story. Under this main theme were some detailed chapters.

4. High Solution Rate with Few Levels

Some chapters were concrete, such as the management team and office arrangement. Unlike other businesses, the Wuhan Plaza didn't have separate offices. Instead, it adopted a centralized and open office floor plan. Pink separator panels as high as the shoulder divided the floor space into regular office cubes. In the cube, every management team member was equipped with a desk, a computer and a telephone. Each cube was independent, yet it was part of the entire management team.

Under the gentle and bright fluorescent lights, with modern communication and office equipment, the employees would feel the need to control their thoughts and behavior. As a result, the busy office work was carried out in a light-hearted tension, calm amid bustle. The biggest advantage of the open yet centralized office space was that everyone was part of the whole, yet relatively independent at the same time. It was compatible with our networked management style and was easy to supervise. It also saved the office space, which was no small matter. As General Manager, I had to maximize the shopping floor space, allowing every square inch to generate profit. I had to be most calculating.

Out of this calculation, we optimized our organization structure. The basic purpose was to build a simple, lean and responsive structure. My strongest feeling from my reading and my visits in the past few years was that we had entered an age of ten-fold speed, in which our living and business activities were continuously picking up speed. The fast pace brought up a challenge: problems should be solved quickly. This required fewer administrative levels, centralized power and lean management.

The issue of centralized power was the focus of heated debate from the very beginning of the Reform. It was at the center of the discussion on manager's responsibilities. As the product of the planned economy, collective leadership and supervisory control used to reject individual power and functions. All this was gradually giving way to a system where the individual would bear the responsibility and consequences. An economic model where a strong individual played a critical role began to take root, following conventions of the market economy.

I often wondered why foreign market economy could produce the "strongman phenomenon," why individual values and beliefs were encouraged, and why the individual enterprise was applauded. The conclusion was all this was necessary for the life-and-death battle on the market. Battles on the market demanded full individual freedom and rapid response, the ultimate sense of responsibility in the event of a crisis, and a strong will, as well as minimum deployment of human resources for the sake of profit. Our economy in transition was developing a complete support system for the market economy, including individual power, concepts and values. This was the very reason the Wuhan Plaza insisted on abolishing deputy positions. Looking back on it, this decision shouldn't have been disputed. The right way to go was trimming the management structure continuously.

The Wuhan Plaza cut (or saved) at least five senior manager positions by eliminating deputy managers.

How did we manage the increased workload with fewer people? Through high technology, of course. Computers could replace some people. On the other hand, the idea that more people were needed to handle more work was mistaken.

I liked the remarks by Sam Walton of Wal-Mart, the world's retail giant. In his autobiography, he mentioned that when a company ran into problems, the usual solution was to add a department with some people. In his opinion, the problems should be dealt with at their roots, that is, to fire the negligent employees.

These remarks reflected more than the iron hand of the modern businessmen. The positive side was its emphasis on the quality (not the quantity) of people, on the potential of people under pressure, on the efficiency that responsibility was likely to bring about, and on the positive function of encouragement rather than routine management.

After absorbing these positive points, the Wuhan Plaza's organization structure became highly streamlined. On each shopping floor, you would never see the offices of floor managers next to the shop-

STRIVE FOR EXCELLENCE   155

ping area as in other stores. One level management was implemented at the Wuhan Plaza. The top management team directly looked after operations at the grass-roots level. This structure saved manpower. We had eight shopping floors. Generally a management team of five members or more would be set up for each floor. We ended up saving the cost of forty managers.

The point did not stop at using less manpower. We had the "warlord economy" under control and reduced physical clumsiness in business warfare. The so-called "warlord economy" referred to the contractual system at the department or floor level in some stores in the past ten years. This system was necessary when market economy was first introduced. The biggest problem of the system was that each department had its own re-stocking channels. It became self-sufficient and would withhold some of the profit. If each floor bargained with the top management, we would end in a situation of "rich monks in a poor temple." In business wars among these small groups, the rich monks would only care for their own interests and refuse to be directed by the company, leading to "weak marshals with strong generals." Orders would be ignored, and battle readiness weakened.

Someone might ask, "Can we keep a departmental management team without a department system based on contracts?"

Even this alternative was considered superfluous at the Wuhan Plaza. At least there would be 40 extra managers, posing more obstruction to the rapid response and the high solution rate as required by the market.

Someone might ask again, "Without departmental management, how can a shopping center of 76,000 square meters be handled by only one upper management?"

My answer would be that even though the management structure was flat, we had built vertical functions and could manage with the computer network.

Generally, the management structure in a shopping center is shaped like a pyramid. The upper level management functions manage through corresponding departments in the middle, and corresponding staff at the bottom. The management structure at the Wuhan Plaza was different. Though there was only one level, a management grid was built. This grid had vertical and horizontal lines in a general framework. The vertical lines were thick, from top down, while the horizontal lines were connected through proper work procedures. The pyramid pattern features solidness, with closely packed staff. In contrast, the grid pattern features elasticity, with flexible staffing. The operations are flexible and rapid.

This pattern was designed to prevent management at the Wuhan Plaza from walking the old path in new shoes. The "old path" refers to the common fault of the state-owned enterprises in their management structures. Because their rights and responsibilities were not clearly defined, no one was willing to appear offensive on management structure and staffing issues. Consequently, many positions were set up at different levels to please everyone. This problem was sometimes so serious that the ratio of management to front line workers fell to 1:1 or 2:1, or even 3:1. We were a new company, with clear definitions of rights and responsibilities. We could not set up positions to accommodate people.

The market is ruthless. It calls for maximum profit with minimum manpower, facilities and expense. Otherwise, we would suffer a crushing defeat.

For this reason, the management structure of the Wuhan Plaza must part with tradition. Vertical management was implemented through the vertical lines, and horizontal procedural connections were made with the optimal horizontal lines.

Our vertical lines were the specialized departments.

When we started to set up departments, different plans were presented to me. We were extremely cautious. For example, how many departments should be set up in the management structure? How flat should the structure be? The public relations function and the planning function were essential to the company. Should they be set up as independent departments? No, they shouldn't. The reason was straightforward. They didn't have the vertical down-reaching function. As an independent department, they should be staffed at least with a manager and a worker. Two employees or more were to be hired. I put these two functions under the General Manager's office. Two positions were eliminated: the managers of the two departments. In another case, we discussed repeatedly whether the Supervising Department should take over the management of sales. I thought the crucial point was not its name, but the definition of its function. If named Sales Department, it should manage corresponding business management offices on each floor. On the other hand, the function of the Supervising Department was to inspect the shopping area. Its staff would walk all the eight shopping floors, dealing with various problems on the spot. Finally we decided to name this organization as Supervising Department, because it better described the nature and scope of work of the vertical line. Following this principle, our management structure was simplified to the bottom line. There was only one level of management structure, which consisted of six departments, one office and one center, in this shopping center with 3,000 employees. The management team counted a little over 100 people, taking up 5% of the total staff. The ratio was fairly optimal.

More importantly, these departments all had vertical management functions. For example, the Supervising Department managed all the eight shopping floors. The Merchandise Department managed merchandise of the whole shopping center as well as goods from every vendor. The Accounting Department managed all the accounting activities, from the enterprise assets of hundreds of millions to every cash register.

Most importantly, these departments, the vertical lines, all ended up in the General Manager's Office. They formed the key links of the company.

Whenever the General Manager pulled on the key links, the whole company would react. The entire company moved in lockstep, with a concerted will. According to *The Art of War* by Sunzi, "If the entire army acts with one will, they will win."

The Wuhan Plaza acquired the capability to respond quickly in the fast changing business landscape, and the flexibility vital to business wars.

5. Leave No Room for Fraudulence

Of the single-level management of the Wuhan Plaza, the most distinguishing feature was the management of merchandise. Usually retail businesses have the same group of people handling purchase and sales of merchandise. This was a tradition dating back to the 1950s. During my ten years in the retail business, I watched this system up close and saw its problems. Combining purchasing with sales would easily lead to fake goods or business for favor. The person in charge would be much too powerful. The vendors would have to seek favor from him or resort to kickbacks and bribery.

Because of these disadvantages, suggestions were made early on to the Board of Directors to adopt the international management model in having purchasing and sales separated. Buyers would work in the Merchandise Department and sellers would be placed in the Sales Department, each with their own responsibilities and each watching out for the other. This specialized role expanded the responsibility of buyers for merchandise purchase. During the selling process, sellers would test the vendors and goods that buyers brought in, forcing the latter to study the market, to rotate vendors and merchandise, and to stay oriented to customer needs.

In the Wuhan Plaza, constraint on buyers was achieved not only through the system but also through technology. We had a special procedure for inspecting purchased goods. It was the staging area, also called the "customs office" of the Wuhan Plaza. The staging area had very tough rules. Our own goods, as well as the goods brought in by vendors who contracted our counters, must pass the inspection in the area before they were sent to the counters. We did this because we had made our promise to the customers on quality and service. We must keep our promise. We wanted to make every day March 15, the Consumer Rights Day.

Out of this ultimate sense of responsibility for the customers, the inspection program of the "customs office" ran like this. For merchandise from new vendors, a form must be filled by buyers, which would then be reviewed and signed by the manager of the New Merchandise Acquisition section. This was the first step. Then, the manager of the Merchandise Management Section would start to check the samples and verify the paperwork. The paperwork must include vendor information, merchandise QA reports and description of the merchandise against other goods in the same category. Only when samples passed the examination of the experienced eyes could they get through the second step. Verified by the Merchandise Department, the merchandise would be sent to the counters for evaluation on their quality, pricing and market prospect. If they met the standards, a senior manager of the Merchandise Department would give his signature and let them pass through the third step. The fourth step was performed by the General Manager's Office, which would verify all the necessary documents and audit the overall merchandise structure. The fifth step was for the Merchandise Department to sign contracts with the vendor, which would specify that the quality and style of the merchandise should remain consistent, with full post-sale service and satisfactory sales revenue. Rewards and penalties would be stated in the appendix. Only after all these steps would the merchandise be registered, entered into the computer system and provided with a barcode number. Then came the sixth step. The Confidential Secretary would verify the computer entry, sign the required documents, and deliver them to Special Merchandising for it to receive the merchandise, to the Accounting Department for it to review the contract and computer data, and to the Human Resources Department for it to arrange training. Only then could the merchandise officially enter the store. Sales on the shopping floor would be the seventh step.

I am going into all the details of the workflow of our "customs office" here in order to make this point: it was extremely difficult for anyone to cheat with these seven steps.

These steps left no room for fraudulence. On the contrary, they built the credit for the company, and provided guarantee for customers.

Due to this unique separation of purchasing from sales, the Wuhan Plaza enjoyed a high reputation among the customers, attracting a daily customer flow of 300,000.

In fact, the "customs office" guarded the life line of the company. This guard was not temporary, but persistent and dynamic.

When I turned on the computer and started my applications, summaries of the sales data would come from the shopping floors. The dynamic curves based on the data would determine whether rewards or warning would be issued to the buyers. They would also decide the fate of the merchandise from vendors doing business in the Wuhan Plaza. Merchandise with many customer complaints would have no place in our shopping center, and merchandise with little sales revenue would be phased out according to our evaluation system.

With the rules and regulations and the numbers, even I could not step in to make exceptions. The management principle of the Wuhan Plaza was "Rules are higher than the General Manager." I refused many requests for my personal intervention. Taking a leather product company for example. They had just gone through the seven steps. Their goods were accepted by the Wuhan Plaza and the sales were good. Perhaps because of this, when their own products went out of stock, they hurriedly collected products of similar styles and color from other vendors and put them on sale as their own products. This trick fell through the first day: when inspectors of the Merchandise Department toured the shopping floors, they discovered the faked items at first sight. Faking was an absolute taboo at the Wuhan Plaza. As a result, the problem was reported to the upper management. According to the contract, the upper management ordered the vendor to pay a penalty and pull out of the Wuhan Plaza. The vendor panicked. They asked for another chance, but the Wuhan Plaza was not entitled to forgiving their fault. The power lay with the customers.

Moreover the Wuhan Plaza couldn't afford to allow for an ant hole of faking. Otherwise, the ant hole would grow into a funnel, which in turn would grow into a break, washing away the whole dyke.

We turned their request down. They were refused access to the Wuhan Plaza the following year. The reason was that the quality of merchandise was associated with the morality of the people. When people lost their credit, the merchandise would lose its charm, too.

Talking about charm and morality, we were really grateful to the hard-working and alert staff in the Merchandise Department, not only for their sense of duty working at "the customs office" day by day, but also for their flexibility and initiative under special circumstances. "Special circumstances" refer to unexpected business events and unexpected seasons. Under such circumstances, following the established procedure would miss business opportunities.

The regular duration for merchandise to pass through the seven steps was a half day. In order to seize business opportunities, stocking plans were often made two months in advance, which were then sent to the vendors. It was proved by our operations that this proactive planning covered 95% of all the business scenarios. But plans could never keep up with changes. For example, the hot summer in 1997 arrived very early without any warnings and the high temperatures lasted for a very long time. Customers were dying for air-conditioners, which were in great demand all over the country. The situation was even reported on China's Central TV.

Under such circumstances, it was not very sensible to keep air-conditioners in the staging area.

The Merchandise Department went out of their way to move in air-conditioners from all possible sources. In the meanwhile, they exempted products from brand-name vendors, to rush them to the shopping floor directly.

The management team entered serial numbers of the air-conditioners into the computer, and checked their documentation on the counter. All worked together to expedite quality air-conditioners to the customers.

Later, I told the management staff involved that making exceptions under special circumstances indicated a sense of responsibility, for customers' needs as well as for the company.

Making exceptions under special circumstances also indicated a kind of capability, the capability to follow principles while showing flexibility.

Profit depends on capabilities of the employees. Only people with good capabilities can generate good profit. For this reason, the Wuhan Plaza came up with a principle: professionals first; profit second.

6. Human Resource Development – a Permanent Task

At the end of 1997, we generated a profit of RMB 127 million. When the statistics were released, the retail business and the public were shocked. Some said that this number was highly desirable even in the developed countries. Some carefully studied how we reached this goal. They finally discovered that there was only one simple reason: giving priority to the management, use and training of the employees.

Talking about our employees, most of the 3,000 who labored day and night for the grand opening of the Wuhan Plaza have now become the backbone of our company. When the Wuhan Plaza started its business, more than 80% of the management team were new hands; some had never worked in the retail business before. Their rapid progress and great improvement were due to the positive environment at the Wuhan Plaza. They were thrown into work, which sometimes was a kind of training in itself — training under pressure to bring out the full potential.

The most important means to develop human resources was a competition system at the Wuhan Plaza. I was aware of the "catfish effect." It told about a boat carrying fish across the oceans. It was found that the fish became weak and died out in large numbers on the long journey. Then someone suggested putting some catfish into the fish tanks. When the catfish came in, the other fish swam hard all the time for fear of being eaten. This way, not a single fish died later on. The "catfish effect" was proven: the weak could improve themselves when challenged by the strong.

Since this effect was proven, we might as well make people feel the pressure of competition all the time.

We announced publicly that five to ten percent of the management staff would be rotated every year, to keep the team refreshed and to apply the "catfish effect."

The rotation rate was not high. We were experiencing a shortage of human resources. There was a shortage of both qualified management staff and ordinary workers. It was not uncommon to find people with outdated ideas, old knowledge, traditional styles, who trusted their own feelings and experience and acted on impulse.

Besides, we are living in an age of ten-fold speed. Knowledge renewal is accelerating. Only those who can keep up with the age will survive.

Competition, however, was only one means in human resource development. The secret of the Wuhan Plaza was to offer training to everyone. We always believed that competition on the market in modern times was the competition among professionals. We should see employee training as a strategic task. Few businesses cared for employee training as we did. At the Wuhan Plaza, one of the most influential principles was "professionals first; profit second." While we minimized the management structure, a training center was established, with a scientific, strict and logical training system. The company saw the training center as a profit center rather than a cost center.

The training system was characterized as all-directional, multi-level, multi-perspective, rotating and composite. Every employee, from senior managers to front-line workers, was expected to receive training without exception. Take me for example. My many job responsibilities could be summarized into three simple categories: planning, supervising and training. I took pains to train myself. I insisted on reading for more than an hour every evening and appointed a team for recommending books and articles to me. When I took part in computer and management training, I told my secretary to turn down telephone calls, visiting guests, or requests for business talks. I would compare myself to a sponge: the more water I absorbed, the more saturated I would grow, and the more water I could squeeze out to refresh the staff and the company. Apart from the continuous on-the-job training, the Wuhan Plaza provided the staff with training classes. There was a three-month training class for senior managers. I did sixty percent of the lecturing. I felt happy when preparing for the lectures. Every stroke of my writing felt like rewarding cultivation. Whenever I stood before the students, I would brighten up. In my opinion, a modern entrepreneur should also be a good speaker, good at expressing her ideas, concepts, methods and expectations through her speech, to encourage people, unite with them, improve them and mobilize them.

Since training was given such priority, Training Manager Yan Jianming lost himself in it. He read many books and wrote 15 kinds of textbooks totaling 112,000 words, six handbooks for training the management staff, and 200 case studies sorted into 23 categories. He went twice to Hong Kong, three times to Shanghai, north up to Beijing and south down to Guangzhou, to learn the latest training technology and methodology, both foreign and Chinese. Because of our collective efforts, the Wuhan Plaza developed a whole set of training principles: every manager at the Wuhan Plaza was a training manager; every counter leader was a training leader; untrained staff were not allowed to take up their positions; the promotion of the management staff was related to the training work in their department. We had two types of training, continuous on-the-job training, and regular training, which included six categories:

- Basic training. When new employees started out, they must obtain the Certificate of Qualification issued after basic training before they became qualified for work.

- Occupational raining. The employees must acquire required knowledge before taking their positions.

- Training for transfer (promotion). No matter how well the employees did in their original position, they must pass training and certification for the new position.

- Correctional training. For common issues and problems, special training with specific purposes was offered.

- Training for improvement. New knowledge and new concepts were introduced based on the new situation. For the employees with great potential, improvement training was provided to bring it out.

- Re-training (including military-style training). At specified intervals, the employees would take turns to get re-trained, to overcome the influence from past experience and inertia.

The company made it clear that these six types of training would be conducted after work, because they were preparations for the knowledge, skills and mentality required for their positions.

To improve our training techniques, we borrowed Harvard's teaching methods. When the bell rang one day and the trainees were all waiting to start the class, a young lady and a middle-aged woman entered the classroom shouting at each other. The young lady said the store was selling fake merchandise; the woman said the young lady didn't know what she was talking about. Everyone was surprised, only to find out later on that the quarrel was part of a simulated training class. We often offered different alternatives for the same issue, so that the students could do their own analysis and reach their own conclusions. After that the teacher would give his comments. This active and efficient teaching method proved more effective than the traditional teaching method of lecturing. The trainees indeed benefited from it.

Of course, employees of the Wuhan Plaza received training at work more often than in the classroom.

This should be credited to our on-the-job training. Our belief was that work was training in itself.

We required every manager to train the counter leader in their daily work. Similarly every counter leader should train their own team members.

Any fault of the team member could be seen as the result of imperfect training by the counter leader. This applied to every level of management, so that all the levels would place training in high priority.

A small incident revealed how the training principle worked. We promoted a young man to the counter leader position. As usual, he would call a team meeting everyday before work started. As a rule, the Training Center provided him with training for transfer. But he spoke in a very soft voice, probably out of nervousness or shyness. He was unable to overcome this problem in spite of two days' training. On the third day, his voice was as soft as ever at the meeting. As a result, the Training Manager was issued a warning note.

The reason was clear. His inappropriate behavior indicated improper training by the Training Center. The Training Center must learn from this incident and fulfill their responsibilities.

The purpose was clear, too. We wanted to emphasize the importance of training, reinforce the training system of the company, and build a well-trained team of workers.

These efforts naturally produced positive effects. In a most typical example, a drunk customer started trouble at the Wuhan Plaza. He even broke the wrist of a security guard. Remembering our rule of "no fighting back when attacked by a customer, and no talking back when insulted," the security guard continued patient persuasion while fighting the pain.

While serving a German tourist who wanted to buy a traveling suitcase, a sales assistant gave airlines' check-in luggage size from her memory. The customer purchased a thirty-inch suitcase with many thanks. This was but one small example.

7. Rules Are Higher than the General Manager

The results of good training could be seen everywhere at the Wuhan Plaza. When the doors opened in the morning, the courtesy team would make a deep bow to the first customers. During business hours, whenever a customer approached a counter, she would hear a warm "Welcome" in standard Chinese. The customer would never have to wait more than two minutes at the cash register. The request for returns would always be served with patience.

With this uniform, pleasant attitude, the staff at the Wuhan Plaza transformed into a smiling army. The army was sometimes called the "profit software" of the Wuhan Plaza, sometimes called the "profit hardware." Whether it was hardware or software, the fact was that our emphasis on the development of human resources was generating profit indeed. Of course, training contributed to profit, but it was not the whole story.

People need to be disciplined, as much as they need to be educated. Discipline is realized as rules and regulations. There are two elements in the human nature, the good and the evil. Education can bring out the good, and rules and regulations are used to discipline the evil. In our changing times, the task to restrain the evil is more arduous, because old traditions, old beliefs and old orders will resurface as the society began to transform itself, before new beliefs, new orders and new ethics have a chance to set in.

Out of this consideration, we formulated the principle that "Rules are higher than the General Manager." It meant that the rules were ruthless, regardless of the positions of the people involved, or the importance of the issues. I believed that the higher the position, the more rigorously the rules would be applied. Otherwise people in lower positions would not be convinced. Regarding the importance of the issues, I believed that rules should apply to the least significant issues. Otherwise the big issues would be hard to handle.

As an example of attending to the less significant issues, the Wuhan Plaza fired three workers who hid themselves in the restroom for a smoke. They violated the no smoking rule of the company, exposing the company to the risk of fire.

To justify the disciplinary action, the Human Resources Department quoted a case in history. Before the Jiawu Sino-Japan Naval Battle, a Japanese naval admiral went to visit a naval base of the Chinese Qing Dynasty. Finding oil stain under the warship's guns, he predicted that the naval force of the Qing Dynasty would be defeated. It turned out that he was right. This case proved the risk of overlooking slight defects.

The Wuhan Plaza couldn't forgive any small violations for another reason, which was the "butterfly effect" discovered by the American meteorologist Edward Laurence. After a long-term research, he found that a butterfly flapping wings in Singapore could have some impact on a hurricane in North Carolina.

We didn't need any hurricane. So we must watch out for the butterfly effect.

I denounced the "butterfly effect" as the enemy of our rules and regulations before the whole company. Meanwhile, I talked about the "cup theory," which only considered the result, not the process. When a cup was broken, it was your fault, no matter how it was broken.

These two management theories were known to everyone in the company, who tried their best to avoid violating the rules and regulations, but violations happened anyway.

These violations despite the heavy penalty could be attributed to our inertia. A Hong Kong friend had told me a story. When American restaurants looked for dish washers, the Japanese would be their first choice. Next came the Chinese from Hong Kong and Taiwan. The Chinese from Mainland China would be the last choice. The Japanese would wash the dishes as many times as required, without exception; most of those from Hong Kong and Taiwan would do the same, too; but people from Mainland China would cut some corners in general and laugh at the honest Japanese.

I felt sad though it was only a story. On the other hand, it alerted me to the danger of inertia.

One event could be considered as a typical case of fighting the inertia. It happened during the National Day holiday in 1998, a peak season for the whole company. A counter leader wanted to finish off remodeling at home during this time, but he knew that any request for a leave without special reasons would be turned down during the holidays. So he left work without permission several times during the three-day holiday. To our surprise, all the attendance records indicated that he was there all the time, and the floor manager made up for the leave permit for him later. When this incident was tipped off, the Human Resources Department was shocked. This was an incident of rule violation involving several people.

Other companies probably would have brushed it off as insignificant, but we were different. There were three things that would not be tolerated at the Wuhan Plaza: first, cheating the company; second, stealing the property of the company, be it a piece of paper or a packaging bag; third, fighting or quarreling with customers or colleagues. The offenders in this incident dared to behave the way they did perhaps because they thought "the law would make exceptions when many are involved." They were wrong. The company applied the rules without any hesitation.

The main offender, the counter leader, was fired.

The floor supervisor who didn't fulfill his duty during his inspection was dismissed from his position.

The floor supervising manager was demoted.

The floor manager was demoted and transferred to another position.

The attendance record keeper was demoted to a sales assistant.

The incident involved several managers, and someone suggested leniency.

The Human Resources Department replied that everyone was equal before the rules and regulations. Managers were no exceptions.

One might be curious whether there was any resistance in implementing the rules and regulations. The answer is yes. There was. The traditional Chinese culture emphasizes "mediocrity," "propriety" and "harmony." Before penalty was dealt out, many would lobby on behalf of the offender. Take the one who was fired for smoking for example. Someone said to me, "Isn't it too much to fire an employee just for smoking?" That afternoon, a leader from the Wuhan Department Store Group called me about the incident. When I returned home, my husband wanted me to give the employee another chance because the family members of that man had talked to him. In this case, I had to confront the challenge of the traditional culture, and to make a choice between the rules and human relations.

I knew that any slight back down would produce the "butterfly effect."

Finally, the Human Resources Manager announced the decision to the employee with tears in the eyes. I also felt bad, because this employee had sweated with us for the opening of the Wuhan Plaza. But even the General Manager could not override the established rules. At the Wuhan Plaza, "Rules are higher than the General Manager."

Harsh penalty was necessary sometimes. Traditional enterprises couldn't maintain rules because they were not serious about looking into the lapse of the staff, and they could not make up their mind to fire those responsible for the lapse. As a result, they became weak and undisciplined, falling apart in the end.

The Wuhan Plaza fired that employee without hesitation.

Of course, in punishing those who violated the rules, we offered to help first. For instance, one afternoon in the summer of 1998, I received a complaint that a senior manager had bought some clothes at the wholesale price without authorization. Obviously, it was against the rules of the company.

This was a colleague who had been working at the Wuhan Plaza since the very beginning, one of those who worked out the rules and regulations for the company. Why did she go against the rules to save a few pennies?

I sent for her and reprimanded her harshly.

That day we had a long talk and I didn't try to hide my anger.

She didn't talk back, just listening to my angry talk in silence.

At last she said, "Chief Hu, don't pick at me anymore. I was on my way to find someone at the time. It so happened that on the third floor, I saw the blouse on sale, which I had always wanted but didn't have time to buy. I lost my senses and asked someone to buy it for me. Now I know I was wrong. I will return it and pay my penalty."

Her "losing her senses" reminded me of the root causes of such violations and the difficulty to eliminate them.

Many of the violations were not on purpose. Rather, they were motivated by the subconscious.

After the talk, she was issue a severe warning. Twenty percent of her yearly bonus was deducted with an additional fine. The fault and the penalty were entered in her personnel file. Besides, she was required to exercise self-criticism.

This punishment was next to dismissal from the company.

In view of her status and prestige, it was decided that the punishment wouldn't be made public on the bulletin board in the passageways used by the staff. It would be announced only to the management team.

The manager proved to be very sensible. She knew I did not bear any grudge against her personally. I was just doing my job.

Doing one's job without personal grudge meant impartiality. Only with impartiality could we stand by the rules and regulations, building a knowledgeable and well-disciplined army with harsh measures.

8. Seal off Cracks through Making Rounds

Talking about punishment for violations, some might be curious, "How do you find these violations?" This question is easy to answer, because the Wuhan Plaza had a special management term "making rounds." What is "making rounds?" It means that for every job, we would ask the employees in charge to follow up, supervise and ensure its solution. Making rounds in the Wuhan Plaza was more than a method in work; it was a company rule, a dynamic management concept.

Making rounds was established into a rule to deal with the defects witnessed in many companies these days. They were not short of good planning, good systems and good measures. What was missing was aggressive implementation. In this light, we emphasized confronting problems, solving them and finding new problems, all through a dynamic mechanism. We went to such an extreme that the Training Center went in and measured steps around the shopping floors, and specified that every floor supervisor must take ninety steps every minute. They must continuously inspect the area under their supervision, to forestall mistakes that violated company rules and regulations. Ninety steps per minute did not seem to be a big deal, but taking every step at 0.8 meter, six hours a day, the supervisor would have to walk 25,920 meters, or 25 kilometers. Apart from the supervisors, this rule also involved a large group of floor managers and mobile security guards. That is, quite a number of people in the Wuhan Plaza had to walk 25 kilometers each shift in their supervisory work.

This was strenuous, but necessary.

What is management? It involves sorting out the details and dealing with them. Management is strenuous and detailed by nature.

With more high technology and fewer layers, management work requires more people making their rounds, to spot and stop possible cracks and leaks.

Computers and a flat organization reduce the management head count. The benefits are higher efficiency and less manpower, but it has its own problems. Making rounds can straighten out our operations.

What was the advantage of making rounds? Here is an example. In the winter of 1996, two months after the grand opening, I walked around the store as usual. In the shopping area of the first floor, I found the marble floor was not as clean and shiny as it should be. Floor maintenance was the responsibility of the cleaning company. According to the agreement, 50 barrels of imported wax should be used up every month, and the marble floor must be waxed once and polished twice every week. I asked the Property Management Department to look into the matter. They discovered that the workers of the cleaning company had been cutting corners. They had waxed the floor only twice in the past three weeks. Polishing was even more of a shame.

Without making rounds, I would not have discovered the problem. Now that the problem was found, I fined the cleaning company RMB 5,000, as specified by the contract. The senior manager of the Property Management Department had 5% of his salary taken out that month.

The floor marble slates were imported across the oceans from Italy. According to our plan of property management, the value of property should increase through careful maintenance. If I resigned from my position one day, I would like to leave a clean and shiny property to my successor.

The breach of contract terms by the cleaners was undermining our property management plan. It had to be penalized.

Here is another example of management through making rounds. One night, the manager of the Human Resources Department went to the employee passage on the first floor, only to find it noisy and crowded when the employees went off work. What was the matter? After some investigation, we learned that all the employees must change their uniforms in the locker rooms along the passageways when they came in or went off. The rule was right, but one issue was overlooked: the employees came in one by one but went off work all at the same time, which led to the confusion. This problem could be solved by adjusting the peak flow. I had the off-work time changed for each floor. The store music was used as an indicator, to inform the employees of their time of exit, starting from the highest floor. The time gap between different floors provided a solution to the disorder and confusion at the rush hour.

I liked the comments of Mr. Wallace, President of Coca Cola. He said that a large amount of information was vital for decision-making. The kind of CEO staying high up was fading out, to be replaced by the platoon leader type of CEOs.

A platoon leader (not to mention those under him) would have to charge at enemy positions on the battlefield, and make his due rounds.

"Making rounds" developed later on into another management principle: follow-up.

Many things at the Wuhan Plaza would open up the eyes of business visitors, from the company structure to the spotless environment. When they inquired about our success story, all the employees would mention: "follow-up."

"Follow-up" sounds like a military term in Chinese. I like it because it refers to the coordination of military operations among various groups, one formation following another.

Commercial competition is warfare without gun smoke. It calls for follow-up, too.

Throughout all these years, I have realized that running a company is sometimes more nerve-racking than fighting a war. You must exercise great caution in dealing with everything, big or small. Never expect your directives to be carried out completely the first time you give them. You must follow everything up. For that reason, I advocated "follow-up" in the company, and made it into a principle to be enforced.

We required the upper link in our chain of work to follow up on the lower link. Nobody should feel that their job was done when a task was passed downstream. The upper link must follow the progress and result of the task. Failure to follow up would be considered neglect of duty. I told the staff that "follow-up" was the reflection of one's proactive attitude. I also said that dynamic thinking was the mental basis of "follow-up," which would reflect one's flexibility.

Under the pressure of the principle of follow-up, our management improved substantially. A small incident proved it. In 1998, summer came very early in Wuhan. In order to save energy and prevent the hot air outside from coming in, I asked the Property Management Department to close the employee passageways that had remained open. The Property Management Department promptly came up with a plan, informed every floor and every department, and installed springs on the doors in the passageways. It seemed that the issue was taken care of, but I did not dismiss it from my mind. I made some follow-up inspections as I always did.

A few days later, during my inspection, I found many doors were still open in the passageways. I sent for the Property Management Department.

They had discovered the problem, too. They followed up, re-numbered all the doors in the passageways, and installed the springs of better quality.

Then they followed up even further, specifying which door could be opened and which doors couldn't, and posting the notice "Please close the door" on every door.

Now the issue was taken care of in a perfect way. This perfection was due to continuous follow-up.

Since the positive effect of follow-up impressed the staff, and since follow-up was made into a principle, specific follow-up measures were drawn up for all the tasks at the Wuhan Plaza. The Merchandise Department consistently followed up on all the introduced brands. If a vendor failed to reach the anticipated sales volume in three months, it would be advised to consolidate its business. If the consolidation did not work, it would be asked to pack up and leave. The Human Resources Department regularly followed up on the performance of the employees. Every month, 50 best performers and 50 worst performers would be selected. Every six months, an evaluation would be conducted on every employee. Every year a comprehensive review would be performed. The Accounting Department always followed up on all the expenses. Because of their follow-up with constant alerts, our travel expenses were controlled to less than one million *yuan* per year, in contrast to several million *yuan* per year by other large-scale shopping centers. The Computer Center constantly followed up on all the software and hardware, minimizing the downtime of the hardware and developing new software at the same time.

Without follow-up measures, business management could only be loose and inefficient.

Our goal was optimal management, which required follow-up.

It was proved that intensive follow-up activities were required by intensive management, as were intensive work, concentrated technology and rich human resources.

Follow-up meant implementation and execution. It was stimulation, encouragement and alerting at the same time. The significance of follow-up was that it ensured our success as a top-class enterprise.

9. Work While Standing

Both following up and making rounds require the standing position. The standing position has the advantage of fostering an active attitude and discouraging weariness. It puts people in a motion to keep them alert, which would in turn boost their efficiency and responsiveness. To bring out its advantages, the Wuhan Plaza deliberately enforced a standing work style. It included two sides. One was the physical position. The other was the mental "standing" state to respond at any time. The physical position was easy to describe. It was visible everywhere at the Wuhan Plaza.

There were no chairs or benches inside the counters at the Wuhan Plaza. Not only that, the sales staff were not allowed to lean on the counter to relax. Sales assistants were required to stand in a standard posture throughout their work shift. This requirement was made to present a new working style in our shopping center as well as to show respect to our customers. More importantly, it put sales assistants in a working mental state, ready to serve the customers at any moment. To ensure the best service, cups and mugs were not allowed inside the counter. They were left in the employee rest area, where there were no chairs to sit on for drinking either. In the rest area, there were all kinds of cups in the cupboards, high, low, made of glass or ceramics, all huddling together, like shelves in a convenience store, or terra-cotta warriors ready to march.

The office of floor manages didn't have chairs, either. Why? To encourage them to make their rounds, promoting the style of working on site. Sitting down could lead to inactivity and reluctance to return to the shopping floors. The office environment would shape up people's behavior, which in turn would induce a certain mental state. We removed all the chairs to create an environment which would encourage a dynamic work style.

The employees were required to stand through their shifts as well as through meetings before and after work. Ranks in good order at the meetings took on the looks of a military force. We made the rule on purpose. I was for the military views on formation drills. According to these views, formations were no longer useful in the war. The purpose of formation drills was to train soldiers in team spirit and strict discipline.

The management team stood through meetings, too. The meeting would last for three to five minutes, at most ten. People were required to stand through meetings because we wanted to encourage short meetings, so that focus would be put on actions and practical issues, not on talks and formalities. Standing through meetings would also cultivate a "sense of ranks," so that the management team would feel used to taking orders from their superiors.

Of course, it was tiring to stand all the time.

But in my opinion, tiredness was part of the work. After all, work was not rest or fooling around.

Human beings are highly flexible. The key is to build up a behavior pattern. When they get used to standing, they will feel uneasy sitting down.

We would do well by building readiness for business wars and mechanism for efficiency and profitability, from the perspectives of culture, psychology, behavior, and system.

In this regard, I would like to touch upon the mental "standing" state that we emphasized. At the micro level, this mental standing state banned tea cups and newspapers from the desks of employees (senior managers included), in order to overcome the traditional corporate epidemic of "with a newspaper, a cigarette and a cup of tea, gossip for half a day." At the macro level, it generated the staff rotation system. At the Wuhan Plaza, few would work for more than two years in the same position if they are really good. Hired as the supervisor in the cashier section the first year, an employee named Zhu Jianwen was promoted to the floor manager position the second year, and to the senior manager position the third year. It was not unusual to see employees in their 40s managed by young people not yet 20 years old, and old timers in the retail business managed by new hands just hired from outside.

One purpose of the rotation system was to develop multiple skills among the employees. Another purpose was to create a sense of crisis, so that they would not take their position and salary for granted. They ought to keep a watchful eye from time to time, to see where they would land soon. If they did not stay alert mentally, they might go downhill the next day. The only choice for them was to respond to the ever-changing situation with a dynamic mentality. They had to fight hard and be prepared to move on at any time.

The ancient Chinese scholar Han Feizi often talked about "laws, methods and tendencies." We were pushing for a tendency.

Encouraged by this tendency, the Wuhan Plaza management team often stayed on until 8 or 9 in the evening. They were not asked to work overtime; they simply felt that they must finish the work at hand.

There were a great number of such selfless examples at the Wuhan Plaza. For instance, in order to make a video tape named "Handbook of Sales Assistants," a manager gave up a business trip to Beijing during which he had planned to help his daughter change her major in Beijing Broadcasting College. Feng Jinlin, a manager of the Supervising Department, sent her mother to a nursing home in October, 1996 to devote all her time to work. She said to her mother before leaving her, "Mom, I will bring you home when I feel at ease with my work."

The staff were very hard-working, with high efficiency. The tendency we pushed for trained them, in line with the development of the times.

In front of the standing employees, I believed that I was giving them the mental preparation for and a real feeling of reform, a mental "standing" state — ready to go at any time. This would benefit them forever.

President Clinton once remarked that life depended on exercise, and yet exercise must be moderate; life existed in the form of work, and yet caution must be given to the work method; life was shaped by the spirit, and so we must cheer up. I still remember these remarks till this day.

10. Show Affection in Rewards and Penalties

The tough discipline, the rapid pace of work, and the high coordination at the Wuhan Plaza appeared frightening to many people. When the Wuhan Plaza was first built, some of the employees at the Wuhan Department Store felt nervous when they heard that they would be transferred to the Wuhan Plaza, fearing that they couldn't stand the harsh work. In fact, this was misunderstanding. We were indeed very demanding at the Wuhan Plaza, but we were not lacking in affection. As General Manager, I had too many responsibilities to be emotional. Nevertheless, as a woman, I was very affectionate inside my heart.

When we were preparing for the opening of the Wuhan Plaza, the Women's Day came and the Labor Union bought some gifts for our female employees. I found the packaging was not good enough. I had the gifts packed into exquisite boxes, tied up with a fancy silk ribbon, to let the female staff members feel they were appreciated. After the Wuhan Plaza opened to business, we made a rule not to be altered under any circumstances. On his/her birthday, the Human Resources Department would present the employee with a card and a flower in the morning if he or she worked in the office. For sales assistants, charming birthday songs would be broadcast over the loudspeakers during the morning meeting. The employees said that flowers were nothing unusual, but they showed affection, and that songs were heard everyday, yet they sounded the most touching on their birthday.

Affection is our spiritual support. It is what our heart craves for. In an enterprise, affection is also a very important cohesive force, the green shade very much needed in the laborious trudge. I agree to the remarks by Toffler, the American futurologist, who said that in the age of high technology and high pass rate, intensive emotion was in great demand. Out of this conviction, when Teng Yubei, a student studying at an American university, sent me a long letter about humanistic management, I took time to read it in detail, and adopted several reasonable suggestions.

I said "several" instead of "all" because I thought the major management problem in China now was not lack of affection, but insufficient rules and regulations. We should focus on the solutions to this problem. But it didn't rule out the need to show our affection at the same time. Sometimes we must insist on our own opinions while presenting an amiable public image; sometimes we must show our affection while adhering to the principles. The Human Resources Department disciplined quite a few people in the past few years, but there were no hard feelings. The reason was simple: everyone understood we did so for the benefit of the company, and we showed our affection in rewarding and disciplining the employees.

To show our affection while punishing the employees, we must guide them to the proper behavior. This would be good for them and for their interests in the long run. To show our affection while rewarding the employees, we must take their special needs into consideration.

One evening in October, 1998, I saw two middle-aged employees sitting and talking on the landing of the staircase between the sixth floor and the fifth floor. I was just passing by, but they got up and ran when they spotted me. Perhaps they knew that they violated the rule that banned gossiping during the business hours. I asked them not to run, but to take their time. Then one of them said anxiously to me, "Chief Hu, I am having a bad time. I felt worried and wanted to talk it over with someone." I asked them to take the matter to the floor manager on duty. On the next day, the floor manager presented his opinion to the Human Resources Department. The two employees had a serious fault recorded in their personnel files.

After reading the report from the Human Resources Department, I sent for the department manager and asked her to find out what difficulties the employee ran into. It was discovered that her family was in deep financial trouble. Her husband had lost his job. In addition, she and her husband each had a parent sick in bed. She had borrowed RMB 3,000. Now it was time to pay the interest. She was very upset and wanted to talk it over with the other woman, before I saw them.

I felt disturbed, and immediately sent a senior manager in the Human Resources Department and the floor director of human resources to her home, to find out the details. It turned out that the real situation was even worse.

I couldn't sit still any more. I asked the Human Resources Department to extend our concern to her family. They visited her home, bringing RMB 200 as relief, together with milk powder and other nourishment.

When I came back home at night, the face of that employee was still in my mind. RMB 200 wouldn't go far in such an emergency.

The next day, I called a managers' meeting and described the situation of that employee, suggesting that every senior manager contribute RMB 100. All together RMB 1,000 was collected and given to the employee. Meanwhile, I discussed the issue with the Human Resources Department, the Labor Union and floor managers to make a long-term relief plan. The employee was deeply moved, and later did outstanding work. She wrote a thank-you letter to me, saying that I was cold as ice to mistakes, and hot as fire to the staff.

In a similar case, the "rules, reasoning and affection" principle in implementing company policies was better represented. One morning, the shopping center was about to open. I was inspecting the third floor, and found a male employee in his 30s sitting on the floor, lost in thoughts. This behavior was banned by the company rules. I went to him and asked why he was sitting there. He threw a glance at me and said bluntly, "I am weak. I didn't have the money for breakfast."

At the time, I felt something was wrong. I found the floor manager and asked him to handle the matter. The floor manager reported the second day that, according to the rules, the employee had a serious fault recorded in his personnel file and was fined RMB 50. He had to hand in a written explanation in self-criticism. It seemed that the incident was over, but I followed up further and found out that man's wife had given birth to twins recently, and had lost her job. He was having a hard time, feeling rather agitated. Now the rules were conflicting with human emotions once more.

I felt that it was correct to discipline that employee. It was good for the company and for the employee himself as well.

But did we have the responsibility to lend him a hand during his hard time?

The contract did not spell out this responsibility loud and clear. But considering our human nature and human feelings, the responsibility was clearly there.

Employees go to work in a company day by day, spending most of their time there. What do they expect? They wish to be part of the company, to obtain financial security and emotional support.

Then the conclusion was very clear. We wanted him to feel the power of our company in his difficult times, and feel that the company was behind him. I asked the Human Resources Department to implement the following decisions: (1) the employee would be fined for his behavior; (2) the Labor Union would go and visit him at his home, bringing gifts for his twins; (3) starting from that month, a special subsidy of RMB 100 would be provided to him each month; (4) he would be transferred to another counter with better profitability and benefits. After this incident, the employee improved rapidly. He said, "I almost gave up. It was the rules, reasoning and affection from the company that pulled me back. The company treats me with feelings. I will surely pay back."

Did the company have feelings? Of course. Out of our affection, we later on established a system to show our concern for our staff. It was the General Manager's Reception Day. On that day, I did nothing but to receive the employees, listening to their stories and difficulties. During the day, little trifles were sometimes brought up, but I didn't feel bored. Instead, I was very happy. I felt it was necessary for introducing democracy and humanity into the company.

The reception was not just for show. When I finished the day, the Human Resources Department would take over and solve the problems for the employees.

Modern enterprises must establish a management mechanism of "rules, reasoning, and affection."

Rules mean the corporate policies. Reasoning means training. And affection means showing our concern and support.

Only with the combination of these three elements can an enterprise be powerful, mobilizing the staff to strive for first-class profitability.

In terms of affection, besides random cases, we should watch out against offering only small favors, not substantial ones, which an ancient maxim warned about, because "people wouldn't obey without small favors."

"Without small favors" implied that it was difficult to benefit everyone with small favors. Without them, people would not follow.

This required that we set up a general provision to spread out our affection to every corner.

We had many provisions like this: the provision to present a flower to employees on their birthdays, the provision to celebrate newly married couples with songs on demand, the provision to visit families in great difficulties, the provision to offer medical insurance to employees, the provision to award outstanding employees with paid travel or education, the provision to encourage criticism from employees, the provision to grant rewards to employees with great contributions, to name a few.

We even went so far as to invite a psychologist (a Harvard graduate) from Hong Kong to give psychological lectures to the employees, to show our consideration for them.

Psychology is considered one of the most popular sciences in the 21st century. It is an important remedy for diseases in the future, a new perspective for examining the relation between human beings and the environment, and a philosophy about life that can improve the quality of people.

The Wuhan Plaza should shape many healthy, beautiful and strong minds for the upcoming century!

(Endnotes)

[1] This is a line from the National Anthem of China.

[2] *The Book of Songs* was the first anthology of poems in ancient China, compiled more than 2,000 years ago.

[3] *Pingtan* is a kind of story telling and ballad singing in the Suzhou dialect in southern Jiangsu Province.

[4] It is a folk art form popular in the northwestern part of China. Hundreds of performers in formations perform to the beat of drums and gongs strapped to their body.

[5] Huang Chao and Li Zicheng were leaders of large-scale peasant uprising in the Chinese history.

[6] *Chi* is a Chinese measurement unit of length, a little more than a foot.

[7] *Li* is a Chinese measurement unit of length, about one third of a mile.

5

Clone the Wuhan Plaza

> Knowledge expansion precedes capital expansion.
> Why can't we exchange knowledge for capital?
> — Author

1. A Priceless Model

When the Wuhan Plaza was marching to success, a wind blew up in the retail business. It started in this 76,000 square meter area of ours, hovered along the daily customer flow of 300,000, and then broke loose from its breeding ground onto the outside world with a powerful force. It shook the retail business, attracted the media and drew attention from high officials. In 1997, a year after we started our business, someone commented that a "Wuhan Plaza hurricane" was taking shape in the retail business. It had the potential to lead and push forward the reform in China's retail business. Meanwhile, we stopped with some success the advance for more grounds by foreign retail companies through competing with them with our achievement instead of through government intervention or whining for mercy.

These comments came from someone with authority, and they were supported by evidence. At the end of 1997, in a weak market, we made a profit of RMB 127 million and topped China's retail business in profitability. Our performance was evaluated against the top retail businesses in China, including Chinese businesses, businesses with foreign investment and joint-venture businesses. This meant that in a fair competition in market economy, we gained a dominant position with our convincing financial statistics. Moreover, all this success was achieved by a group of Chinese.

When our performance data was released, our office became really busy. Wave after wave of messages arrived at my desk through telephone, fax and Internet. We were receiving more than 20 groups of visitors a month, and numerous prize cups and medals appeared in the conference room. Chinese businesses and researchers showed enormous interest. Many experts and scholars turned up in person.

In June, 1998, an advanced seminar was held in Wuhan. This seminar, named "Seminar on the Wuhan Plaza Model and Renovation of Large Shopping Centers," was co-sponsored by the Chinese Society of Commercial Economy and the Research Institute of Finance and Trade under the Chinese Academy of Social Sciences. Well-known universities such as the People's University, the Beijing Business Management College, Wuhan University, and the Zhongnan University of Finance and Economy took part in the seminar. Dozens of experts and scholars discussed our development with elation. The Wuhan Plaza model was formally established in the Chinese retail business, as evidenced by various documentation.

The issue under frequent discussion in the seminar was: What had the Wuhan Plaza achieved?

The conclusion was that the Wuhan Plaza not only achieved some advanced benchmarks, which were open to competition from other companies, but also built a development model integrating advanced management in the world with the Chinese reality. This model included a series of business concepts, systems, market strategies, market orientation, management mechanism, high technology utilization and humanized relationships.

Another issue was also raised: What was the significance of the Wuhan Plaza model?

The conclusion was that it arrived just in time. It would be a motivating role model for the Chinese retail business, because at the threshold of the 21st century, new concepts, new thoughts and new breakthroughs were desperately needed!

If concepts, thoughts and breakthroughs could be compared to a flowing river, one of the most significant accomplishments of the Wuhan Plaza was to freeze this river with a thick pile of Total Quality Management documents.

The tangible and the intangible are different. The intangible are random and accidental, difficult to capture and model on. The tangible are systematic and scientific, ready to be operated on and transplanted.

When the world entered the late 20th century, science created a standard human environment. Everything can be transplanted. A Siemens mobile phone can be used in Asia or in Africa. Bill Gates' computer software can be used worldwide. Panasonic color TVs can receive programs anywhere. Standards (or models) make it easy to transplant. They are promoting transplanting.

The success of cloning in biological engineering proves that almost everything can be cloned now. The main consideration in cloning is no longer technological difficulties, but the justification for it.

Following the first wave of visitors, well-known shopping centers in China, such as Xidan, Wangfujing and Xi'an's Minsheng also sent their teams over. They did not act on government calls. They were totally market driven, which revealed the urgent need of these companies to seek new directions. This convincingly proved our value. I was so distracted entertaining these visitors that I began to worry about the profitability of the Wuhan Plaza. We could not afford to forget our own business because of the visitors and watch our profit go down the drain.

The search for profit was forever the main theme of a market economy. I needed to watch out for the gain and loss of the Wuhan Plaza in this tidal wave of business visitors.

I saw that visitors came not in response to government requests, not because they had to make the trip. They came entirely for the sake of the profit of their own companies.

When their eyes brightened up after they touched the shiny hand-rails, when their heart warmed up at hearing the greeting "Welcome to the Wuhan Plaza," their preoccupation was how to copy all this to their own companies, in order to improve the profitability.

When I looked into the areas of interest of these visitors, I realized that most of the visitors belonged to two categories of companies. One was the state-owned large retail businesses. They accounted for 70% of all the visitors. These old companies were doing business in the 1990s with the concepts and the management models from the 1950s and 1960s. Facing a new situation, they felt the crisis in their survival. They wanted to find new ways out. The other category was large real estate development companies. They built many high buildings recently, and the bottom floors were usually designed as stores on the street. Their initial intention was selling the stores, but it was not easy. So they were forced to manage the stores themselves and grope in an unknown business area.

A broad demand for management surfaced in the analysis.

I found myself staring at another market opportunity.

This market is not the merchandise market, but the market of management.

Now that we had created a top management model, why shouldn't we go and grab this market?

We decided to treat our documentation on the management model as intellectual property, and put a price tag on it, RMB 600,000.

In my opinion, free transfer of knowledge and experience was history as the planned economy was transformed into a market economy.

Another set of game rules appeared in the emerging market economy. They were a system of elimination as well. The stronger would have the right to survive, while the weaker would have to reconcile to their bad luck.

To achieve a powerful position, unprecedented wars flared up in the world, price wars, technology wars, wars over human resources, management wars... You name it.

Under such circumstances, we were not obliged, nor could we afford, to give away our management information, leaving ourselves at risk.

We had spent a great deal of money, manpower, energy, labor and time on this set of management documents. According to economic laws, where there is investment, there should be rewards.

We are in a knowledge economy, where knowledge is no longer remarks that can be casually given out. It is a resource, a productive force, and another form of capital investment. Meanwhile, it is also an important force to change the world.

For retail businesses, adapting to the knowledge economy, increasing the percentage of knowledge in our business structure, and generating added value through knowledge in our daily operations, these will pose new and serious challenges.

2. Export Management for More Turf and Profit

I asked myself how we could achieve even higher after taking the first place in profit in the Chinese retail trade.

On my notebook appeared a logical thread like the following:

Exporting commodities was the goal of the traditional retail trade, the basic level of business.

Exporting management would be the goal of the present and future retail trade, a higher level of business.

In line with this logic was a new expansion and integration principle:

Integration of commodities. This was the first level of expansion.

Integration of retail businesses. This was the second level of expansion.

Integration of management. This was the third level of expansion.

We must keep moving and we must expand. Then, my thoughts became clear. It was not fantasy, but a necessity. It all boiled down to a very simple question: How to export management? Another related question: How would a single business entity expand?

The expansion model of the traditional single business entity was to continuously pour funds into the original locale, to expand the scale, and to maximize the varieties of merchandise (for instance, the two major renovations of the Wuhan Department Store in the 1970s and 1980s). But this kind of expansion was not the direction to go, because this maximization was limited by the space. It could not be repeated infinitely. Meanwhile, it required the investment of a large amount of money and time.

Recent approaches to expansion by single business entities could be summarized as follows: on the basis of a single entity dealing mainly in one trade, attempts were made to expand into other trades to achieve business diversification. (The Wuhan Department Store had recently expanded into real estate, transportation, restaurant and garment manufacturing.) This diversified expansion was less limited by time and space, but I didn't intend to follow it, because sometimes it would have some negative impact on the main business, bogging us down in an unknown terrain. Besides, it required large investment, too.

Worth noting was another kind of expansion now popular in the world. For example, Wal-Mart had 3,000 chain stores in the world. This kind of chain expansion, limitless in time and space, could replicate itself infinitely. However, it required considerable resources and a fast expansion rate based on the resources. It was in fact a kind of "capital + model" expansion. I envied it, but I thought, "Is there a type of expansion that requires minimal investment, with the potential to expand infinitely?"

Was it fantasy? Was I wishing for a free lunch? No, I wasn't. We did have our assets, which were the Wuhan Plaza model. We had a model project. This was the existing Wuhan Plaza. Although our assets were not physical, they were in line with the principle of capital expansion in the knowledge-based economy. We could explore a new approach for expansion.

There was a market for management consulting out there. That would lead to a lot of opportunities. In fact, we had started on this path already.

At the end of 1997, Hami's Daqiao Department Store in Xinjiang heard our story and paid us a visit. These people, having weathered desert winds and sand, were determined to break through geographical isolation and catch up with the rest of the world under the leadership of their general manager.

The mirror-like smooth floor, the spotless shopping space, the methodical management and well-trained employees riveted their attention like magnet.

They wished to learn from us. When Yan Jianming, Senior Training Manager at the Wuhan Plaza, briefed me on their intention, I told her to explore the possibility of exporting management with some compensation.

The general manager of the Hami department store understood this concept. He was willing to spend some money and learn some shortcuts.

The first deal to export management with compensation was closed.

We were very serious about this deal. We must win the first battle. We gave them the whole set of management documentation, and offered training to their management staff. We helped them plan for the remodeling of their store, and supported their renovation project. We flew to Hami to follow up and offered management consulting. Our management export achieved such an effect that whenever the department store had a serious problem, the general manager would yell, "Those who were trained at the Wuhan Plaza, step forward!" And these people always succeeded in solving the problems despite immense difficulties. After that, the Wuhan Plaza's management model gained appreciation far and wide. It was indeed invaluable.

The news went round fast, and the media began to talk about it. Systematic export of management with compensation was undoubtedly a new thing in China, a valuable piece of news to be elaborated on. Various newspapers and periodicals in China carried articles to report and discuss it. The hot headlines caught the attention of the public. Here is a list:

- November 7, 1997, the *Market Guidance* had this headline, "Xinjiang Businessmen Came to Study at the Wuhan Plaza"
- November 11, 1997, the *News Digest* had this headline, "The Wuhan Plaza Won't Accept Students for

Free. They Said 'Management Export with Compensation' Should Become New Concept"

- December 22, 1997, the Hong Kong Ta Kung Pao had this headline, "The Wuhan Plaza Exports Management with Compensation; Made Profit of 100 Million in the First Year"
- March 23, 1998, the *Xinmin Evening News* had this headline, "Experience Is Treasure; You Have to Pay to Learn It"
- April 2, 1998, the *China Commercial News* had this headline, "Should We Pay to Learn from Others?"
- May 14, 1998, the Central People's Broadcasting Station had this headline in its news section, "The Wuhan Plaza Demands Compensation for the Chance to Learn"
- June 10, 1998, the *Securities Times* had this headline, "The Hubei Wuhan Department Store Sells a Special Commodity — Experience"
- June 29, 1998, the *Guangming Daily* had this headline, "How Did the Wuhan Plaza Make Money?"

In the frenzy of the media, the public began to take note of us. First, the Wuhan Municipal Commerce Committee invited me to give a speech. Well-known universities such as the Huazhong University of Technology and Wuhan University sent their invitations, too. They believed that our concepts and approaches were very powerful, which would bring fresh air to China's retail business. I agreed to the invitations in spite of my busy schedule. One of the speeches was reported on the front page of the *Changjiang Daily* as follows:

"Yesterday, the Wuhan Plaza Experience-Sharing Meeting, which was sponsored by the Municipal Commerce Committee and Commerce Association, generated strong interest in the retail business in Wuhan. In the morning, the auditorium of the Municipal Commerce Committee with a capacity of 250 people was densely packed. The organizers hung up some loudspeakers outside the auditorium. Late-comers could only sit and listen in the open. The organizers mentioned that it was very rare to see this enthusiastic response in the last few years. General managers and other top officials from more than 130 retail businesses took notes while carefully listening to the report. Some even recorded the report..."

The same situation occurred when I gave a speech at the Huazhong University of Technology. In this enthusiastic response, I felt that we were on the right track again. The Wuhan Plaza made a splash in China's business world. Or in other words, China's business world had been waiting for this moment for a long time. Our next step was to seize more turf and profit in this "Wuhan Plaza tornado."

On June 2, 1998, it was reported by *Changjiang Daily* that "Beijing's Xidan Friendship Group spent a large sum of money purchasing management experience from the Wuhan Plaza." When the information was released, it sent a shock wave through China's retail business. The Xidan Emporium was one of the best-known retail giants in China, with a long history. It was not easy to understand why it spent a large sum of money to learn from this little brother that had been in business for less than 2 years. Some people asked me about this. My explanation was that the event was not as strange as it seemed. On the one hand, it showed the ups and downs of various retail businesses; on the other hand, it had its ultimate internal reason against a broad background.

The ultimate reason was that China's retail businesses were looking for breakthroughs in response to the challenges of the new century.

The broad background was that in the process of looking for breakthroughs, many companies paid a horrific price. Taking a well-known department store in Beijing for example. It spent three million U.S. dollars introducing the foreign management model. It turned out that though the foreign management model was good, it didn't work in the Chinese environment.

As the call for a Chinese solution was rising, people turned their eye to us. Xi'an's Minsheng Group Co. Ltd., as the "Northwestern King" in the retail business and as a publicly-traded company, spent hundreds of thousands of *yuan* purchasing our model. Through scientific verification, they concluded that the gross margin would grow dozens of millions of *yuan* if the Wuhan Plaza model was implemented.

Our fraternal company, the Wuhan Department Store, made a profit of more than five million in 40 days after implementing the Wuhan Plaza system. And past issues such as obstruction to orders, growth of small group interests and erosion of profit at the company level were brought under control.

In this situation, we decided to further push for the management export. The purpose was to achieve mutual benefits, to bring the retail business to a new level and to improve management and profitability of the retail business in China.

Then, we registered the Wuhan Ruitai Commercial Management Co., Ltd. with new Internet, fax and telephone connections. We signed contracts of paid management export with more than twenty large department stores in Chongqing, Shenyang, Shijiazhuang, Nanjing, Jinan, Shanghai, Beijing, Xiamen, Shenzhen, Mudanjiang and Xi'an in a short time. This "soft business" realized our dream to open the door to wealth using our knowledge.

3. Expand with Entrusted Management

The more than 20 department stores that introduced our management model were located all over the country on the map.

They showed an ensuring radiating pattern. Meanwhile, an issue rose to our attention: control.

Not to control the business operations of those companies, but to control the survival rate and success rate of our model among them.

We could solve this problem through continuous consulting and follow-up, but this was not the optimal control method, because the model was being implemented by people, and people were so different.

A year after the Wuhan Plaza exported our management model with compensation, I began to reflect on the approach. Self-reflection is always a must for an entrepreneur, because it involves summarizing our experience and filtering out successful stories and fail-

ures. It is like climbing a spiral staircase. After all, everything pro-
ceeds spirally. In my reflection, I discovered that the past export
activities were still based on trading. Only the goods traded for were
something special. Business expansion achieved by management
export was an expansion of quantity represented by the increasing
sales revenue. There was no fundamental difference.

From another perspective, although that single entity of ours was
very big, it was still a single entity. In order to have multiple entities
through the export activities, which would bring about expansion
in its true sense, we must rise to a new level.

What would be the new level? Entrusted management.

What was entrusted management? It was to manage other companies with our staff and our management model.

This was a strategic leap, a new and complex operation. Although
there were cases of entrusted management in the world, few had
happened in China. Entrusted management looked similar to con-
tracting, including the pledge to achieve certain financial targets.
But it was essentially different from the latter. A contractor wouldn't
lay any claim to the credit of success, nor would he be required to
bring in a certain model. All he would do was exchange his labor
for financial rewards. The most important feature of entrusted management was the introduction of intangible assets. It was a type of
profit sharing based on investment. Of course, the investment was
in the form of intangible assets such as the brand name, knowledge
and method. It was one of the operating principles of the knowledge economy: exchange knowledge for profit.

The Wuhan Plaza took to the fast lane: it ranked first in profit in
China's retail trade within one year after it went into operation. It
began to export management in the second year. It was to expand
through entrusted management in the third year. Three leaps in three
years.

The plan for entrusted management needed an opportunity to be
tested out. In 1998, this opportunity was created by the market.
Market was like a magician. Wherever there was demand, there
was supply. At that time, Hong Kong's Anderson Group Limited
was investing in real estate in Tianjin, and had completed several
development projects there. As a rule, a large shopping center was

built, with a space of 120,000 square meters. The Xinan Commercial Group Co. was set up for its management. Real estate developers were stepping into the retail business.

It was not difficult to imagine how tough it was for them to enter an unfamiliar terrain.

On a casual occasion, leaders of the National Economy and Trade Commission suggested they make a trip to the Wuhan Plaza.

Following that advice, Mr. Chan, General Manager of Xin'an, took his team to the Wuhan Plaza. Once in the Wuhan Plaza, they found themselves in an internationalized shopping center, experiencing our high quality and outstanding management.

Mr. Chan was a businessman from Hong Kong. It was significant that he was utterly convinced by the achievements of the Mainlanders. Equally significant was the fact that although Mr. Chan learned about the Wuhan Plaza by accident, it was no accident that real estate developers were seeking help from retail businesses. We had long expected it.

We sat down to talk.

The solemn conference room, the comfortable leather sofa, the thick notes of our talks and the gentle light all bore witnesses to the negotiations.

Mr. Chan was in his prime years. He had seen international cases of entrusted management and was open to new management concepts. He accepted our intent for entrusted management in principle.

In December, 1998, we signed the Letter of Intent.

Eighteen days into the new year of 1999, Wuhan Ruitai signed a contract of entrusted management with Tianjin Xin'an:

- Xin'an would entrust an area of 100,000 square meters to be managed by Wuhan Ruitai. They would accept and pay for the general manager we would appoint for them as well as our complete management model.

- Xin'an would accept and pay for the use of our name Ruitai. The company under entrusted management registered as Xin'an Ruitai Shopping Center.

- Xin'an would accept and pay for the use of our computer software.
- Xin'an would accept and pay for our market positioning and vendor recruitment activities.

Of course, these compensations were subject to a series of restrictive provisions. We promised to build Xin'an Ruitai into a shopping center based on the Wuhan Plaza model, which would meet the needs of the 21st century.

If market is an invisible hand, knowledge is the magic wand in that hand which can turn stone into gold. In the cooperation between Xin'an and Ruitai, the main means of our profit and expansion was knowledge and intellect, not investment or physical labor. "Software" gained access to "hardware" in this case. The basis of our agreement was the sincere desire for mutual benefits.

Mr. Chan was shrewd. He had the foresight of a strategist and the carefulness of an accountant. He made a secure move.

We should make the next move in response. In other words, after the contract was officially signed on January 18, 1999 by both sides, it was all up to us.

We selected eight managers and sent them to Tianjin. They made elaborate and precise plans and schedules, set up a supervisory department to monitor and support operations, and built a recruitment team which plunged right into action.

This was like gambling, but I felt that I had to gamble under certain circumstances. I remembered a speech made by Mao Zedong before the Huaihai Campaign in the movie *Great Decisive Campaigns*. "A decisive battle is a gamble. The word 'gamble' doesn't sound good, but it is a gamble, a gamble on the fate of the army and the nation." After the speech, Mao Zedong started the Great Decisive Campaign in a grand scale. I was deeply impressed by this speech by Mao. Yes, on entrusted management, we must have the guts to gamble.

Because its success or failure would determine the fate of a new expansion approach.

This approach had a broad market in China with a lot of potential. It had the Wuhan Plaza model as the means of operation. What we needed now was just experience.

Success depended on caution. It also depended on courage. We had already done our cautious planning. Now let's strike out bravely.

China's business has to be renovated, and China's economy should interface with international economy. For this reason alone, we should go for this gamble!

4. Run a New Huangpu Military Academy

Although I decided to engage in this gamble, I was rather nervous when the appointed general manager flew to Tianjin.

I understood that from now on he would determine to some extent the success of entrusted management and the new expansion approach.

The world-famous Fortune magazine once published the result from a survey. Presidents of 500 top enterprises in the world were surveyed. When asked about the key to success, the presidents unanimously pointed to good leadership.

Models cannot replace the work of people. Good models are created by people. They have to be operated by talented people.

The issue of human resources is forever a strategic issue. Panasonic has a popular slogan, which states that enterprises must "set goals on human resources, focus on them, organize them and find out ways to train them." When the Wuhan Plaza project was still in the planning stage, we decided on the principle of "professionals first; profit second." We were badly in need of professionals at that time. But the thirst for professionals then was no match for our need now. I was acutely feeling the need of a large group of professionals in a rapidly expanding company, a large group of senior managers and general managers.

The problem looked upsetting. If we had two, three or even a group of companies for entrusted management like Xin'an in Tianjin, would we have enough general managers to send out? Would the shortage disrupt our expansion plan?

Before sending out the general manager to Xin'an, we first selected three candidates out of the entire company and then eliminated two of them. The only one left was Zhuang Xianmin, Assistant to General Manager of the Wuhan Plaza.

But we must have a larger pool of professionals to meet the challenge of expansion.

A plan took shape in my mind: run a Huangpu Military Academy.

During the military-style training before the grand opening, I was told that our training was like that in the Huangpu Military Academy. The staff that underwent training at the time joked that they were the first Huangpu class. Our training had a good reputation. Many new companies paid us to train their staff, calling it Huangpu training. Our Training Department was very proud of this reputation. Of course, this pride was over-optimistic, because what we ran at the time was only a junior class.

Now we needed to run senior classes, to train senior managers and general managers.

With the continuous expansion of the company and the development of our age, there would be greater demand for senior professionals.

Who could offer a solution to such urgent needs? We must pull ourselves together: we could only depend on ourselves.

Could a company offer training to a large group of general managers? It was a new challenge.

I once read a book written by an American. The gist was like this: The purpose of education was to prepare professionals for the future. Subjects should be forward-looking and anticipatory, and contents should be operable. In his opinion, our current education was lagging behind the times, the contents not operable. So he suggested removing all the present schools and creating company schools and network schools.

His opinion was quite radical. But education should prepare professionals for the future. Contents should be operable. Companies should act like schools.

Our company certainly should become the Huangpu Military Academy. We had our teaching syllabus — the Wuhan Plaza model; we had our teachers — all levels of managers who had grown rapidly under the concept "every manager should be a training manager." But where were the candidates?

An idea struck me: could we solve the candidate problem through promotion level by level?

It meant that we would train outstanding workers into counter team leaders and supervisors, team leaders and supervisors into managers, managers into senior managers, and senior managers into general managers.

The issue of finding training candidates for senior managers and general managers was solved. Now we had one final problem. If we started to train the badly needed senior managers and general managers right away, gaps might develop in management staff because of the rapid promotion on all levels.

The way to fill the gap was to promote candidates internally and recruit them externally.

With this in mind, we put ads in newspapers once more to recruit senior management candidates.

Hundreds of people sent in their applications. Through two rounds of examinations, more than a dozen senior and middle management candidates proved their capabilities.

On the New Year's Day of 1999, I sat once more with my senior assistants along the big conference desk in the conference room for the final interview.

Thick carpet, gentle light, elegant high-back chairs, and a big desk, behind which sat a line of examiners. In front of the desk was a chair for the interviewee. It was a solemn occasion. Stacks of forms and answer sheets circulated among us, and interviewees were led to the seat one by one. They were very young, all college-educated. Many had worked in middle management positions in joint-ventures, experienced and energetic. We asked them all kinds of questions. They would join those promoted internally, serving as a pool of talents for future expansion. They would take over senior or middle management positions so that the experienced, capable managers who were familiar with the Wuhan Plaza model could go to the "Huangpu Military Academy."

Eighteen future general managers would emerge from our "Huangpu Military Academy."

They would be trained for 3 to 6 months. "Huangpu" should have a quick turnover, three months each class.

"Huangpu" was officially named as Training Class for General Managers.

The general managers trained here would not become the Wuhan Plaza's general managers. They would be general managers of the entities after future business expansion.

The only main course of "Huangpu" was the Wuhan Plaza model.

In a sense, there was more than one course at "Huangpu," because in addition to the required knowledge, general managers must have the right demeanor, the right cultivation, the right style and the right values which were behind all this.

Our values advocated individualism, because it was the basis for market economy. Our future general managers should have the mental aptitude to lead a company individually.

The Training Department had these contents in its teaching syllabus: future general managers should be prepared to take on the worst hardship in playing the leading role; they should have an enterprising spirit; they should have the bravery to break into unknown territories; they should be bold enough to talk about profitability openly; they should take the initiative to compete and to promote themselves; and they should be able to survive adverse circumstances.

These ideas looked unconventional, but in fact they were not. Groups are made up of individuals. Strong individuals will make strong groups. As permanent employment fades out, as planned economy gives way to market economy, the collective psychology of following the crowd and doing what is told is losing its appeal. Market operations are supported by new concepts, new morals and new ethics, and this support depends on the individuals.

Everything was ready. "Huangpu" was about to open. The classroom, teaching aids and teaching materials were all in place. The teaching materials were composed of various management documents, abstracts from magazines and periodicals domestic and abroad, video and audio tapes, and case studies carefully compiled by the Training Department. They were a unique combination. We followed Harvard's teaching methodology, spending most of the time on case studies to develop their abilities. I would deliver more than 50% of the lectures, helping candidates understand the thoughts and methods of a general manager, and the way in which a general manager handled daily operations.

Based on our rules, the trainees must pay fees for their study. The reason was simple. If one wanted to be a general manager, it was necessary to make some investment. Knowledge learned at a cost would be retained longer.

Upon graduation, the trainees would be issued certificates with the term Ruitai on them. Though the certificates were not approved by the government Department of Education at any level, we strongly believed that in the near future, they would be accepted by all the businesses in the retail trade. They would become proof of qualification for general managers in China's retail business and passport to senior management positions, because they were issued by the Wuhan Plaza, an enterprise which was seeking excellence and which achieved excellence to a high degree.

In fact, it was impossible and unnecessary to be approved by any government Department of Education. "Huangpu" was totally new in its goals and operations. The present education system did not have a place for it yet.

We took the lead again. It was good to act quickly. Our leading role would be acknowledged as time passed, because it was born out of a market demand that became more and more pressing.

5. The First Management Company in China

Applying the management of the Wuhan Plaza across the retail trade marked the generalization and commercialization of our export operations.

These operations should be managed by a specialized company. Then another idea struck me: could we set up a specialized management company?

This inspiration was not only touched off by logical thinking. The increasing talks and business activities on management export also brought home the need for a special organization. Specialization would lead to perfection.

This type of company specializing in management was unprecedented in China, not to be found in the catalogues of Chinese enterprises, or on the Internet.

China's governments had long been running business operations, and planned economy was a tradition. The public service industry was in a primitive state, and the business service industry was but a recent development. In the past fifty years, social services were identified with restaurants, hotels, transportation, department stores, barbershops and photo studios. Services for business activities were not included. After the Reform, the business service industry emerged. Auditing, accounting, assets assessment, and sales brokerage were separated from government-run enterprises. At a closer look, these business services were limited in scope to technical functions and purchase/sales. This business service industry could not generate service strategies at advanced levels. It could not come up with pioneering originality, nor would it provide a powerful bird's eye view of the past and future.

The specialized management company in planning obviously belonged to the higher level in the business service industry. But there was no such entry in catalogues of China's enterprises.

Traditional concepts were another cause of this absence. In the past, the government had been the driving force for disseminating new management styles and beneficial experiences. They were considered government functions.

It was unimaginable for a business organization to drive these activities. People would ask in bewilderment: without administrative resources, without the official authority for dissemination, how could our model and experiences be marketed?

Misconception and the gap in our economic development put our management company in a unique situation.

It was so unique that when we went to ask about registration at the Business Administration Bureau, the workers there didn't know how to define our line of business even with a thick book of business categorization. Was it a trading company? Or a service company? They couldn't figure out. If it were a trading company, the commodities we sold could not be categorized as any type of materials. If it were a service company, our service was not included in the scope of traditional commerce. It did not even resemble new fashions like information brokerage. It seemed as if we were offering service to something intangible and blurry.

We, and the governmental institutions as well, both faced an awkward situation. We could not define a pioneering, cross-trade organization that defied any categorization and engaged in multiple business activities.

Since there were no precedents in China, we turned our eyes overseas.

Foreign business service companies offer many services: supervision, management, advertising and public relations, and business consulting.

All this broadened our vision. Our company in planning should integrate trading and service. We would trade in a special commodity — our model, and we would provide service in a special area — management.

Our registration with the Business Administration Bureau was thus completed without any problem. We set up Wuhan Plaza Ruitai Business Consulting Co., Ltd. In the Scope of Business section, we put down the following services: business planning, human resource training, entrusted management and consulting.

We placed a whole-page advertisement in the newspaper, expressing our conviction to pioneer in this business.

The advertisement was designed like this: on the open ocean, a gigantic steamer named Ruitai was sailing on. On the deck were not ordinary engine rooms and cabins, but high buildings named Wuhan Plaza, Wuhan Department Store and World Trade Plaza. The implication of the advertisement was very clear. Ruitai Co. would carry China's large retail businesses into the 21st century. It was obvious that the advertisement made use of computer technology to combine two different groups of images, to create an imaginary steamer carrying many buildings on it. The advertisement was chosen from many draft designs. I picked it because of its pioneering design and the enterprising spirit through computer integration.

I liked the pioneering design. With this design, we officially announced to the public that the first business management company in China was born.

We didn't indulge in the poetic romance. We plunged into action immediately.

The first promotion materials by Ruitai presented a grave, life-and-death picture to the readers. It said, "As a general manager in the retail business, you must have felt the growing pressure of competition. There are more and more competitors. The profit margin is declining, while business expenses are shooting up. Customers are harder and harder to please!"

We were telling the truth, because only the truth was sharp enough to wake people up to the importance of management.

Our management was in fragments, with gaps and ditches underfoot, and howling wind and galloping clouds overhead. This was the status of management in China.

The agricultural tradition for thousands of years was the root cause of this status. The government running business and planned economy further aggravated the situation. Before the Reform, there were studies on government, but no theories on management; there were rules to govern the people, but no means to manage the economy; there was random management, but no scientific management.

The failure in management became an enormous black hole in the Chinese economy. The black hole swallowed orderly development, profit and the effort to catch up with the rest of the world.

We should fill up the black hole now. We had a sense of mission. There was no more time to lose. We started the work at once.

The first thing was to decide on the mission of our business. We came up with this one: "Design a new management model for China's retail business in the 21st century." It should be internationalized, and applicable to the Chinese cases as well. As a "commodity," the model came in various forms, including the shopping center model, the department store model, the chain store model, the cash-and-carry store (or discount warehouse) model, the supermarket model, and the specialty store model. The value of this "commodity" was to help retail businesses improve their adaptability and competitiveness in the market, standardize their management, and increase their profitability — the ultimate goal of all the other measures.

The second thing was to publicize our goals. In addition to the whole-page advertisement mentioned above, we released the news in all kinds of media including the Internet, printed many promotion materials, informed other companies in the retail business, and reported to the government agency in charge. Our news release was multi-channel and comprehensive, but the tone was low key. Management was careful and solid work by nature. Noisy bragging sounded out of place.

We believed in "honest business" which had become the convention in the world.

Honest business aims at achieving good results with honest motives, honest styles, honest manner and honest operations.

To engage in honest business, we strengthened our research, training and monitoring systems, established several departments, worked out a number of detailed procedures, and trained some staff in preparation.

Planning for the battle was our principle. Our major planning activity focused on the Wuhan Plaza. It was a model project and a training base. Other preparations included measures mentioned in the previous paragraph, as well as an emphasis on professionalism, hard work, enterprise and creativity.

We devoted all our resources. This devotion was witnessed in our patient talks with the customers, in the night oil that we burnt, in the frequent travels to our customers' sites for detailed investigations, and in the individualized designs we worked out through sleepless nights. This high investment resulted in rewards as anticipated. Our success was proved by more than a dozen customers from Shenzhen, Jinan and Shanghai, and the entrusted management case in Tianjin. In connection to the case in Tianjin, I would like to return to the issue on the right to use our company name. We insisted on this right because we wanted to meet our responsibilities, because we wanted to publicize our name, and also because we wanted to put this first management company in China under the scrutiny of the public and of history.

It was an honor to be the leading pioneer. I said to all the staff of Ruitai, "You should value this pioneering role."

To ensure the success of our pioneering work, I formally signed my name in the "Corporate Representative" field in the business registration documents.

Pioneering work would never be easy. I would encounter numerous new challenges and new issues.

But I love the pioneering role, because our times need pioneers and are producing them one by one and group by group, who will push China towards new summits.

6. Please Give Me Your Tuition

When we were cloning the Wuhan Plaza or exporting our management model, I often said to the customer, the public, and myself, "Please give me your tuition."

I was not marketing Ruitai. I spoke from a deep concern in my personal experience.

A friend told me about the fate of patents. He said that China was not short of inventions and patents, but few of them were marketed. The rate of patent utilization in developed countries was 10% (almost 20% in Japan). Ours was less than 2%.

Strangely, the obstruction to the marketing of patents in China was the traditional reluctance to pay for them. People would repeat the research process for the same patents, or resort to piracy, rather than buying them.

In traditional concepts and behavior, time and manpower did not count as money. Rules and regulations did not have any monetary value. Failures in explorations did not seem to have financial consequences. The leaders of some companies lived in the 1990s, but their mental state was just like that of a peasant fooling around. You asked him to buy some fruit. He replied that he knew how to grow them. You wanted to give him some fruit. He said, "I don't mean to trouble you" and promised to get them himself. He looked this way and that way, without finally setting his foot into the door. This led to a sad phenomenon. On the one hand, a lot of fruit were wasted; on the other, people kept complaining that they didn't have good fruit.

I thought about patents because as an intellectual product, our model's fate was similar to that of patents. I often saw perplexed and shocked looks after we offered our quote. I also met some open-handed general managers who bargained over pennies in negotiations over the price tag for management export. A general manager proudly announced on the first day of his visit that he had spent hundreds of thousands of *yuan* on business tours to determine the market position of his company. But he kept his mouth shut when we discussed our priced management export.

It was not because he disliked our model. He was very excited when he arrived at the Wuhan Plaza, as if seeing a lover he had been seeking for a long time.

In fact, our quote was not very high.

Was he thinking about risks? No, he knew how serious we were, and, he understood we could add terms of compensation.

He simply didn't want to pay. I would very much like to say at that time, "Please give me your tuition!"

Many of our business leaders are spoiled by a tradition in which knowledge and experience are transferred through the government free of charge. They are spoiled to such a degree that they take university classes or have professional training at the expenses of the organization. Their textbooks, teaching materials and stationery are all reimbursed. I am not sure whether it is a kind of corruption, but it is clear that this learning experience will not help them respect the value of knowledge. Before the concept is established that knowledge has value, the knowledge economy will run into barriers in its operation.

The reluctance to spend money on knowledge among many business leaders is also due to lack of demarcation of responsibilities and property rights in our enterprises. I had taken part in an investment project. The prospect of the project in the market was uncertain, and sales contracts were yet to be signed. Participants in the project were all inclined to hold back for some time. But the big boss broke out, "No big deal. Let's go for it! If the worst happens, we would take the loss as our tuition. Just a few million *yuan*." I was really shocked. If he were to spend the money out of his own pocket, would he say so?

I believe he wouldn't. My hypothesis does not make sense anyway. Because up to now we do not have a system to investigate those guilty for errors and failures, or to punish those neglecting their duty. The consequence for the knowledge economy is that these people would rather grow fruit than buy them, because there will be no punishment even if no fruit is grown. In fact, it is better for them to buy fruit. It is fast, and the quality is evident. If ever there is a problem, it is easy to identify who is at fault.

Fortunately, there are still many sensible people around.

The Reform pushing through the past twenty years has shaken and changed traditional concepts with some success. It has broadened our mind, created a group of modern entrepreneurs, and, through violent market clashes, brought about a sense of crisis and a need to look for new directions.

Needs are always more powerful than concepts. Needs can break old concepts and create new ones.

In particular, the need to survive can stimulate people's intelligence, open-mindedness, and even the willingness to give in temporarily.

This helped our operations to clone the Wuhan Plaza. It brought us in contact with leaders with insight, such as general managers of the Tianjin Anderson Group, the Xidan Friendship Group and Xi'an's Minsheng Group.

I said to them, "Please give me your tuition." They smiled, "OK. We will."

We were joking and serious at the same time. We were relaxed, but we were also heavy-hearted. We knew what was important.

We left the details to our subordinates. As general managers, our job was to work out the guidelines.

We all understood that, with tuition in our left hand, we would give what they needed with our right hand.

6

Worry in Success

> Worry in success;
> Worry in reclusion;
> Then when would one feel relieved?
> — "Notes on Yueyang Tower" by
> Fan Zhongyan

> If Andrew Grove, founder of Intel,
> often worries about the future even
> under favorable circumstances, how
> can we feel secure in adverse con-
> ditions?
> — Author

I like the term "sense of crisis." I also like the saying "planning ahead." I believe there is some connection between them. A sense of crisis would lead to planning ahead, and planning ahead would bring about a sense of crisis. It is uncertain whether these should be on the mind of every business person. But one thing is clear. They are good for studying all kinds of strategic turning points and controlling them.

The term "strategic turning point" was created by Andrew Grove, founder of Intel. It means that, due to the changes of internal and external forces, one's (or the company's) position would change.

The moment changes take place is the strategic turning point. Mr. Grove mentioned that most of the strategic turning points approach quietly. They would not arrive with fanfare. At the beginning, they are just like a distant and indistinct image on the radar screen. Generally speaking, one would not be able to see their existence very clearly except in retrospection. They are usually some details that seem insignificant but imply that the competitive situation has changed. In Grove's opinion, when the changes of external and internal forces go out of the range under one's control, the strategic turning point has arrived. As a neutral expression, the strategic turning point may indicate positive or negative turns. What's important is to be sensitive to it.

In fact, I experienced three major strategic turning points in the past ten years, and the Wuhan Plaza also experienced three minor strategic turning points. Of my three major strategic turning points, one took place in 1988 when I left the Organization Division of the Communist Party's Commerce Committee to become the Deputy General Manager of the Wuhan Department Store; another happened in 1994 when I left the Wuhan Department Store to lead the preparations for the Wuhan Plaza; the last one came at the end of 1998, when I was promoted to the General Manager of the Wuhan Department Store Group, to manage the first public company in the retail business in China. Of the minor strategic turning points, one took place in 1996, when the Wuhan Plaza opened to business; another one was in 1997, when the Wuhan Plaza ranked first in profit in China's retail trade and turned from merchandise trading to management export; the last one happened in 1998, when management export was replaced by entrusted management and the first management company was set up in China. We made the right decisions at both the major and minor turning points. We saw the turn of trends ahead of others and adjusted our strategies to follow the strategic turning points. In another perspective, it was the trends of the times that pushed us to success, as Tagore said, "I didn't choose the best; the best chose me."

But we can't sit back and relax. Mr. Grove specifically mentioned that success could lead to some "success inertia." In this chapter, I will address some concerns and worries, in the spirit of Fan Zhongyan's "worry in success."

1. Tornadoes of Ten-Fold Speed

In recent years, I had the feeling of trepidation.

This feeling was stimulated not just by my sense of mission, but to a larger extent by the grave life-and-death situation.

I always feel that in the 1950s, 1960s and even 1970s, everything around us was so stable, solid and everlasting. For example, whenever I walked out of the side street where I lived, I could see the familiar department store and grocery store. They sold the same goods day after day, year after year. The fat shop assistant was forever smiling and happy.

But suddenly, everything changed. There were tornadoes around us. The wind blew ice cold into my heart.

Our environment started to look strange. It changed into kaleidoscopic images that dazzled us. New commodities rushed in, wave after wave. First came tape-recorders, color TVs, then computers, with individualized clothing styles. Merchandise was sold through multiple channels: street peddlers, markets, business streets, big plazas, supermarkets, cash-and-carry stores, and shopping centers. Prices varied; advertisements were individualized; shop decorations were no longer the same. Everyone was in high spirits, preparing for the upcoming battle. But suddenly, ambitious businesses closed down. Famous brands failed. The rise and fall swept through the society and the business world. Take the many tonic drinks for example. No single brand can hold out for more than five years. Take another look at the electric appliances manufacturers. Wanbao dominated the Chinese market a few years ago, but where is it now? Where is its soul resting?

The movement of the world seems to be speeding up. The life cycle of a brand and a company is shortened, and knowledge is renewed at shorter intervals. Many new words pour in like waves. Before you fully digest their meanings, new waves leave you stupefied. I have realized that we have lost the comfortable and calm life. We can no longer afford to fantasize and stop for a breath. This is our fate.

To look into the fate, I read the trilogy on the future by Alvin Toffler, *The Third Wave*, *Future Shock*, and *Powershift*. I discovered that although what is happening is a personal experience for me, it represents a tendency in history. Toffler advocated changes, asserting that changes were speeding up. He pointed out that it took the human race two thousand years to develop from an agricultural society into an industrial society, five hundred years to develop from an industrial society into a post-industrial society, but it took only fifty years to develop from a post-industrial society into an information society. Societal changes were undoubtedly accelerating. He also pointed out the cause of the acceleration — science and technology explosion or information explosion generated by knowledge explosion. He quoted book publishing as an example. To publish 1,000 titles, it took 1,400 years before the 14th century, 100 years in the 15th century, 1 year in the 18th century, and less than one day now. These descriptions by Toffler gave me a sense of crisis and urgency. As a modern person, as a modern entrepreneur, how should I deal with this tornado of changes? If we don't want to give up and let the tornado blow us away, the only choice is to change with the changes.

To change with the changes is an elusive topic. The elusiveness is borne out by a series of stories that show the ups and downs of our companies. In the early 1980s, a small company called Wanbao in Guangdong Province became a household brand name because the company introduced advanced equipment. It succeeded because it changed with the times. But now, where is its glory and grandeur? For how many years did it enjoy the sweet taste of success?

Meanwhile, a small company named Haier started to grow in the northern city of Qingdao. By that time, a large group of Chinese manufacturers of electric appliances were well established. Haier was having a hard time catching up. But Haier kept breaking new ground and making changes. It finally turned out to be the favored stock in the Chinese stock market. What is the significance of Haier's success?

From a broader perspective, the up and down of the Japanese Yaohan Department Store throws a more convincing light on the need of change. This renowned retail enterprise was founded by Katsu Wada, whom the Chinese know well, and developed from a fruit shop into a retail giant around the Pacific Ocean. A few years ago, it was still busy expanding out of Japan and setting up franchises in Shanghai and Beijing. But the fate was unpredictable. At the end of 1997, it came down with a huge bang. Its sad ending compelled us to consider what changes meant.

From these stories and lessons, it is clear that we cannot resist the law of changes. What we should do is to obey the law of changes, to be aware of changes, and to prepare as many measures as possible to deal with them. Wanbao's and Yaohan's initial success could be credited to their changes, and their failure later on was caused by their resistance to change. When they succeeded, they thought they had everything under control and went off guard. At that moment, their death toll sounded.

Was it fate? No. A more accurate conclusion would be that they failed to track changes all the way down.

This in turn could only result in giving up halfway.

But how can we deal with changes or watch out for them?

I remember a book, *Only the Paranoid Can Survive* by Andrew Grove.

Grove was the President of Intel. He was once on the cover page of the *Time* magazine. His face was covered with computer chips, which conveyed a sense of experience and power. His own life is full of changes, too. Grove was cited by *Time* as Man of the Year in 1997, but this is not the point here.

The point for me is that he has exposed the law of changes through mathematical models. In his opinion, big changes do not happen out of the blue. They are in fact the accumulation of a series of gradual changes. Gradual changes take place this way: if one of the many elements affecting a company starts to change, it will expand at a ten-fold speed, rapidly prevailing over other elements, changing the company's direction and pushing the company to the critical point. Grove called this critical point "strategic turning point," which means that you must change your strategy at this critical moment.

"Ten-fold speed change" and "strategic turning point" are both very important ideas.

Then, how do we guard against ten-fold speed changes, and how do we detect strategic turning points?

Grove believes that we must remain paranoid about the following principles: anything that is possible will become factual; the closer to success, the more crises will be lurking around; success is based on a clear understanding of the reality.

Grove was once considered a paranoid, but I do not see any insensibility in these "paranoid" principles. Instead, they reflect a reasonable soberness, an emphasis on scientific laws, and a philosophical thinking.

Following this "paranoid" reasoning, Grove points out that the strategic turning point refers to this situation: if changes in a part of a company exceed the degree the company can usually bear, the strategic turning point has arrived.

This makes the whole concept easy to understand. More significantly, he points out six factors that might bring the company to the strategic turning point:

(1) The power, dynamics and capabilities of existing competitors;

(2) The power, dynamics and capabilities of complementary companies;

(3) The power, dynamics and capabilities of clients;

(4) The power, dynamics and capabilities of vendors;

(5) The possibility that the items the company deals in are provided through other means;

(6) The power, dynamics and capabilities of potential competitors.

Then the logic becomes clear: remain paranoid about the six factors; watch out for the ten-fold speed change of any of them; detect the strategic turning point; change the strategy accordingly.

As a world-class president, Grove tells us his experience and wisdom about how to deal with a world of tornadoes. He also provides a methodology for our enterprise to survive and develop.

Now the problem is what to do when the strategic turning point arrives.

Many actions can be taken in theory, but we don't have a strategy for operations. We are in a world short of strategy.

This is obvious from the fact that many state-owned retail businesses are fighting a losing battle, and that some foreign retail businesses are showing more and more signs of difficulty in China. It is too bad that we find ourselves in a period of historical changes, in a battlefield where Chinese companies clash with foreign companies. For many events, we don't have any preparations in perception and methodology, not to mention strategy.

This is a real risk. As a result, we must watch out for the slightest sign of change, learn from everyone, exercise introspection, continuously improve the successful Wuhan Plaza model, and constantly drive at renovations, in order to engage upcoming strategic turning points. At the same time, we have to keep in mind Fan Zhongyan's well-known line, "Worried in success."

2. Thoughts on China's Retail Trade

These days we don't see many things that can cheer us up. Some events carry a lot of significance in retrospection.

It was a weekend in the top commercial district of China, in the summer of 1995.

In the northeastern corner of the Xidan intersection in Beijing, a brand new modern shopping center was celebrating its grand opening. It was quite a sight. Colorful balloons and signs were floating in the sky. The shopping center was named Xinte.

No one would imagine that only 100 days later, it would close its doors forever.

Xinte closed down.

The bankruptcy of Xinte was a signal, an ominous signal.

In the chronicle of China's retail trade, the Xinte Shopping Center was recorded as a major retail business that went bankrupt in the history of the People's Republic of China. China's retail business was under enormous pressure and was facing great difficulties like never before.

In the following two years, 1996 and 1997, all kinds of retail businesses all over China went through close-down, reorganization, bankruptcy and liquidation, as if to prove the domino effect.

In less than two years, nine shopping centers closed down in Shenzhen. Bad news kept pouring in from Guangzhou, Beijing, Shanghai, Xi'an, Zhengzhou, Shenyang and Shijiazhuang. For a time, disputes arose everywhere; people agitated. Consumers that were hurt, sales assistants that were cheated, vendors that incurred losses, investors and proprietors that were left penniless and disgraced all came together, to form a gray torrent that washed against the establishments of the society, further weakening the fragile social security network.

When Xinte closed down, we were preparing for the opening of the Wuhan Plaza Shopping Center. At the moment, I realized that it marked the beginning of the dark days of China's retail business, not its end.

Many signs had already emerged. The bankruptcy of Xinte was just a reflection of these signs.

There was no strategy at all. The grave market situation was underestimated. Proprietors joined the trade with all kinds of background. Ownership and responsibilities were not clearly defined. Market research, which called for earnest efforts, was ignored. Careful and painstaking research and design of new business models for shopping centers were lacking. There was no accurate market positioning. Vendor recruitment was chaotic. Incompetent retailers were doing business side by side with competent ones. Business management was out of control. Business concepts and management principles were outdated.

Obviously, companies with these faults couldn't get anywhere in a market economy.

Such a commercial treasure land as Xidan in Beijing is the dream of many retail businesses. If Xinte had …

But, history cannot be relived through hypothesis.

We are not prophets; we cannot see into the distant future. But we are concerned about the progress of our life and our undertakings. We cannot quit watching and thinking.

Just like an English poet said, which Hemingway quoted in his novel *For Whom the Bell Tolls*:

> No man is an island, entire of itself; every man is a piece of the continent, a part of the main. If a clod be washed away by the sea, Europe is the less, as well as if a promontory were, as well as if a manor of thy friend's or of thine own were: any man's death diminishes me, because I am involved in mankind, and therefore never send to know for whom the bells tolls; it tolls for thee.

Any failure or loss is indeed the failure or loss of China's retail trade. The alarm has sounded; the pressure is mounting. China's retail business has entered an unprecedented period of historical changes. It will definitely go through great pain and severe tribulation. It cannot get around the iron law: the fittest survive.

The market economy is our judge. Survival or death will depend on our answers.

According to the information from the National Domestic Trade Bureau, statistics in the first half of 1998 indicated that decline in sales did not change significantly. From January to April, sales of consumer goods increased only by 6.9%, the lowest rate in the 1990s. The growth rate slowed down by 3%. It was a landslide!

Looking back, 199 out of the 212 large department stores in China recorded negative profit for the first time in 1996. It was a landslide!

In 1997, among the 249 large department stores in China, the profit margin decreased 0.6% over the previous year. In 133 businesses, which accounted for 53.4% of the group, the profit margin showed severe negative growth. 31 stores or 12.4% of the group started to show loss, doubling the number in 1996. A bigger landslide!

In Zhengzhou, Henan Province, the Zijingshan Department Store, which was known as the first retail business to reach RMB 100 million in sales in China, now has more sales assistants than customers.

Shanghai is the traditional commercial center of China. In the 1990s, it took the lead in strengthening commerce and promoting reform. Still the retail business in Shanghai is challenged by declining profit. In the first ten months of 1997, the average profit margin in retail sales was only 1.22%, dropping 0.01% over the year before.

Wuhan has always been known for its violent business wars. Its geographical location as "a passage to nine provinces" determines the openness of this city in the heartland of China. The retail business in Wuhan has ranked among the top class in China for a long time, but after 1996, sales began to decline. Competition intensified. Some newly opened stores slipped right into weak sales after the promotion month.

More businesses result in worse competition. They compete with all kinds of means, including suicidal means and illicit means. The result? All involved are hurt badly. There are no winners.

It is difficult to stop the decline.

The decline is like an infectious disease. One sneezes and another catches the flu.

What is wrong?

The worldwide depression, the Asian financial crisis, competition from multinational corporations, unemployment caused by social changes, higher interest rate and less money available, these can all be considered as the cause. Insufficient governmental regulation and slow response have resulted in the structural imbalance in the total number of department stores in China, which has created an over-supply of department stores in big cities.

The top cities in the world such as Paris and New York have less than 20 large department stores.

Tokyo, capital of Japan, has a population of 12 million, with a strong commercial economy. It has about 50 large department stores.

In Beijing, China, there were 180 large department stores up to the first half of 1998, in operation or under construction. In Shanghai, there are more than 100 large department stores.

When we examine the contrast of these two groups of statistics, don't forget the huge gap in the city size, gross national product, and average income level between the Chinese and foreign cities.

I am in pain for our country. If we have to pay some price for the Reform, this price is too high. Once more we have wasted the precious time and resources; once more we have taken a long and muddy zigzagging path. We are far from being mature. Qualifications of the decision-makers leave a lot to be desired. They are shortsighted, neglecting even the basic investigation and research.

The childish and blind optimism and the lust for grandeur and success have also contributed to the runaway situation at the macro level.

We are presented with a high price tag for this blunder, and it will take a long time to pay for it.

For a long time, the traditional state-owned retail businesses were spoiled by the leisurely and carefree days. Under the system of planned economy, the department stores had no sense of crisis. The unified seller's market enabled the retail business to stay carefree.

In the good old days, the sky was blue, and clouds white. Every retail business was having a good time. When some commodities were in high demand, customers would even come and beg for them. Everything was planned. It did not matter, though, if you did not complete the plan. No one would give you a bonus if you did, and no one would give you a hard time if you did not.

Some people miss those days very much. The memory is deep in their bone marrow.

Later, the good old days were gone forever.

It is definitely a turn for the better. It indicates that the shortage economy gave way to an economy with sufficient supply, and that the seller's market turned into the buyer's market. We are making progress.

The reform of China's retail trade has made some headway.

Retail was one of the first trades in China that embraced reform. It is also one of the trades with the most extensive reform. We can say that the retail trade re-invented itself.

Apart from some isolated commodities (such as gold) which are still regulated by the government, all the commodities are now in open circulation. The retail trade has 60 public companies. The market share of privately owned retail businesses is rapidly expanding. They have taken over state-owned retail businesses in terms of percentage in retail sales revenue.

The retail trade in China is trying hard to remold itself.

The change to the buyer's market from the seller's market cannot be reversed.

This situation makes us happy and proud.

But our retail trade paid a very high price.

This is because the retail trade achieved fairly substantial results at the beginning of the Reform, and those working in the retail trade really benefited from the Reform.

Many people, therefore, concluded that they would always have sunny days on the road of the Reform.

But the situation took a turn later on. The changes were dramatic, and the inertia against changes was strong.

In this period of real changes, China's retail trade trudged on a muddy path, braving harsh storms, bruised all over, as a line in a song describes, "A pain is spreading over the city."

Because the initial reform was carried out in a relatively closed environment, it didn't meet strong resistance and obstruction. The progress was stable and smooth. Business was easy. Sales revenue of almost every department store was more than promising. More and more people had money in their pockets. They were exposed to the outside world and had new and higher demands. As soon as the department store opened, customers would come in for shopping. It would not be an exaggeration to describe the scene as "jammed with people." Farsighted managers started to plan for more funds and the renovation/expansion of their businesses, which looked a little out of fashion now. They increased investment and expanded sales areas. Everyone was excited.

In the 1990s, reform in China's retail trade suddenly accelerated. In this process of rapid development, the goal became more and more clear: to line up with the international retail trade. Foreign investment was allowed to enter China's retail market, though with some restrictions. Foreign retail businesses had been craving for this day. So foreign investment poured in, and they acted very quickly. In a very short time, department stores backed by foreign investment appeared "fresh and flashy."

They were really flashy. Luxurious decoration, bright halls, famous brands, meticulous service, efficient management... Everything was different, so fresh, so exciting, so appealing, and so conformable. Even the background music in the store was so gentle, considerate, refreshing and elevating. With a happy heart, you couldn't help spending some money shopping around. The more you shopped, the happier you would feel.

After a purchase, the sales assistant would bow to you, saying, "Thanks," and "Please come back again."

People felt they were appreciated. They could find here the happiness and dignity of being a human.

This was the shock that foreign investment brought to us.

China's retailers were convinced. Foreign investment introduced China to modern retail business. They broadened our view.

Foreign investment introduced even more.

They brought in totally new business operations:

Department stores could be chained together.

Merchandise could be divided into different categories and sold in franchised stores and specialty stores.

Merchandise could be sold either in large supermarkets with many brands or in small specialty mini-markets.

Commodities could be piled up in an area as large as a soccer field. Customers could choose at their own will. Everything was so cheap that you might wonder whether they were mispriced. But, if you wanted to go in for shopping, you must first of all purchase the membership card. They called this "cash-and-carry stores" or "warehouse stores."

Most striking was the gigantic shopping center. It had everything in it, stores, restaurants and play areas. You could buy whatever you wanted. If you were to explore every corner, you could spend a whole day there.

Undoubtedly, they showed us how plentiful and attractive the retail business could be. When we exclaimed with admiration, most of us realized that they introduced challenges and threats as well.

As a result, China's retail trade cried out: The wolf is here...

Amid this cry of "The wolf is here," the opening China was still pressing forward.

The Reform in China could never be reversed.

China is not a narrow-minded nation. China accepted different cultures in Han and Tang Dynasties, and had a history to embrace different schools of thought in Wei and Jin Dynasties. It had the tolerance to accommodate and study everything, enriching itself in the process.

In this light, China's retail trade was "Dances With Wolves," to borrow from an American movie.

Right at that time, Deng Xiaoping's speech during his inspection tour to South China refreshed everybody's mind. Market economy was no longer talked about in private; it was officially endorsed. To solve problems in the system, we must adopt international conventions. From then on, reform and pressure in their true sense started to emerge in China's retail trade. This marked the intensification of the Reform.

A few days ago, I watched an episode in a TV series named "Powerful Events in the Past Century," produced by Yang Lan Studio of Hong Kong's Phoenix Satellite Television. That episode told some stories in Japan's economic recovery after WWII.

What impressed me most was the story of a Japanese shipyard making a concerted effort to build the first 10,000-ton oceangoing freighter after the war. At the launching ceremony, the general director worked on the dock and directed workers to remove the supporting frame so that the freighter could slip off the dock into the sea. That was the most critical moment. The freighter would tip over if not properly handled.

That general director hid a sharp knife and a dagger around his leg and waist. He was ready to kill himself should the operation fail. I was shocked by his behavior.

I always remember the scene. That was a determined spirit of no turning back. I could understand him. I could also understand the determination and tenacity of the Japanese nation. This determined spirit paved the way for Japan's economic miracle after the war.

Climbing uphill with heavy loads, we also need this spirit.

We need tenacity and perseverance.

We should be prepared to sacrifice everything.

Because our reform and our cause have reached an important turning point. Any hesitation and slack could undermine our great cause.

Apart from loss of control over the overall capacity, the difficulties of China's retail business can be attributed to the system and influence from traditional thinking.

The traditional retail businesses are still using the old management model in planned economy. This model has tied their feet in the operation of a market economy.

Unfortunately, these businesses are the backbone of China's retail trade. They are giants with clay feet.

Ways of thinking and concepts are more problematic, so are the general qualities of our people. If their own interests are jeopardized by the reform, the reformers would immediately stand up against it. The peasant ideology, agricultural traditions and traditions of small production have prevented us from internationalizing our retail trade. The underdeveloped market support systems and the social security system are obstructing efforts to change this situation. One consensus is that without mature market support systems, we would not have a real market economy or concepts and standards on human resources.

Laziness, lack of enterprise, shortsightedness, narrow mind, jealousy, closed mentality, and conservatism are enemies of our reform and open policy.

Outdated thinking and concepts will definitely lead to outdated management styles and management technologies.

Not to mention outdated business concepts and business technologies, outdated marketing concepts and strategies, outdated methodologies and equipment, and lack of creativity.

Shortage of professionals also undermines our reform in terms of sustainable development and competitiveness. Professionals cannot be trained overnight; it takes a long time and enormous efforts.

The internal fight in China's retail trade generated a chaos, which shattered the weak ranks.

Our starting point and capacity are no match for the experiences and capacity in Western developed countries. For instance, the total sales revenue of Wal-Mart in 1997 was $120 billion.

All this means that we still have a long way to go. The pain will be with us for many years to come.

Up to the spring of 1999, China's retail trade is still trudging along.

While Western developed countries are feeding on the luxurious feast of the knowledge economy and information age, our country is marching with a heavy load, on its way to the entrance of the 21st century.

Yet we have not lost our confidence. Although our circumstances are far from encouraging, we know that the dawn of the new century will shine on the faces of all human beings.

It is hard to judge who will be asleep or awake at the turning point of the upcoming century.

3. Uncertainty to Expand to the Suburbs

With the 21st century turning around the corner, China's retail trade is facing many more challenges.

One particular topic is the issue of decentralizing commercial centers by expanding into the suburbs.

After Deng Xiaoping's tour to South China in 1992, the real estate business took off in a big way. Blocks after blocks of high buildings appeared in the suburbs of many old cities. Residential communities with 100,000 to 200,000 inhabitants were developed. Satellite cities gradually sprang up around big cities. An issue started to develop.

Why? Suburban residential communities needed supporting commercial facilities. So the retail trade had some new space to expand into. There appeared new demands for the retail business.

This was good news for the retail trade. It also represented the trend of the international retail trade. Many Western sociologists predicted two developments for future cities: they would have a super size, and would shift around. The super size is achieved with continuous expansion of the population. When the traditional agricultural society transforms into a modern society, the appeal of metropolises as the center of information, culture and business will become irresistible, attracting more people from the countryside. "Shifting around" means that under the pressure of a large population, the traditional metropolitan centers will be displaced. Satellite cities will take over some of the functions of the metropolis. The predictions by Western sociologists have been proved to some extent. These days, an office worker who works in New York or Tokyo can live a hundred miles away from his office. He works under the fluorescent lights in the skyscrapers during the day, and breathes fresh air in his suburban home in the evening.

Following this development, the retail trade in those countries has moved to decentralize their operations and expand into the suburban areas. The fact that Wal-Mart grew out of a small town indicates that the town was characteristic of satellite cities and represented the trend in social development. Wal-Mart accumulated some capital by riding with this trend. Later on it cashed in on this trend, successfully building 3,000 chain stores.

This trend impacted the form of business as well as the whole commercial system.

To deal with the shifting trend in cities, developed countries established large commercial distribution centers in key cities. When I went to the United States on a business trip in June, 1996, I visited a huge distribution center in eastern U.S. It stored all kinds of commodities in large quantities, as the logistics center for the decentralized retail trade.

Meanwhile, the function of the retail trade began to change dramatically for the first time in human economic activities. It is no longer the end link of social production and distribution. Instead, it has become the first step. In fact, large companies such as Wal-Mart are integrating the entire production process. They have replaced suppliers' brands with their own brands. They issue purchase orders to the suppliers, asking them to set up branches in designated locations to produce commodities to their specifications, in order to supply the decentralized cities directly.

Urbanization enabled the retail trade to intervene in production. It is a good opportunity for the retail trade and an interesting development as well.

But stop! Don't feel complacent too soon. In China, maybe this is just a faint dream; maybe it is even a pitfall.

When the theory of commercial decentralization and suburban development was introduced in China, the retail businesses felt excited for a moment, but soon their enthusiasm dissipated.

The excitement had a simple motivation. With intensified competition and diluted profit, a big investment would be needed to do business in the much-coveted commercial areas in the center of the cities. Going to the suburbs and decentralizing the business would cut the cost of the building and other business expenses. This translates into more business space and more profit.

Out of this consideration, a number of large department stores were built in the residential communities in the suburbs. The pioneers were foreign businesses who had experiences and the guts.

I have seen this kind of department stores in the Pudong and Hongqiao districts of Shanghai, in the Bao'an district of Shenzhen, and in the Shunde district of Guangzhou. I have also seen similar cash-and-carry stores and supermarkets in Wuhan. They are all having a hard time. I feel worried for the investors.

Are our consuming habits rejecting the decentralization and suburban development of the retail business? Or is our economic development not advanced enough for them to take place?

I read an article about urbanization in China published in the UNESCO periodical, which was written by Guo Youzhong, Vice Mayor of Wuhan. Mr. Guo is a well-known mathematician. A visiting professor to several prestigious universities, he used mathematical models to demonstrate that the agricultural population of China was not developed enough for large-scale immigration to cities.

This is to say, urbanization still has a long way to go in China. The urban development in China possibly will not follow the model of super-sized cities or shifting commercial centers as in Western countries. Its vast territory and huge population might lead to scattered developments.

With scattered developments, the suburban-oriented and decentralized models of commercial activities would run into a dead end. The prospect of the distribution center system and the integration of production by the retail trade become questionable.

Even if China develops along the path as predicted by Western sociologists, the timing for decentralization and development into the suburbs has to be carefully watched for because of the slow progress.

Why? Because if you build a department store in a remote place, how can people go shopping without a public transportation system or private cars?

You can invest hundreds of millions in these places. However, the market will teach you that illusions would not bring about any rewards.

Our retail businesses still find themselves in an awkward situation: competing with numerous rivals in a limited narrow space.

The competition sometimes turns suicidal. For example, right at this moment when I am writing my thoughts, Wuhan's retail businesses are engaged in the first round of promotion campaign in the spring of 1999. Some businesses offer a prize worth RMB 60 or 80 for commodities priced at RMB 200 only. How can anyone make a profit like this?

At the beginning of 1998, a department store in Shenzhen was reported to have closed down because its promotions went out of hand. The news shocked all the retail businesses in China.

We cannot go in the direction of suburbanization and decentralization. On the other hand, the intensified and concentrated competition leaves everyone bruised. The room for doing retail business is very restricted.

Probably the opportunities we are looking for lie in the "soft" part, not in the "hard" part.

The "soft" part — concepts, management and systems — is a long stormy path we should follow with relentless reform!

4. Threat from the Web

When we talk about the "soft" part, it is not possible to leave out computers or a term that became popular recently: hackers.

Hackers are intelligent criminals that commit crimes using computers. They usually enter the computer network without permission, steal computer instructions and disrupt computer programs. They are called "killers on the network."

Because the computer network of the Wuhan Plaza is an isolated one, we are not worried about hackers for the time being. But honestly, I do feel another threat from the Web.

Online shopping has already been very popular in developed countries. It has made its appearance in our country, too. As its pioneer, TV shopping has been acclaimed for some time.

A book named *A Woman Who Made Money in Pajamas* written by an American describes a Web age. In this age, you can make money without a company, a store or a warehouse. Through the computer at home, you place purchase orders, which will be sent to the suppliers via the well-developed computer network. The suppliers will produce, assemble or allocate the products on your demands, and deliver them to your customers. At this moment, the payment will be transferred to your online account through the Web, making it possible to work at home, i.e., making money in your pajamas.

Is it science fiction? No. If this book appeared twenty years ago, you could have considered it science fiction. But now, it is increasingly turning into reality. I checked some statistics on the Internet. By February, 1998, there were altogether 113 million Internet users in the world, including 62 million in the US, around 30% of the U.S. population; 9 million in Canada, 31% of the Canadian population; 8.84 million in Japan, 6.4% of the Japanese population; 6 million in England, 10.25% of the British population; 5.8 million in

Germany, 12.1% of the German population; 1.4 million in Norway, 32.5% of its population. With access to the Internet, these users started online shopping. Take the U.S. for example. 30% of the families, which translate to around 30 million people, did online shopping in 1998, a 50% increase over 1997. Besides, these families did online shopping 1.7 times in the first six months, as compared to once in the same period in 1997. According to statistics, in the first two months of 1998, online shopping revenue reached $4.3 billion in the U.S. Experts estimate that another 41% families are also interested in online shopping, and that by 2002, online shopping would generate a revenue of $54 billion in the U.S.

It is very likely that online shopping in the U.S. today will take place in China in the near future. I feel happy for the progress when reading these statistics. It is really exciting to have technology take care of our daily needs. All we need is a computer. It is a time of great changes. The computer technology is barely 50 years old, but it has already changed our life at an unprecedented speed.

But to tell the truth, as an entrepreneur in the retail trade, I cannot feel happy for the news. It tastes bitter: we are destined to be born to an ever-changing age. How many means should we prepare to deal with the challenges that keep coming up?!

Obviously, online shopping is no good news for the traditional retail trade. This unique way of shopping not only changes our shopping style, it will also bring about a revolution in production, circulation and distribution. The issue is very simple. If the buyer and the seller can meet directly through the Internet, the traditional intermediaries would be largely useless. Now that the purchase and sale of merchandise is done through a few clicks of the mouse, the package and display of the merchandise would no longer be important. Generic stores and generic merchandise would appear in force. Consequently traditional circulation links such as purchase, sale, shipment and storage would be functions of manufacturers. And businesses with zero stock and zero storefronts would challenge all existing department stores like hurricanes.

Existing department stores must have been chilled by this challenge. The reason is simple. They cannot mount enough resistance.

They usually appeal to customers with hundreds of millions in investment, make a profit by subtracting cost from the selling price, and solicit returning customers with post-sale services. Now these means don't appear attractive any more. Those luxurious department stores would probably collapse like cardboard houses. This in turn would expose the huge investment to unprecedented danger. The weapons that online shopping uses to fight the traditional retail trade are not complicated. They are just simple things like "convenience" and "price."

When it comes to "convenience," online shopping removes the need to spend time strolling around the stores. Customers never worry about being cheated by fake merchandise. They don't have to hesitate facing dazzling choices. By pressing on the computer keyboard a few times, genuine vendors would deliver genuine merchandise to their home. It is really convenient.

The advantage in pricing is even more evident. Without the property investment of big department stores, without salaries of the large workforce in distribution channels, without the added value by various traders in between, the price is definitely cheaper and customers will certainly benefit from it.

An advertisement described Seiko watches as having "irresistible charm." In my opinion, online shopping fits the description, too.

The retail trade will be thrown into deep trouble: it faces a real crisis brought about by variables other than business methods, business forms, or management models!

How serious is the crisis for us in China? Let's look at some statistics.

According to information available through the Internet, there are currently 2.1 million Internet users in China, 0.11% of the total population. The number doesn't seem very big, but it has the potential to expand at ten-fold speed. If we consider the dissemination rate of the computer and the fact that the Internet was introduced into China not long ago, and if we refer to the dissemination rate of the mobile phone and color TV (for which China already ranks third in the world), we should feel duly alarmed to online shopping.

Experts believe that online shopping will become popular in China sooner or later.

The consensus is that this will come about in five years. It means that we will face the challenge of online shopping in 2004. It also means that we have only five years to get prepared for dealing with online shopping.

I am very reluctant to use the phrase "deal with," but I can't find better words to express my ideas. I don't mean to treat online shopping as enemies. As a member of the human race, I would hail this achievement in our civilization. We should investigate the future direction of the retail trade, and determine the concepts, models, business forms and means we will adopt. We must be positive when confronted with the crisis, and try our best to save shopping centers with hundreds of millions in investment from being trashed under our management.

Once more, we need to patch up the roof before it rains.

Once more, we must prepare our strategic weapons before the "strategic turning point" arrives.

In my opinion, our strategic weapons can only be prepared with a proper assessment of the situation.

The situation is that although online shopping has many advantages as a progress in consumption stimulated by technology, it lacks the sense of culture valued by human beings.

Obviously, the merchandise menu on the Web can never replace the real feeling produced by a superb collection of beautiful merchandise. The convenience to have merchandise delivered directly to the door can never replace the pleasure of strolling around a shopping center. The cheap price can never replace people's desire for refinement. Saved time and energy can never replace a sense of leisure to enjoy shopping after work.

Ikeda Daisaku, a Japanese futurologist, pointed out that the future would bring along more sense of leisure. High technology would not squeeze feelings out of people and make them bored. Instead, it would stimulate more attachment to affections.

This means that online shopping will shake the existing retail trade, but not replace it. The existing retail trade will have to be reformed and revamped, but it will not disappear. The most likely scenario is that both business forms will co-exist, to meet the different needs of customers.

This is in line with the future tendency of diversification. It also demands that the existing retail trade take on many new features with respect to the capacity, size, form, function, management, and, in particular, culture.

Retail that is based on high culture is yet another new topic. If we don't understand it or get prepared for it, we will probably run into dead ends.

5. The Issue of Professionals Revisited

When designing the strategy for the future retail trade, we are often gripped with the shortage of quality planning and execution professionals.

I was deeply struck by an event which keeps reminding me of my situation: a gap in the structure of human resources.

After the Wuhan Plaza started its business, we planned a big promotion. The promotion site was the square in front of the shopping center. Since we had to conduct sales on the square, and since it was not possible to move cash registers out, we decided to collect payment manually. The procedures for payment collection by the staff were announced at a meeting. The issue seemed very simple, but the simple issue went wrong.

When the promotion was over, it turned out that the receipts couldn't be entered into the account. Receipts from cash registers always had an item number on it. In the meantime, the cash register would automatically record the commodity's sales volume, sales revenue and quantity in stock. The manual receipts left out the item numbers. The system of purchase, sales, and stock was completely messed up. If we didn't straighten everything out immediately, the whole management system would have to be suspended, or sales would have to be stopped.

It went without saying that the management system couldn't be suspended. The only alternative was to sort out the account with existing receipts.

It took three days to sort out each item based on the amount on the receipts, and each item number based on the item. The numbers then were entered into the computer.

There was such a mess for so little a thing. Why? It was due to the simplistic thinking and slack management styles of those responsible for the activity.

Their oversight and lack of professionalism threw us into a difficult situation in our business. The gap in the structure of human resources was thus presented to us, catching us by surprise.

It would be assuring if the gap were scarce or limited in scope. The real problem is that it has always been there, quite universal. It has become a potential stumbling block for the retail trade and a barrier to the building of a modern commerce. To put it bluntly, the qualifications of the existing ranks in our commerce are far from satisfactory. They don't have an advanced knowledge structure, or a matching professionalism. The situation is much worse than in other trades. I am not bashing my own profession. I know the truth. Among the ranks of workers, peasants, soldiers, academics and merchants, merchants have the lowest qualifications.

What was the cause of all this? It resulted from the long-term emphasis on agriculture over commerce, on production over circulation. Before China started the Reform, professionals with high qualifications never considered commerce as their career. Students went to commerce schools usually because they were rejected by other schools. Workers needed science and technology. Farmers needed astronomy and geography. Soldiers needed military strategies and tactics. Scholars needed extensive and detailed knowledge. It seemed that elementary arithmetic was all that merchants needed. Empiricism and low technology dominated the trade for a long time. In order to cover up these problems, the mysticism that "it would take three years to become a scholar, but ten years to become a businessman" was very popular in the retail business.

The situation was changed to a certain degree with the Reform. The massive rush to take up business brought in all types of characters. "Intelligent businessmen" and "scholar businessmen" started to appear in our business. Professionals with advanced knowledge structures were streaming in.

But the improvement is too slow for the rapidly changing situation in the retail business.

Modern commerce is involved in ten-fold speed life-and-death competition. Investment of millions of dollars, dazzling business models, complicated and instant decision-making, careful and scientific operations, all this has to be supported by professionals.

But well-trained professionals are hard to find.

Talking about well-trained professionals, I often remember an article "A Letter to Garcia." The author of this short article was Elbert Hubbard. It was published in 1898 and has been translated into almost every language in the world. The Penn Station in New York printed 1.5 million copies and gave them out. During the Japanese-Russian War, every Russian soldier had the article with him. When the Japanese found the article on Russian captives, they believed that it must have been a treasure and had it translated into Japanese. Later, by the order of the Japanese emperor, every Japanese government employee, soldier and civilian was required to have this article. The article had been printed for more than 100 million copies, breaking the world record.

The article described an event in the Spanish–American War. America wanted very much to contact Garcia, leader of a rebel army against the Spanish government. But where was Garcia? No one knew it. No letter could be sent. No phone call could be made. Then the American President was told that he could send a man named Rowan to look for Garcia. He found Rowan, gave him the letter and asked him to take it to Garcia.

For a mission like this, the usual attitude was to refuse to take it. But Rowan took the letter, put it in an oil paper envelop, sealed the envelop and hung it on his chest. He took a boat and landed in Cuba on a dark night before disappearing into the woods.

Even if people knew where Garcia was, execution of the task would have been difficult. But in less than three weeks, Rowan walked across the jeopardous Cuba and took the letter to Garcia, thus bringing back his troops.

No one knew how he found Garcia, but we can imagine that he must have endured great hardships in accomplishing the task with his capabilities and resolve.

When I read this article, the greatest revelation was that we needed an elite army of professionals like Rowan for our business warfare.

He must have a sense of mission, professional ethics, and the discipline to obey the superiors.

He must have the ability and, more importantly, the will to solve problems independently.

He must be prepared to brave all the hardships.

He must have the ability and resolve to survive in a desperate situation.

Obviously, these qualifications can only be found in professionals.

That's why we need an army of professionals urgently right now.

These professionals can be acquired through training within the company, but companies usually cannot afford to offer massive training.

This is because the training of professionals can't be completed in a short time. The training of specialized professionals requires special circumstances, special approaches and special courses.

Are there any professionals in China now? We should say that they are making their appearance.

Most of them work in joint-ventures. They have benefited from the free movement policy,[1] management training provided by foreign or joint-venture companies, and a two-way selection system.

I visited a number of world-famous companies on purpose, including two visits to IBM Beijing. The professionalism there impressed me deeply. From the very moment I stepped into their reception room, I could feel the exquisite professional handling of everything, including what paper cup the visitors would use, what to drink, who to receive those visitors and where. Everything was arranged meticulously and carefully in a professional manner.

To bring up professionals, we must deepen the Reform, reinforce the free movement system, the system of selection based on competition and the management system.

We should make great efforts to add this function to our companies. A modern company should have more functions than traditional companies, including the education function and the learning function.

In fact, professionals are growing up in our company. For example, we have a manager who picked shoes up three times after the customer threw them down. We have a security guard who didn't bring it out on the customer when his wrist was seriously hurt. We also have a supervisor who apologized to a customer at his home despite the customer's rude behavior.

But our professionalism is not very high yet. We still feel the gap in the structure of our staff. We do not have the capacity to meet the needs for professionals of the society.

Without professionals, China's retail trade would never be stable. An unstable retail trade would never make any progress. Out of the concern for China's retail trade, I want to call on the public in general and on our educators in particular: focus on the training of professionals!

6. Fatal Shortage

The issue of professionals brings up the issue of knowledge. We are experiencing a shortage in knowledge.

Ten years ago, who heard of cash-and-carry stores? Who heard of chain stores? Who visited supermarkets?

It seems that no one did. At that time, most people only went to department stores for shopping.

In just a few years, all kinds of retail businesses made their way into many cities in China. The development was so rapid that people were dazzled.

As an ordinary consumer, I am very pleased to see so many places for shopping. But many business owners would feel terrified and threatened. After the 1980s, we already found ourselves in a knowledge explosion with the rapid development of the computer technology and the extensive application of the information technology. A slight letup and we would be washed away by torrents of the knowledge explosion.

Among business people, the greatest fear is being left behind the mainstream and losing the competitive edge. Consequently, they have a strong desire for new knowledge. Old knowledge is problematic. Traditional ways of doing business through experience and relations led to contempt for knowledge, science and technology. What little knowledge we had looks so insignificant against the rapid progress and great change of our times. The 1990s saw the building of huge shopping centers, dozens of or even hundreds of thousands of square meters in space. For these super-size shopping centers, market positioning and business strategies are crucial. We are at considerable risk without acquiring new knowledge.

Current risks aside, we will bog down further down the road without new knowledge. Futurologists have pointed out that the past 30 years generated as much knowledge as in the past two thousand years. By 2003, the knowledge in the world will double what we have now. In 2050, our current knowledge will account for only 1% of the total. This means that without acquiring new knowledge, we would become blind.

This is no exaggeration. These days we cannot do business with foreigners without knowing foreign languages. We must work on computers to process daily work promptly and to avoid waste of time. Without any idea of the networked and paperless office, improving the office environment and following international standards would remain as empty talk. "Modern illiterate" or "functional illiterate" are real life dangers hovering over us.

According to the definition by UNESCO, "modern illiterates" refers to those who cannot identify modern information signals and graphs, and who cannot use computers to exchange and manage information.

This definition will rule out quite a few people around us as illiterate.

In addition, the knowledge economy is storming over like a hurricane. We all have to treat it and its power seriously.

As corporate managers and leaders, as companies dedicated to modernizing and internationalizing the Chinese retail business, and as entrepreneurs eager for new ideas, we must pay full attention to the knowledge economy.

Because when the knowledge economy comes along, we will have to face more challenges, with more worries and a sense of urgency.

What is the knowledge economy? In short, it is a form of economy, under which all the resources and elements of production must be assigned on the basis of knowledge, and all the economic activities must be carried out focusing on creation.

What should we do? We should follow the advice of Dale Neef, editor of the book *The Knowledge Economy*, that development relies on creation and creation calls for knowledge.

The key to future competition is our continuous learning and use of new knowledge and new business concepts. The more knowledge and business concepts we have, the better chance to win out in the competition.

7. China Needs a General Manager Class

Coming hand in hand with the knowledge explosion is the global economic integration.

Knowledge explosion spreads the fragments of information all over the places, which are then collected by the computer network. Closed mountain villages and isolated cities disappeared from the earth.

Global integration is a chance as well as a challenge to China. It is a chance because Chinese businesses will gain access to the world. It is a challenge because access is no guarantee of success.

The current situation is that we are having a hard time accessing the world. Economic integration has proved a bitter experience for us. More often than not, we become the target of integration, unable to bring our economy out to the world.

Apart from weak groundwork and outdated concepts, a very significant factor is our shortage of a strong group of professionals.

A group of professionals that can represent the management level of our country; a group of professionals specialized in the study of international trade; a group of professionals capable of solving business problems at any time and place; a group of professionals with strong appeal and power.

I am talking about professional entrepreneurs and a Chinese general manager class made up of them. To our regret, in the 20 years of reform and opening up, the many entrepreneurs that emerged were anything but professional, not to mention forming a strong group. Some top businessmen made their appearance and then quickly fell into oblivion. Those that survived are scattered around like sparse stars. Taking Chief Mao for example. He was one of the four representatives of the first group of top businessmen in Wuhan. But today, one of the four has retired; another has washed his hands; yet another has gone abroad. Only Mao is still running full speed ahead. But what about his successors? No one has followed up. There is a big gap. Our forces are not combined, and our army has not taken their positions. As a result, the Chinese companies cannot muster the power of a team when they charge into the world, and fail to build a solid and extensive Great Wall to ward off the intrusion of foreign companies.

Don't we have the need for this group?

Yes! The reform of state-owned enterprises is calling for a large group of executives from this class, who can jump in and take the lead right away.

The successful negotiations at the Uruguay Round and the approaching admission of China into the WTO also call for a large number of competent business professionals from this class.

A group of businessmen can build a company or even an industry, boost the economy in a region or a trade, improve the management level within their power, lead a company or an industry into the international market. Everyone knows this.

But, what should have grown out of the need did not come up; what was understood has not been implemented. It can only be concluded that the current system has prevented the general manager class from taking shape.

This leads to another question: Under what conditions can a general manager class grow?

There are many required conditions: an encouraging policy, support from the public, an understanding attitude, real separation of government functions from businesses, comprehensive assignment of responsibility, power and profit, and the clarification of the relationship between ownership and business management, etc.

But the primary condition must be the understanding that a general manager is a natural person that can make their own professional choices.

The current problem is that general managers in almost all state-owned businesses are appointed by the government, and once appointed, they become the legal person. As such, they have to take on many undefined responsibilities for the company, and can be removed from office at any time. There is no guarantee for his position in business operations, let alone the corresponding power and compensations.

General managers are controlled by a network of strings. They virtually become marionettes.

I don't like to be controlled. When the Party's Municipal Commerce Committee and Mao Dongsheng, Chairman of the Board, wanted me to be the general manager of the Wuhan Department Store Group at the end of 1998, I told them that I would like to resign my public office[2] first and sign a contract with the Group as a natural person, so that we could make my obligations, power and responsibilities clear from the legal perspective.

Some people didn't understand my move to give up the public office and take the risk to compete in the business world.

But I insisted on my idea, because I intended to fight for the interests of professional general managers. I was exploring a way for the growth of the Chinese general manager class. In my opinion, to compete in business, we must first of all conquer ourselves, getting rid of all the weak points in ourselves that could be exploited by our competitors.

Fortunately, this request was understood by the government. Zhang Daizhong, Vice Mayor of Wuhan, and Wu Yumei, Director of the Party's Municipal Commerce Committee, both showed their appreciation for my act.

Mr. Zhang said, "In the reform of large state-owned enterprises, we are at a loss about how to introduce entrepreneurs. If we follow the general practice, the legal person doesn't have to be held responsible for what he does. Contracts based on high compensations would lead to pay raise at all levels. Your act solves every problem."

I resigned the public office without hesitation and signed the contract with the Wuhan Department Store Group as a natural person. Perhaps I was the first one to do so in Wuhan and in Hubei Province.

I have to admit that I was very lucky. When I took the office of the general manager, the Wuhan Department Store Group was already reformed into a stock company, with clear demarcation of ownership and business management, allowing me to hold the office as a natural person.

Maybe other general managers or would-be general managers don't work in stock companies. I understand from this that only intensified reform would bring up a general manager class in China.

The growth of a social class requires specific climate and soil. With the current political, economic and cultural situation in China, the formation of the right climate and soil will take some time.

The reassuring thought is that the Reform has passed the point of no return despite obstacles and controversies. Conditions for the growth of a general manager class are listed on the agenda, such as the setup of a shareholding system, the separation of ownership from management, and the system in which the general manager will be given the full power and held solely responsible for business operations. What remains to be done includes analysis, transformation, thorough implementation and integration.

The time for integration should not be too far away, because the bell for the new century will soon ring out. A new round of international competition will start shortly. It is the demand of history that professionals take to the stage.

General managers will brace themselves up, too, and help to usher in the moment with their competence, achievements and courage.

China needs general managers, a group of people who devote themselves to the Reform with enormous intelligence, courage, ethics and skills. If our general managers cannot contribute to the early arrival of this moment with their competence, they are not worthy of their office.

With the gushing torrents and storms in our age, I would like to shout a line from our National Anthem, "Arise, ye who refuse to be slaves! With our flesh and blood, let us build our new Great Wall!"

(Endnotes)

[1] For many years in the planned economy, people were assigned jobs in China. They could not look for employment. Changing jobs was extremely difficult. The "free movement policy" allowed job seekers to quit or choose their jobs.

[2] In China, once you become a government employee (a cadre), that status will remain unchanged wherever you work, even in the private sector.

Epilog

When I finished the last line, the anticipated feeling of relief didn't occur.

On the contrary, many fragments from the remote memory and from my past life showed up before my eyes, some full of sunshine, some like an old film with numerous scratches.

Maybe that is the way of life. You wish for a clear and happy morning, only to run into endless rain.

Or when you are feeling downhearted, a rainbow rises into the sky.

My superiors and colleagues are the first to appear in my mind. Among them are Qian Yunlu, Secretary of the Party's Municipal Committee; several mayors of Wuhan; Wu Yumei, Director of the Party's Municipal Commerce Committee and Mr. Liu, Director of the Organization Division, as well as the staff of the Wuhan Plaza: Zhuang Xianmin, Zhang Xurui, Xiao Yuhua, Yan Jianmin, Xiao Zhouyun, Chen Mulan, Chen Shaohe, Tu Wuyi, Pan Hanlin, Li Lifen, and Li Yunbo. Next come Mr. William Choi, General Manager representing the Hong Kong side; Ms. Choi Kwai Cheung, Deputy General Manager from the Hong Kong side; general managers of Beijing Lufthansa and Shanghai Hualian; founders of the Huaxin Real Estate Co., Ltd. and all the employees of the Wuhan Plaza. Without their support, I would never have had the stage to perform on, and would never have had so many thoughts and experiences. Mao Dongsheng, Chairman of the Board of the Wuhan Department Store Group, can be regarded as the ultimate motivator of this book, because his persistent understanding and guidance shaped several episodes in my work, thus giving life to this book.

I want to express my hearty thanks to these people. At the same time, I miss my family so dearly. I miss my daughter who is on the other side of the Pacific. She was still a teenager when she had to travel thousands of miles, to face a life totally unknown, all by herself. Yet she often called and wrote to me to inquire about my career. My parents, with their love for me, never tried to pull me back, not even when they were sick. They gave up the last days of their life to me, to the growing Chinese retail trade. I will always feel guilty to them, especially to my mother. I always wanted to take off some time to have dinner with her, to stay by her side in the hospital, but I was always so busy that she passed away in solitude.

Time passes quickly. Before I noticed it, many experiences and stories turned into footprints in the past. Hardship and setbacks, pleasure and comfort, all were gone with the wind in lingering streaks of smoke.

I have to move on before I can stop and indulge in my sentiments.

The goal I set for myself is still out of sight.

The Chinese wisdom has it that a man becomes established at thirty, enlightened at forty, and resigned to fate at fifty.

On a quiet night, I suddenly realized that I was approaching the age of resignation. There is no way to stop the flow of time.

On an afternoon of bright sunshine, the ancient Chinese master thinker Confucius went to watch the swirling water of the Yellow River and philosophized, "Time goes by like this."

Indeed, our life goes by just like that big river.

Most people of my age have seen the turbulent times, have experienced all kinds of frustrations and setbacks, and have had the opportunity to witness the dramatic turns in the society and the Reform which started 20 years ago.

Maybe our experience will never be understood by our descendents. Every one of us has our own stories, miraculous or mundane, working on something good for the society and for ourselves.

Since I set my foot in the retail business in the fall of 1988, I have had the chance to see the great changes and challenges in

China's retail business, and have had my own moments of shock, meditation, struggle and endeavor.

While experiencing the shocks of these great changes, I have been trying hard to find solutions, like climbing steep, unknown mountains.

Because of this, I have always wanted to record these moments, to write down my thoughts, my perplexity, my pleasure, and my setbacks, so that I can share and discuss them with my friends and colleagues.

I believe this is valuable, because we are living in a valuable golden age.

I hope my story can provide some help and inspiration to my readers.

More Titles from Homa & Sekey Books

**The Haier Way: The Making of a Chinese Business Leader
And a Global Brand** by Jeannie J. Yi, Ph.D., & Shawn X. Ye, MBA
ISBN: 1-931907-01-3, Hardcover, Business, $24.95

Ink Paintings by Gao Xingjian, the Nobel Prize Winner
ISBN: 1-931907-03-X, Hardcover, Art, $34.95

Splendor of Tibet: The Potala Palace, Jewel of the Himalayas
By Phuntsok Namgyal, ISBN: 1-931907-02-1, Hardcover
Art/Architecture, $39.95

Flower Terror: Suffocating Stories of China
By Pu Ning, ISBN 0-9665421-0-X, Fiction, Paperback, $13.95

The Peony Pavilion: A Novel
By Xiaoping Yen, Ph.D., ISBN 0-9665421-2-6, Fiction, Paperback, $16.95

Butterfly Lovers: A Tale of the Chinese Romeo and Juliet
By Fan Dai, Ph.D., ISBN 0-9665421-4-2, Fiction, Paperback, $16.95

Always Bright: Paintings by American Chinese Artists 1970-1999
Edited by Xue Jian Xin, et al. ISBN 0-9665421-3-4, Art, Hardcover, $49.95

Always Bright, Vol. II: Paintings by Chinese American Artists
Edited by Eugene Wang, Ph.D., et al. ISBN: 0-9665421-6-9
Art, Hardcover, $50.00

The Dream of the Red Chamber: An Allegory of Love
By Jeannie Jinsheng Yi, Ph.D., ISBN: 0-9665421-7-7, Hardcover
Asian Studies/Literary Criticism, $49.95

Dai Yunhui's Sketches
By Dai Yunhui, ISBN: 1-931907-00-5, Art, Paperback, $14.95

Musical Qigong: Ancient Chinese Healing Art from a Modern Master
By Shen Wu, ISBN: 0-9665421-5-0, Health, Paperback, $14.95

Surfacing Sadness: A Centennial of Korean-American Literature 1903-2003
Edited by Yearn Hong Choi, Ph. D. & Haeng Ja Kim, ISBN: 1-931907-09-9
Literary Anthology, Hardcover, $25.00

www.homabooks.com

Order Information: Within U.S.: $5.00 for the first item, $1.50 for each additional item. **Outside U.S.**: $10.00 for the first item, $5.00 for each additional item. All major credit cards accepted. You may also send a check or money order in U.S. fund (payable to Homa & Sekey Books) to: Orders Department, Homa & Sekey Books, 138 Veterans Plaza, P. O. Box 103, Dumont, NJ 07628 U. S. A. Tel: 800-870-HOMA, 201-261-8810; Fax: 201-261-8890, 201-384-6055; Email: info@homabooks.com